Redesigning Professional Education Doctorates

REDESIGNING PROFESSIONAL EDUCATION DOCTORATES

Applications of Critical Friendship Theory
to the EdD

Edited by

Valerie A. Storey

palgrave
macmillan

REDESIGNING PROFESSIONAL EDUCATION DOCTORATES

Copyright © Valerie A. Storey, 2013.

All rights reserved.

First published in 2013 by
PALGRAVE MACMILLAN®
in the United States—a division of St. Martin's Press LLC,
175 Fifth Avenue, New York, NY 10010.

Where this book is distributed in the UK, Europe and the rest of the world,
this is by Palgrave Macmillan, a division of Macmillan Publishers Limited,
registered in England, company number 785998, of Houndmills,
Basingstoke, Hampshire RG21 6XS.

Palgrave Macmillan is the global academic imprint of the above companies
and has companies and representatives throughout the world.

Palgrave® and Macmillan® are registered trademarks in the United States,
the United Kingdom, Europe and other countries.

ISBN: 978–1–137–36093–9

Library of Congress Cataloging-in-Publication Data is available from the
Library of Congress.

A catalogue record of the book is available from the British Library.

Design by Newgen Knowledge Works (P) Ltd., Chennai, India.

First edition: December 2013

10 9 8 7 6 5 4 3 2 1

This book is dedicated to my Critical Friends

CONTENTS

Illustrations

Figures

Tables

Acknowledgments

The author wishes to acknowledge all those colleagues and friends who have contributed in one way or another to the writing of this book. I have learned from critical friends in my own institution; from the Carnegie Project on the Education Doctorate (CPED) consortium members; and from participants at conferences both in the United States and the United Kingdom. Specifically, I would like to thank Dr. David Imig and Dr. Jill Alexa Perry, codirectors, CPED, for their continued vision and support as higher education institutions domestically and internationally work to implement innovative professional practice education doctorates. Scarlet Neath at Palgrave Macmillan provided expertise regarding the book's organization and formatting and graduate student, Brendan Richard, assisted with editing.

FOREWORD

Dean Fayneese Miller

We view the doctorate as a degree that exists at the junction of the intellectual and moral. The Ph.D. is expected to serve as a steward of her discipline, dedicated to the integrity of its work in the generation, critique, transformation, transmission, and use of its knowledge.

—*Lee S. Shulman*

In 2006, Chris M. Golde and George E. Walker edited a book entitled *Envisioning the Future of Doctoral Education: Preparing Stewards of the Discipline.* The authors of the chapters represented the following disciplines: chemistry, neuroscience, mathematics, English, education, and history. Each author was asked a series of questions including, "How ought PhD's be educated and prepared" and "If you could start *de novo*, what would be the best way to structure doctoral education in your field to prepare stewards of the discipline?" (p. 9). In the two education chapters, one by Valerie Richards and the other by David Berliner, the focus is on what *should* or possibly *could* happen in doctoral education programs.

While one might argue that the questions raised in the 2006 volume are similar to those raised by Valerie A. Storey in the *Redesigning Professional Education Doctorates* edited volume, to do so would lead one to miss the nuanced way in which Storey and Richard ask the questions. Instead of focusing on the "what if," Storey, along with the chapter writers, use work they have done or are doing as part of their participation in the Carnegie Project on the Education Doctorate (CPED) initiative to illustrate the importance of a critical friendship framework for both rethinking how candidates in education professional doctorate programs are prepared and, second, implementing the proposed changes.

Central components in the critical friendship concept for CPED institutions are constructive critique, reflection, and support. At each of the higher education institutions represented in the volume and part of the CPED initiative, faculty engaged in a systematic and constructive critique of their program, and asked, "How are we doing preparing professionals who will engage in the practice of education or do research on or about the practice of education? What needs to be in place to ensure that candidates in education doctoral programs are engaged in and practice innovative practice? What structure or mechanism should be in place to support candidates as they prepare for leadership roles in K-12 or higher education?" Many questions are asked and several examples are presented as to how some higher education institutions are attempting to address the myriad of challenges that have arisen as well generating new questions yet to be answered.

Storey's book is the first look at what higher education could do to better prepare leaders in K-12 and beyond. Instead of attempting to replicate theoretical or empirical-oriented research PhD programs, the focus is on how we improve programs geared toward those who will engage in the practice of education.

Shulman, as stated in the earlier quote, sees those with doctorates as serving as stewards. He has proposed that stewards are those who are expected to ensure that programs of education maintain quality and those prepared to work in education have integrity. Some have interpreted this to mean that the faculty and candidates in education be scholars who actively work to generate new knowledge and transform what they know through scholarly writings, teaching, and the application of the knowledge. The authors in this book epitomize what Shulman expected of those in higher education who are preparing leaders in education. They are stewards who are acting as Critical Friends in the development, restructuring, and implementation of high quality professional doctoral programs in education. Those who they prepare to engage in the practice of education are also stewards in that they too are expected to generate new knowledge and use that knowledge to improve leadership in education or innovations in curriculum and instruction.

As with the notion of stewardship, I believe the notion of Critical Friends encompasses two roles—one that establishes the roles and skills needed to innovate, to generate new knowledge, to serve; and, two, one that is grounded in notions of moral purpose and principles. Although many of the chapter authors focus on the support nature explicit in the notion of Critical Friend, a moral component is implicit in much of what is discussed.

As many of the CPED institutions engaged in the work necessary to transform their programs, they did so with a belief that they have a moral obligation to provide a quality educational experience for those whose job it will be to educate our nation's future leaders and workers—to prepare those who will become intimately involved in the inner workings of a civil society by virtue of their citizenry. The work to transform programs is hard, especially when there are those who prefer to view and act as though the preparation for work for those who will practice and those who will serve as university-based scholars should be the same. What should be the same are the principles they will be expected to uphold, not the roles they will hold or the expectations associated with the roles. Because the roles and the settings are different, the way we prepare them should be different, in some ways, from a typical PhD program.

CPED, by virtue of the fact that there is more than one cohort of colleges of education, serves as the "place" for the Critical Friends network. It is through CPED that faculty and administrators engaged in the work to rethink and restructure their doctoral programs can receive critiques of and feedback about their plans. Information is shared, qualitative databases built, and new knowledge generated about professional doctoral programs. And, programs are engaging in critical reflection and receiving objective feedback from those involved in similar work in colleges of education. The work itself, in my opinion, suggests a moral responsibility felt by those in colleges of education that extends far beyond the ivy leaden walls of higher education.

Storey proposes that the Critical Friends model is far broader, and possibly more appropriate, than mentoring, when involved in rethinking academic programs in higher education. The Critical Friends model is similar to what researchers and scholars do as they begin the work on a new article or book—the work is provided to a mentor or colleagues, feedback is solicited, and then shared with others across the profession. The Critical Friend is a trusted colleague who provides objective feedback, identifies challenges and opportunities, and raises more questions—questions that should strengthen what one proposes to do or sharpen one's thinking. A mentor is one aspect of the Critical Friends model as it is for the scholar who looks for guidance from a more experienced colleague. The Critical Friend offers both intellectual and moral support.

The culture of higher education is undergoing major changes. It is opportune that colleges of education have begun to rethink its various academic programs, especially its professional practice doctorate, and ask whether or not they are as relevant today as yesterday. Have we held on to a model of the doctorate that is no longer, if it ever was, all encompassing? Are we doing the "right" thing in the way we prepare those who will do the hard work of educating our children and youth? Are we being morally responsible to those who pay or have their employers pay the higher education bill by making sure they are ready to do the work that is necessary? It is clear from the chapters in this book that the authors feel a moral obligation to continue to improve upon their programs and prepare K-12 administrators who are ready and able to do the work necessary, to think critically, encourage innovation, and provide support to colleagues at the same time.

The redesign of professional education doctorate programs, using the Critical Friends model, is reminiscent of the words of Virginia Gildersleeve, a past dean at Barnard College. She said, "The ability to think straight, some knowledge of the past, some vision of the future, some skill to do useful service, some urge to fit that service into the well-being of the community—these are the most vital things education must try to produce" (Gildersleeve, 1959, p. 422). This, I believe, is what those involved with CPED hope to accomplish and what the Critical Friends model, ultimately, is all about.

REFERENCES

Gildersleeve, V. (1959). *Many a good crusade: Memoirs of Virginia Gildersleeve.* New York, NY: Macmillan.

Golde, C. M., & Walker, G. E. (2006). Envisioning the future of doctoral education: Preparing stewards of the discipline. Carnegie essays on the doctorate. San Francisco, CA: Jossey-Bass.

Critical Friendship: Facilitating Innovative Doctoral Program Adoption

Valerie A. Storey

A central theme of this book is the application of Critical Friendship (CF) theory to the adoption of innovative approaches to the (re)design of scholarly practitioner doctoral programs, teacher leadership programs, and principalship programs.

A "Critical Friend" is usually a person who provides constructive critique through a mix of both support and challenge and has been in use since the late 1970s (Heller, 1988). Early publications (1990s) focused on developing the CF model by identifying roles, protocols, and reactions (Costa & Kallick, 1993; Cushman, 1998; Handal, 1999). Once these had been established scholars focused on implementation of the CF model and observed outcomes (Bambino, 2002). While papers and articles have been published in a variety of disciplines (Swaffield, 2005) and the concept applied on various continents, for example, The Annenberg Institute for School Reform, United States; Schools Innovation in Science, Technology and Mathematics (ASISTM) Project, Australia; School evaluation, United Kingdom, Australia, and South Africa; Supporting teachers professional learning, United States, United Kingdom, and Australia, there has been an absence of higher education literature centered on the concept. This book addresses the gap through its description and analysis of CF's theory in the change process.

In the foreword Fayneese Miller, dean of the College of Education and Social Services at the University of Vermont (UVM), since 2005, and professor of human development, discusses the importance of becoming part of a national conversation on the education doctorate (EdD) through the Carnegie Project on the Education Doctorate (CPED) initiative. She highlights the significant role of Critical Friends Groups (CFGs) as they enabled faculty to benefit from supportive yet challenging dialogue about professional practice doctoral planning and program (re)design as part of a national team ensuring that (re)designed programs are of high quality and meet the needs of professionals in education.

As a conceptual framework, this book draws from seminal and contemporary literature on CFGs, mentoring, institutional change, diffusion of innovation theory, complexity theory, and social learning theory; exploring the antecedents, moderating and mediating factors, and outcomes of implementing CF theory at institutions of higher education across the United States. Furthermore, the book seeks to enumerate and categorize the benefits of the application of CFGs, and the challenges encountered in implementation. Finally several chapters are focused on examining and comparing specific instances where CFGs were applied. These cases incorporate feedback from a variety of stakeholders involved in the CFGs process, including, but not limited to superintendents, nonprofit and community-based leaders, executive leaders, and district leaders such as directors, coordinators, and mentors. From these case studies we are able to present recommendations for improving the application of CFGs going forward.

This book is organized around three major sections. In part I, "Theory and Action Framework, Opportunities and Threats to the Developing Role of Critical Friendship Groups," the chapters examine the underlying structure and development of CF theory, the inherent benefits of using CFGs, the potential of CFGs as a method of diffusing innovation, and the threats to successfully implementing CFGs at institutions of higher education.

In chapter 1, "Critical Friends: Moving beyond Mentoring," Storey and Richard provide an overview of extant literature on CFs with specific focus on its foundations in peer mentoring and the developments that led to its current configuration and protocols. The overview begins with a description of theory and context, providing a review of the mentoring literature, before moving onto the CF protocols, and a framework for action in educational leadership. The framework is influenced by and is targeted toward CPED, and its member institutions, as they are collectively at the forefront of the effort to (re)design and implement an innovative professional practice education doctorate. This chapter sets the stage for the remaining chapters in the book.

In chapter 2, "Critical Friends and the Education Community's Role in Program Development," Taylor and Marsh provide an overview of the role of CFs in the (re)design of two EdD programs—one in a large public university and one in a small independent university (Taylor & Storey, 2013; Storey & Taylor, 2011), both being phase-one institutional members of the CPED. The overview addresses the role of CFs as they provide a lens for objective feedback and reflection. Extending the role of CFs beyond colleagues in CPED institutions to the broader education community is also discussed. Results of the three-year implementation are provided as support for the potential of CFGs and engagement of the education community to be strategies for innovation in development and implementation of doctoral programs. In chapter 3, "Critical Friends Groups from Afar: Can Long Distance Relationships Work?," Belzer describes the sound foundation developed by CPED for CF encounters—CPED website, FIPSE visits, mentoring structure of Wave 2 institutions, prework, and CFs convening activities. She then explores the obstacles that impede true enactment of the CFG model and offers solutions to these barriers from an institutional context by identifying structures to facilitate CFGs, potentially increasing the rate of diffusion of CPED's EdD design.

In part II, "Role of Critical Friend Groups on EdD Program (Re)design," the chapters provide examples of research institutions that are engaged in research in the field to enhance the (re)design of their EdD and chronicle each institution's experiences in these endeavors. The collection of chapters provides insights into the role of CFs in both academia and clinical practice as drivers of systemic change in PK-12 educational renewal.

In chapter 4, "Critical Friends' Perspectives on Problems of Practice and Inquiry in a EdD Program," Dr. Sands and her team from the University of Colorado Denver: Blunck, Davis, Fulmer, Leech, Ruiz-Primo, Shanklin, Tzur, and Zion, report on the efforts of faculty from an EdD program that looked to their partners to better understand the nature of their work and how inquiry at a professional practice doctoral level, can, and should support their work. As a result of their research, interviews were conducted which incorporated CF protocols to ascertain the views of superintendents, leaders from nonprofit and community-based organizations, executive leaders from higher education contexts, and district-based leaders such as directors, coordinators, and mentors on those questions. Those data were then used to modify the nature of their dissertation in practice as well as the courses required to develop students' knowledge and skills to carry out the respective inquiry. In chapter 5, "CPED as an Incubator for a Clinical Practice Approach to Professional Teacher Preparation at Washington State University: Finding and Promoting Mutual Contexts of Change," Sawyer presents a case examination of the relationship between Washington State University (WSU) and CPED as WSU planned and adopted a clinical practice approach to professional teacher and practitioner education grounded by research increasingly recognizing the necessity of intertwining theory and practice in the preparation and professional development of teachers. This approach holds exceptional promise as a way that colleges of education can meet the challenges of the twenty-first century facing K-16 education. Research questions in the study included the following: (a) What was the change process? (b) What supported it? And, (c) what hindered it. Framed by CF theory, diffusion of innovation theory, and complexity theory, the study presents both description and analysis of the change process. The chapter's discussion considers how the CF's approach may be useful in a conceptual framework as a catalyst for further change, both at WSU as well as other institutions. In chapter 6, "Growing Organically: Building on Strengths to Modernize the University of Vermont's Doctoral Education Program," MacKinnon discusses how University of Vermont's (UVM) Educational Leadership and Policy Studies Program have proved to be an incubator of innovation in problem solving where leaders from pre-K-12 schooling, human service agencies, business, higher education, and nonprofit agencies could come together in a program to tackle the state's problems in a spirit of shared inquiry. This chapter explores the role of CPED CFGs in the evolution of UVM's EdD program, providing insights into the enriching role of supportive and challenging dialogue. The final chapter in the second section of the book comes from Browne-Ferrigno (University of Kentucky). In the chapter "Redesigning Preparation Programs for Teacher Leaders and Principals," Browne-Ferrigno discusses recent changes in programs leading to teacher leader endorsement or principal certification in the state of Kentucky. She highlights significant policy changes that include the elimination of all master's degrees in school administration and specified prerequisites for admission to redesigned principal preparation programs. The Department of Educational Leadership Studies at the University of Kentucky responded to these changes by developing a new Teacher Leadership Program and a new Principalship Program. Throughout the design process for both programs, University of Kentucky faculty engaged with P12 educators who served as critical friends.

In part III, the final section, "Applying the Critical Friend Group Model to the EdD Program," the chapters focus on program (re)design. Universities utilize the CPED framework, and the application of CFGs, to improve various aspects of their programs such as online education, the cohort model, and curriculum. In chapter 8, "Critical Friends Groups and their Roles in the Redefinition of the Online EdD in Higher Education Administration at Texas Tech University," Jones explores how one major research university (Texas Tech University, College of Education) applied CF theory to the redesign of its EdD based on the CPED framework. She explores the strategies and challenges of implementing CF theory in an online environment. In chapter 9, "Using a Cohort Approach to Convert EdD Students into Critical Friends," Hamann and Wunder explore the dynamics of an EdD program's cohort model and the utilization of practitioner's sense of belonging and familiarity to become each other's CFs with specific reference to Lord's (1994) account of critical colleagueship. The authors consider the action steps pursued and the formative evaluative processes that compel minor redirections of courses that have helped convert a collection of advanced graduate students into enduring CFGs. Data include program design elements, and syllabi, but the main source of information are the accounts of the practicing professionals who are pursuing their EdD, that have been collected at regular stages in their journey. In chapter 10, "Criterion-inspired, Emergent Design in Doctoral Education: A Critical Friends Perspective," Reardon and Shakeshaft discuss the applied learnings from CPED's first wave institutions by second wave institutions, and the role of CFs in the knowledge transition, specifically, focusing on embedded field experiences and active learning aspects that are the two signature pedagogies of programs in both CPED waves.

In the epilogue, Perry and Hoffman draw together the various lessons learned throughout the book. Furthermore, they provide an outline for how the application of the CPED framework and CFGs model can be generalized and applied to other fields. In sum, the book focuses on the role of CFs as they support and challenge seven professional graduate programs (re)designed in partnership with the CPED to constantly reflect and reappraise their work. By providing a new viewing lens the CF can provide alternative perspectives by asking questions rather than accepting answers. The chapters illustrate the varying roles of CFs and the importance of context in shaping the relevance of the CF relationship.

References

Bambino, C. (2002). Critical friends. *Educational Leadership, 59*(6), 25–27.

Costa, A., & Kallick, B. (1993). Through the lens of a critical friend. *Educational Leadership, 51*(2), 49–51.

Cushman, K. (1998). How friends can be critical as schools make essential changes [online]. Horace, 14 (5). Available from: http://www.essentialschools.org/cs/cespr/view/ces_res/ 43 [Accessed February 20, 2006].

Handal, G. (1999). Consultation using critical friends. *New Directions for Teaching and Learning, 79*, 59–70.

Heller, H. (1988). The advisory service and consultancy. In H. Gray, (Ed.) *Management Consultancy in Schools.* London: Cassell.

Storey, V. A., & Taylor, R. (2011). Critical friends and the Carnegie Foundation Project on the Education Doctorate: A café conversation at UCEA. *Journal of Alternative Perspectives in the Social Sciences, 3*(2) 849–879.

Taylor, R., & Storey, V. A. (2013). Leaders, critical friends, and the education community: Enhancing effectiveness of the professional practice doctorate. *Journal of Applied Research in Higher Education.*

Swaffield, S. (2005). No sleeping partners: relationships between head teachers and critical friends. *School Leadership & Management, 25*(1), 43–57.

PART I

Theory and Action Framework, Opportunities and Threats to the Developing Role of Critical Friendship Groups

CHAPTER 1

Critical Friends Groups: Moving beyond Mentoring

Valerie A. Storey and Brendan M. Richard

Since 2001, many scholars (Jackson & Kelley, 2002; Shulman, 2005; Murphy, 2006; Walker, Golde, Jones, Bueschel, & Hutchins, 2008) have been urging schools of education to take on the demanding task of developing a distinct Professional Practice Doctorate that provides demanding, rigorous, respectable, high-level academic experience to prepare students for service as leading practitioners in the field of education (Shulman, Golde, Bueschel, & Garabedian, 2006). Shulman et al. challenged members of the Council of Deans from Research Education Institutions (CADREI) to think about how schools of education could unite to reclaim the EdD (Perry, 2012).

In 2007, the Carnegie Project on the Education Doctorate (CPED) was established to pilot efforts to (re)design the Professional Practice Doctorate. Consortium members "commit resources to work together to undertake a critical examination of the doctorate in education through dialog, experimentation, critical feedback and evaluation. The intent of the project is to collaboratively (re)design the EdD and to make it a stronger and more relevant degree for the advanced preparation of school practitioners and clinical faculty, academic leaders and professional staff for the nation's schools and colleges and the learning organizations that support them" (CPED website, 2013). The first 25 institutions in Phase I of the project were very much in the forefront of the field as they struggled to envision a new Professional Practice Doctorate in education (Imig & Perry, 2008). Initial conversation focused on program design principles, components, strategies, and outcomes with further discussion as to how institutions would communicate progress updates. There was an institutional consortium consensus that biannual convenings would be the signature activity of CPED enabling the multiple voices of consortium members to come together to display and discuss demonstration proofs of their progress in professional practice program (re)design grounded on CPED principles (Imig & Perry, 2008). Between convenings, institutions were encouraged to converse online.

In the early convenings the emphasis was on a "bottom up" process (Shulman et al., 2005) thereby ensuring that defined themes, directions, and processes met perceived need rather than being a prescribed top-down standardized approach (Fullan, 2006; Hargreaves & Fink, 2006). As convenings progressed there became an emerging necessity for effective institutional support to ensure that innovative program (re)design was sustainable and embedded in educational practice. Following the third CPED convening in Palo Alto (June 2008), CPED codirectors Imig and Perry observed that finding effective ways to maintain engagement of CPED institutions once they left the convening and faced the challenges of engaging home-institution faculty in the change process was a common problem for all consortium members. Consortium members needed to be externally supported on an ongoing basis which was not a role that could be filled simultaneously by the CPED codirectors for 25 member institutions. In seeking a support mechanism peer mentoring was first discussed. The consortium's dialogue extended to embrace the concept of Critical Friends and of Critical Friends Groups (CFGs) (Storey & Hartwick, 2010) in an attempt to move beyond colleague interaction to a particular form of relationship characterized by trust, provocative questioning, an alternative perspective, constructive critique, and advocacy (Swaffield, 2003, 2005).

In this, the opening chapter of the book, the authors purposefully develop the foundations for the ensuing chapters by first describing to the reader the theory, application, and role of a Critical Friend. Benefits of Critical Friends over traditional mentoring relationships are described and the challenges of applying a Critical Friend approach to doctoral program (re)design are examined. Second, the authors develop a Critical Friends framework to enhance the work of CPED institutions as the consortium continues to grow expanding from the original 25 institutions in Phase I (2007–2010) to over 50 institutions in Phase II (2010–2013). Consortium growth is likely to continue as funding is sought for Phase III of the project. The chapter concludes with some final reflections on the role of Critical Friends in facilitating program change.

CPED EXPANSION: THE NEED FOR SUPPORT

Why did CPED explore both mentoring and Critical Friends? To answer this question it is important to understand not only Critical Friends itself, the "what," but also the "why." CPED, an organization which during Phase I initially had 25 member institutions in its ranks, added 8 new California State University campuses and 27 new universities in Phase II, all committed to continuing the work of the consortium in an evaluative discussion of the EdD (CPED website). Just as an organization finds it difficult in managing the integration of a new acquisition, or the European Union has growing pains integrating new member states, so too does the integration of new member institutions into CPED present challenges to be faced and overcome. CPED faced the daunting task of doubling the size of its organization over the course of a year. It can be seen that CPED therefore was facing both organizational growth and rapid integration issues.

In order for Phase I and Phase II institutions to become a cohesive body, two barriers needed to be addressed. First, integration issues focused on whole group interaction, that is when members of Phase I (insiders) are present, Phase II (outsiders) are likely to behave differently due to identifying differencing institutional characteristics (Abrams & Hogg, 2004). Second, the consortium's culture may be negatively affected as Phase I (insiders) have not developed the same degree of trust with Phase II (outsiders), which may impact the consortium's professional practice doctorate (re)design program.

Anticipating integration issues as a potential barrier to CPED cohesiveness, Phase I institutional members began to plan for the "joining" of 25 additional institutions to the consortium. Phase I (insiders) had a common and agreed-upon vocabulary and could be perceived by nonmembers or CPED outsiders as having privileged knowledge or a prescribed status (Merton, 1972). CPED working principles (October, 2009) and conceptual definitions on which the work of the consortium is grounded had been crafted by Phase I institutions (insiders) after considerable intellectual inquiry and reflection. While history can be shared, the lens for viewing the past differs depending on experience. The richness of the process becomes less important to new consortium members more focused on the outcome, six CPED working principles. The insider/outsider doctrine explains the impact of differing member experience by suggesting that no matter how talented the outsiders (Phase II), insiders believe their group to be superior to all other cognate groups. Caplow (1964) called this the aggrandizement affect: the distortion upward of the prestige of an organization by its members. Outsiders (Phase II) perceive that the insiders (CPED consortium) hold knowledge to cultural truths that they are unable to access and believe is desirable. While Phase I institutions looked forward to the anticipated intellectual interchange with new institutions, and the opportunity to learn from each other, there was an understanding that agreed CPED norms were likely to be questioned. The complex processes that had contributed to consensual decision making, and the introspective shared meanings of experience within Phase I institutions for three years, would not be understood or effectively communicated to Phase II institutional members, despite plentiful information available on the CPED website.

The second identified barrier to CPED cohesiveness was concern with the state of its culture, the culture of the acquisition, and the fit between the two. Research has detailed how poor culture-fit or low cultural compatibility is an antecedent to poor performance postacquisition (Hambrick & Cannella, 1993; Nahavandi & Malekzedah, 1988; Weber & Schweiger, 1992). Every group, in these case institutions of higher education, has a unique culture that is comprised of the history and experiences of its members (Schien, 1985). The result is a set of assumptions that the members share in common. Culture is not only unique; it is embedded, and difficult to change. It is for this reason that when two cultures interact, in this case the integration of Phase II institutions to CPED, they are going to clash.

Research of organizational culture and climate has studied the integration of acquisitions into host organizations (Nahavandi & Malekzedah, 1988). Researchers have proposed that when two differing cultures interact, the similarities between the two cultures and the degree of congruence between the preferred modes of cultural integration are related to the success of the merger. In relation to CPED, it is therefore important to ascertain what the respective cultures of the two phases (I and II) were, how different they were from each other, and their relative strengths. Phase I institutions faced several challenges, revolving specifically around the relative size of the two groups, the inherent strength of the existing culture, and the distance between the two cultures.

CPED's composition during late Phase I (2007–2010) consisted of 25 institutions of higher education (22 public, 3 private), which collectively represented 18 unique states geographically positioned in every region within the United States. Of these 25 institutions, 18 (72%) were members of the CADREI, and 18 (72%) were National

Council for Accreditation of Teacher Education (NCATE) accredited institutions. In contrast, the institutions integrated into CPED during Phase II (2010–2013) numbered 32 (26 public, 6 private), collectively representing 17 unique states, also representing every region within the United States. Of these 32 institutions, 25 (78%) were NCATE accredited institutions (Consortium Members, 2013). Comparing the members added during Phases I and II, it can be seen that they were in fact very similar, both representing a geographically diverse group of predominantly public, NCATE accredited institutions. One area in which the two groups diverge is their average graduate rankings. Using a trusted and long-standing ranking system, US News and World Reports' ranking of graduate educational programs, the average rank of Phase I institutions was 59, relative to the Phase II institutions average rank of 91 (Best Education Schools, 2012).

Program rankings indicate that Phase I (insider) institutions possess a higher level of prestige than Phase II (outsider) institutions. Understanding this unique situation CPED found itself in circa 2010, underscores the impetus for CPED's efforts to put in place a support structure to further the integration process, develop cohesion, and foster a common identity amongst its member institutions. With the understanding that these goals would not achieve themselves on their own, or would take too long to achieve naturally given CPED's timelines and funding constraints, CPED pursued a process to help achieve their goals.

SUPPORTING CONSORTIUM MEMBERS

CPED, desiring to become a cohesive unit, with a strong unified culture, sought out means by which to foster the acculturation process between its far-flung members. In determining which method or methods was the best course of action, specific to CPED's unique circumstances, CPED relied on its members, their knowledge, and their professional experiences. One implemented strategy was the development of Critical Friendships, through Critical Friends Groups (CFGs), as it was perceived that this method would bring together members, develop trust, and bring about the program (re)design that was sought after. At the same time other strategies such as mentoring were also being implemented within the consortium. Why is the Critical Friends method appealing to some institutions and not others? Is the Critical Friends method a beneficial way of bringing together the members, transferring member knowledge and experiences, and fostering program (re)design? To answer these questions we must first explore mentoring practices, both in detail and from a historical perspective.

MENTORING

Mentoring is a process that consists traditionally of two members, the mentor and the protégé. The mentor possesses a greater level of wisdom, knowledge, and experience, whereas the protégé is attempting to advance his or her career, identity, and/or status. The responsibilities of the mentor include being advisor, guide, resource, friend, role model, motivator, and listener (Gold & Pepin, 1987). While the practice of mentoring has been in use for quite some time, the term having come from Greek Mythology, and being first used in the modern age in the seventeenth century (Roberts, 1999), no standard definition has been agreed upon (Galvez-Hjornevik 1986; Stevens 1995; Murphy 1995).

Ehrich, Hansford, and Tennant (2001) explored 151 educational mentoring studies and 159 business mentoring studies conducting a meta-analysis of mentoring literature within the fields of business and education. The study's raison d'être was to establish whether or not mentoring was in fact grounded within a wider theoretical framework. This was in response to Jacobi's (1991) comprehensive review of mentoring in which it was indicated that mentoring research was weakened by a lack of a theoretical and conceptual base. Ehrich et al.'s meta-analysis (2001) found only 15 percent of empirical education studies and 35 percent of business studies included theoretical perspectives on, or contained a definition and/or meaning of, mentoring. Over 40 different definitions of mentoring were identified by Haggard et al. (2011) within empirical literature on mentoring since 1980. The lack of a theoretical framework and an agreed-upon definition make it difficult to study and report on the benefits of mentoring. Hattie (2009), researching the antecedents of student achievement, conducted a meta-analysis, offers a definition of mentoring, "a form of peer tutoring, although it normally involved older persons (often adults) providing academic or social assistance, or both ... but it also occurs throughout adult work situations to facilitate career development," (p. 187). In this definition, the relationship is hierarchical, consists of a pair, and has the primary purpose of providing assistance in one direction, from one participant to the other.

While CPED might not be concerned with the lack of a unifying definition in the mentoring literature, it is understandably interested in the effectiveness of the method, the outcomes and implications of its usage. Protégé development research has found relationships between the mentoring process and job satisfaction, salary level, and promotion rate (Chao, Walz, & Gardner, 1992; Fagenson, 1989; Scandura, 1992; Whitely, Dougherty, & Dreher, 1991). More recently, researcher efforts have focused on amalgamating existing research, factoring in boundary conditions and generalizability, to provide a better understanding of mentoring and its effects. Allen et al. (2004) combining existing empirical research, conducted a meta-analysis on the career benefits obtained by the protégé. The results were "generally supportive of claims associated with the benefits of mentoring but also reveal that the effect size associated with objective career outcomes is small" (Allen et al., 2004, p. 132). Furthermore, the author recommends that pursuing mentoring in order to achieve career success can't be substantiated with empirical evidence.

CPED, and other parties in similar situations interested in program (re)design, should be wary of considering implementing a traditional mentoring process, with mentors and protégés, as it lacks structure, and has a highly variable outcome, depending on the motivations and effectiveness of the mentor in assisting the protégé (Ragins, Cotton, & Miller, 2000). Contrasting the traditional mentoring process with Critical Friends, the relationship is lateral, not hierarchical, and the Critical Friend need not possess relevant experience to that of his or her colleague (Swaffield, 2007). The relationship is long term, based on trust, and encourages reframing and reflecting. The Critical Friend process is a two-way street, in which both parties are encouraged to challenge each other, provide advice, and grow.

Peer Mentoring

Peer mentoring goes beyond traditional mentoring and its dependence on a single mentor to ensure a successful outcome. In peer mentoring, a group of individuals that are typically all at the same level come together to mentor each other. Baker and McNicoll (2006) surmised that peer mentoring's greatest strength is its reliance on diversity. The collective skills, experiences, and resources of the group are above and beyond that of any one individual. In addition, peer mentoring fosters self-reflection, in which individuals utilize critical thinking to assess their actions, formulate new actions, and assess the outcomes. In addition to the increased level of diversity inherent to a peer mentoring group, the power structure is different from that of a traditional mentoring relationship. Instead of a hierarchical structure consisting of a mentor and a protégé, in peer mentoring the participants are of equal status. It has been proposed that as a result of this lateral power structure, trust between participants can develop faster, and that it will enhance motivation that is intrinsically driven.

With all of its advantages over traditional methods of mentoring, is peer mentoring the most beneficial method for CPED to utilize to nurture and spur program (re)design in its member programs? If peer mentoring is more beneficial than Critical Friends to groups seeking to become a more cohesive unit it must not only be structurally sound in its composition, but also deliver results. To ensure a successful peer mentoring process, Baker and McNicoll (2006, p. 30) provide the following list of necessary attributes, "clarity of purpose, clear working agreements/guidelines, clear structures and processes that result in constructive interactions and a commitment from members to collectively maintain the quality of experience." It is not always possible to attain these attributes though, because just like traditional mentoring, peer mentoring lacks a fixed process component, instead relying upon the motivations and actions of its participants. Bond and Holland (1998) support this assertion with their investigation into the British National Health Service's (British NHS) experiences with peer review groups, in which the authors find that failure resulted from a lack of structure, leadership, motivation, and skills. Delving into the failure of peer mentoring to reach its full potential, McNicoll and Baker (2004) explore common pitfalls, noting amongst others: session degeneration into gossip sessions, lack of commitment over time, not providing enough time to properly conduct the sessions, a lack of trust, sacrificing breadth for depth, confidentiality issues, personality struggles, and a lessening of objectivity. It is no surprise then that Baker and McNicoll (2006), in their continued study of peer mentoring, recommended that in order to improve peer mentoring, and avoid the aforementioned pitfalls, peer mentoring groups must focus on building a supportive culture and providing structure to the sessions. It is for precisely these reasons that the implementation of the Critical Friends process can be beneficial to groups working to implement change (table 1.1). While peer mentoring is successful in that it increases diversity of thought, and focuses on action-learning and self-reflection, it also lacks the structure and culture needed to maximize its potential. We propose that CFGs, with their structure and purpose, are the solution to the shortcomings of mentoring and peer mentoring.

THE CRITICAL FRIEND

Critical Friend Theory

The concept of the Critical Friend originated in the 1970s (Heller, 1988) and the term is attributed to Desmond Nuttall's work on

Table 1.1   Mentoring comparison

	Traditional Mentoring	Peer Mentoring	Critical Friends Groups
Number of participants	2	2+	4–6
Power Structure	Hierarchical	Lateral	Lateral
Composition	Internal	Internal / External	Internal / External
Process	Variable	Variable	Fixed
Results	Variable	Variable	Structured

self-appraisal activity. However, the most commonly cited definition is from Costa and Kallick (1993, p. 50) who defined the role as follows:

> A trusted person who asks provocative questions, provides data to be examined through another lens, and offers critique of a person's work as a friend. A critical friend takes the time to fully understand the context of the work presented and the outcomes that the person or group is working toward. The friend is an advocate for the success of that work.

The Critical Friend is a powerful idea, perhaps because it contains an inherent tension. Whilst friends bring a high degree of unconditional positive regard, critics can be conditional, negative, and intolerant of failure (Macbeath, 1998). Originally utilized in the K-12 sector in both England and the United States, the use of Critical Friends is becoming more widespread across a range of contexts, and perceptions of the role vary according to particular circumstances (Swaffield, 2005). As a consequence, our understanding of a Critical Friend is continually being shaped and refined by the experiences of those engaged in the role.

CFG was championed in the United States by the Annenberg Institute for School Reform (AISR) at Brown University as a professional development model. In 1994, AISR designed a new approach to the CFG process, focusing on the practitioner and improving student learning. This model was based on a collaborative effort that allowed for critical feedback in a nonthreatening environment (Bambino, 2002; Costa and Kallick, 1993). In 2000, the National School Reform Faculty (NSRF) program, which undertakes CFG training was relocated to the Harmony Education Center in Bloomington, Indiana. According to the NSRF (2012) the purpose of CFGs is to create a professional learning community in which participants talk about teaching, provide understanding through experiences, work collaboratively, turn theories into practice, and seek to achieve sustained professional development.

While from an external perspective the application of CFGs is a practical approach for CPED to take, as with so many fledgling initiatives, in the early stages of implementation, nourishment is needed for the approach to flourish. This nourishment occurs in the form of CFG protocol training, otherwise successful adoption of the initiative and implementation with fidelity can be spasmodic.

Not only do Critical Friends need to understand the importance of empathy, emotional intelligence, and technical intelligence to the development of effective Critical Friendships but CFGs need to develop accurate listening, reflecting back, reformulating, challenging, and confronting, at times soothing and smoothing (Macbeath, 1998; Swaffield, 2003, 2005). But perhaps the primary requirement is that of reflective practice. Reflection is defined as "a process which involves mental concentration and careful consideration both individually and collectively for the purpose of generating new learning and/or deeper understanding" (National School Reform Faculty, 2012, p. 1). In a CFG, the reflection process is characterized by an in-depth conversation, which contains thorough descriptions, thoughtful listening, and detailed feedback. The feedback itself can be supportive ("warm"), distanced ("cool"), or challenging ("hard"). Providing feedback that is constructive, descriptive, and useful is crucial to supporting greater learning and deeper understanding (National School Reform Faculty, 2012).

Critical Friends Group Protocols

To function with purpose as a CFG there must be a structure based on group norms (Storey & Richard, 2013). A protocol helps support and structure the group to achieve the goal of the session (Franzak, 2002) and assists in the development of a sense of trust in the community of Critical Friends (Coalition of Essential Schools Northwest Center, 2013). Applying protocols to a CFG meeting ensures that the focus is always the issue at hand. This is in contrast to, and a rationale for, the usage of CFG, as opposed to peer mentoring. As previously mentioned, a common pitfall of peer mentoring can be sessions that lack structure and protocols, which can result in a degeneration of meetings into gossip sessions.

Developed CFG protocol generally adopts the charette model, which originates from the fields of engineering, and is used extensively in design, business, and government decision making and planning (Storey & Richard, 2013). Due to its "collaborative" nature, the charette model (Juarez & Thompson-Grove, 2003) is particularly appropriate when the nature of the issue indicates a need for group participants in face-to-face interaction for stimulation and exchange of ideas and views. The ensuing "creative burst of energy builds momentum for a project, sets it on a course to meet project goals, facilitates strategic planning, overcomes conflict, establishes trust, builds consensus, and allows participants to be a part of the decision-making process" (Lindsey, Todd, Hayter, & Ellis, 2009, p. 1). While utilizing the charette model, CFGs differ from charettes in several ways. First, they are formed to accelerate the professional development of the participants and, second, they attribute their existence not to an external event (i.e., a team getting "stuck"), but to the intrinsic motivations of self-development, and extrinsic motivations of career and organizational development (Storey & Richard, 2013). Additional differentiating factors are that "critical friends are more process ... oriented ... tend to be engaged for a longer period of time ... and work with people who are open to fundamental change rather than simply seeking the solution to a specific problem" (Swaffield, 2003, p. 1).

CFG protocol consists of five steps: (1) presentation of the dilemma/ issue/problem; (2) probing session; (3) warm, positive feedback; (4) cool feedback; and (5) challenge. Once the dilemma/issue/problem has been presented CFs ask probing questions to acquire additional pertinent knowledge relating to the presentation. Steps two and three (warm, positive feedback, and cool feedback), are completed with the presenter remaining silent. Finally, a challenge to the presenter ends the protocol. Challenge in this process has a constructivist interpretation and is not meant to be adversarial but rather a stimulation to reflect or act, and a questioning that prompts reasoning and explanation or the consideration of different viewpoints. How something is felt, understood, and consequently reacted to depend on the recipient, not on the intentions of the instigator (Swaffield, 2009).

The Critical Friend and Program (Re)design

Program (re)design is a complex process, with several factors influencing its implementation and likelihood of success. Even when resources, leadership, motivations, and willingness for change exist, faculty may still feel the need for personal support and reassurance, particularly if they are becoming overwhelmed by their own institutional issues.

Critical Friends are in a position where they are able to provide additional support, reassurance, and challenge to address encountered issues, and sustain the organizational change as they are able to view such challenges through an unfiltered lens being slightly removed from the issue or challenge being encountered (Swaffield, 2003).

CFGs, effectively implemented, combine the long-term, trust-based relationship of mentorship, with the diversity of thought and lateral relationships of peer mentoring and the structure and processes of the charette method. The CFG, an amalgamation of mentoring processes, has the potential to bring together program (re)design stakeholders (both internal and external to the program), to fully utilize their contributions to the change process. Each stakeholder possesses a unique perspective on the rationale for program (re)design. CFGs provide these stakeholders not only with the opportunity to express their opinions and in doing so contribute to the (re)design process, but also the potential to develop meaningful relationships with their fellow participants. It is the development of relationships, based on trust, that differentiate CFGs from a mere process. Relationships are crucial because concern for and encouragement of fellow participants allows CFGs to achieve outcomes that would not be possible, were those relationships nonexistent.

In comparing the Critical Friends method over traditional mentoring relationships it can be seen that there is no clear certainty of success irrespective of the method chosen as both involve the needs, motivations, and accessibility of independent individuals. Clearly the benefits of engaging in the traditional mentoring process are by no means universal, due to the dependence of the outcomes on the quality of the mentorship, something that varies significantly between cases. In contrasting Critical Friends with traditional mentoring, the relationship is more symmetrical, being one of challenge and support, motivating Critical Friends to move forward as the predominant mode of operation is "asking" (Harland, 1990), and the Critical Friend's concern goes beyond the individual to whoever else is affected by the particular issue that is the focus. Critical Friends encourage reframing and reflection, enabling colleagues to construct new understanding as they work in their institutions and the CPED consortium to (re)design the professional practice doctorate.

References

Abrams, D., and Hogg, M. A. (2004). Metatheory: Lessons from social identity research. *Personality and Social Psychology Review, 8*(2), 98–106.

Allen, T. D., Eby, L. T., Poteet, M. L., Lentz, E., & Lima, L. (2004). Career benefits associated with mentoring for protégés: A meta-analytic review. *Journal of Applied Psychology, 89*, 127–136.

Baker, W., & McNicoll, A. (2006). *I can get by with a little help from my friends: Peer mentoring—critical friends for the reflective practitioner.* Auckland, New Zealand: HERDSA.

Bambino, D. (2002). Critical friends. *Educational Leadership, 59*(6), 25–27.

Best Education Schools. (2012). http://grad-schools.usnews.rankingsandreviews.com/. Retrieved September 19, 2012, from http://grad-schools.usnews.rankingsandreviews.com/best-graduate-schools/top-education-schools/edu-rankings.

Bond, M., & Holland, S. (1998). *Skills for clinical supervision for nurses.* Buckingham: Open University Press.

Caplow, T. (1964). *Principles of organization.* New York: Harcourt Brace Jovanovich.

Carnegie Project on the Education Doctorate (CPED) (2013). http://cpedinitiative.org/about.

Chao, G. T., Walz, P. M., & Gardner, P. D. (1992). Formal and informal mentorships: A comparison on mentoring functions and contrast with nonmentored counterparts. *Personnel Psychology, 45*, 619–636.

Coalition of Essential Schools Northwest Center (2013). http://cstp-wa.org/resource/coalition-essential-schools-northwest-center.

Consortium Members. (2013). http://cpedinitiative.org/. Retrieved May 20, 2013, from http://cpedinitiative.org/consortium-members.

Costa, A. L., & Kallick, B. (1993). Through the lens of a critical friend. *Educational Leadership, 51*(2), 49–51.

Ehrich, L. K., Hansford, B., & Tennant, L. (2001). Closing the divide: Theory and practice in mentoring. Paper for ANZAM 2001 Conference, "Closing the Divide," Auckland, New Zealand, December 5–7, 2001. Retrieved December 6, 2012 from http://eprints.qut.edu.au/2261/1/Ehrich_NZ_paper_Sept_01.pdf.

Fagenson, E. A. (1989). The mentor advantage: Perceived career/job experiences of protégé's versus non-protégé's. *Journal of Organizational Behavior, 10*, 309–320.

Franzak, J. K. (2002). Developing a teacher identity: The impact of critical friends practice on the student teacher. *English Education, 34*(4), 258–280.

Fullan, M. (2006). *Turnaround leadership.* San Francisco: Jossey-Bass.

Galvez-Hjornevik, C. (1986). Mentoring among teachers: A review of the literature. *Journal of Teacher Education, 37*(1), 6–11.

Gold, M. J., and Pepin, B. (1987). *Passing the torch: Retired teachers as mentors for new teachers.* City University of New York, New York.

Haggard, D. L., Dougherty, T. W., Turban, D. B., & Wilbanks, J. E. (2011) Who is a mentor? Alternative definitions and implications for research. *Journal of Management, 37*, 280–304.

Hargreaves, A., & Fink, D. (2006). *Sustainable leadership*. San Francisco: Jossey-Bass.

Harland, J. (1990). *The Work and Impact of Advisory Teachers*. Slough: NFER.

Hattie, J. (2009). *Visible learning: A synthesis of over 800 meta-analyses relating to achievement*. Abingdon, Oxon: Routledge.

Heller, Harold (1988). The advisory service and consultancy. In H. Gray (Ed.), *Management consultancy in schools* (pp. 117–128). London: Cassell.

Imig, D., and Perry, J. A. (February, 2008). *The Carnegie Project on the Education Doctorate: Envisioning a new professional practice doctorate in education*. American Association of Colleges for Teacher Education (AACTE), 60th Annual Meeting. New Orleans, LA.

Jackson, B., and Kelley, C. (2002). Exceptional and innovative programs in educational leadership. *Educational Administration Quarterly, 38*(2), 192–212.

Jacobi, M. (1991). Mentoring and undergraduate academic success. A literature review. *Review of educational research, 61*, 505–532.

Juarez, K., & Thompson-Grove, G. (2003). The charette: Overview. National School Reform Faculty. Retrieved from http://www.nsrfharmony.org /protocol/doc/charrette.pdf.

Lindsey, G., Todd, J. A., Hayter, S. J., & Ellis, P. G. (2009). *A handbook for planning and conducting charettes for high-performance projects* (2nd ed.). Washington, DC: US Department of Energy.

MacBeath, J. (1998). I didn't know he was ill: The role and value of the critical friend. In K. Myers and L. Stoll (Eds.), *No quick fixes: Perspectives on schools in difficulty* (pp. 118–133). London: Falmer Press.

McNicoll, A., & Baker, W. (2004). The power of peer mentoring. In Proceedings of the 11th Annual European Mentoring & Coaching conference (pp. 198–201). Brussels, Belgium: EMCC.

Merton, R. K. (1972). Insider and outsiders: A chapter in the sociology of knowledge. *American Journal of Sociology, 78*(1), 9–47.

Murphy, J. (2006). *Preparing school leaders: An agenda for research and action*. Lantham, MD: Rowman and Littlefield Education.

Murphy, S. (1995). *The benefits of mentoring from the mentor's perspective*. Toronto: University of Toronto.

Nahavandi, A., & Malekzadeh, A. R. (1988). Acculturation in mergers and acquisitions. *Academy of Management Review, 13*(1), 79–90.

National School Reform Faculty (2012). Retrieved from http://www.nsrf-harmony.org/.

Perry, J. (2012). What history reveals about the education doctorate. In M. Macintyre Latta & S. Wunder (Eds.), *Placing practitioner knowledge at the center of teacher education—Rethinking the policies and practices of the education doctorate* (pp. 51–72). (Educational Policy in Practice: Critical Cultural Studies Series). Charlotte, NC: Information Age Publishing.

Ragins, B. R., Cotton, J. L., & Miller, J. S. (2000). Marginal mentoring: The effects of type of mentor, quality of relationship, and program design on work and career attitudes. *Academy of Management Journal, 43,* 1177–1194.

Roberts, Andy. (1999) The origins of the term mentor. *History of Education Society Bulletin,* No. 64, November 1999, pp. 313–329.

Scandura, T. A. (1992). Mentorship and career mobility: An empirical investigation. *Journal of Organizational Behavior, 13,* 169–174.

Shulman, L. S. (2005, Spring). Signature pedagogies in the professions. *Daedalus, 134*(3), 52–59.

Shulman, L. S., Golde, C. M., Bueschel, A. C., & Garabedian, K. J. (2006). Reclaiming education's doctorate: A critique and a proposal. *Educational Researcher, 35*(3), 25–32.

Stevens, N. (1995). R and R for mentors: Renewal and reaffirmation for mentors as benefits from the mentoring experience. *Educational Horizons, 73*(3), 130–137.

Storey, V. A., & Richard, B. M. (2013). Carnegie Project for the Educational Doctorate: The role of critical friends in diffusing doctoral program innovation. In C. Mullen & K. Lane (Eds.), *Annual National Council of Professors of Educational Administration Yearbook, 2013* (pp. 52–66). NCPEA.

Storey, V. A., & Hartwick, P. (2010). Critical friends: Supporting a small, private university face the challenges of crafting an innovative scholar-practitioner doctorate. In G. Jean-Marie & A. H. Normore (Eds.), *Educational leadership preparation programs: Innovative and interdisciplinary approaches to the EdD* (pp. 111–133). New York: Palgrave Macmillan.

Swaffield, S. (2003, October). Critical friendship. [Inform No. 3.] Leadership for learning. Cambridge: University of Cambridge Faculty of Education. Retrieved from http://www.educ.cam.ac.uk/centres/lfl/current/inform /InForm_3_Critical_Friendship.pdf.

———. (2005). No sleeping partners: Relationships between head teachers and critical friends. *School Leadership & Management, 25*(1), 43–57.

———. (2007, November). Light touch critical friendship. *Improving schools, 10*(3), 205–219.

———. (2009). Headteachers' views of support and challenge, and of critical friendship: Insights from interviews. Paper presented at the 23rd International Congress for School Effectiveness and Improvement (ICSEI), Kuala Lumpur, January 5–8.

Walker, G., Golde, C., Jones, L., Bueschel, A. C., and Hutchings, P. (2008). *The formation of scholars: Rethinking doctoral education for the twenty-first century.* San Francisco, CA: Jossey-Bass.

Whitely, W., Dougherty, T. W., & Dreher, G. F. (1991). Relationship of career mentoring and socioeconomic origin to managers' and professionals' early career progress. *Academy of Management Journal, 34,* 331–351.

CHAPTER 2

Critical Friends: Roles in Doctoral Program Development, Implementation, and Refinement

Rosemarye T. Taylor and Nicole Lea Marsh

Doctoral program design and implementation varies with the context and culture of each institution of higher education. Policies and practices are diverse in criteria and processes for curriculum change, implementation, and refinement. This chapter focuses on the role of Critical Friends in the redesign and implementation of one EdD in Educational Leadership program at a large, metropolitan, public research university, the University of Central Florida (UCF) in Orlando (Taylor & Storey, 2013, 2011). UCF has an annual undergraduate and graduate enrollment of approximately 60,000 in 12 colleges. The scope of the setting is large; the UCF College of Education prepares and graduates more teachers each year than any other public teacher preparation program in the United States.

The College of Education's dean was a founding member of the Carnegie Project on the Education Doctorate (CPED) (Carnegie Project on the Education Doctorate, 2008). As a CPED founding member, the dean invited the educational leadership faculty to participate in CPED meetings and to revise the EdD in Educational Leadership to align with the initiative's philosophy of preparing EdD graduates to improve their effectiveness in the practice of education leadership as scholar practitioners. During 2009, the faculty redesigned the EdD in Educational Leadership to be renamed the Executive EdD in Educational Leadership.

Program data and student data within this chapter were gathered by the authors separately over time. Assertions are supported by program artifacts that includes agendas, minutes, surveys, and available doctoral student data gathered over the four-year time period from design through the writing of this chapter. Much of the data were part of a three-year evaluation of the newly redesigned program's implementation and an Executive EdD in Educational Leadership student's dissertation in practice (Marsh, 2013). The planned data gathering for improvement and accountability is supported by the European University Association's recent publication, *Quality Assurance in Doctoral Education—results of the ARDE project* (Byrne, Jorgensen, & Loukkola, 2013) who advocate for program accountability aligned with the institution's priorities that includes such measures as time until graduation, progress in the program, and career advancements.

Cohort One began the redesigned program of study in August 2010. The number of applications (56) for the first cohort exceeded all expectations and more acceptable applicants (35) than faculty thought were desirable applied for the first cohort and therefore faculty admitted 26. The mean Graduate Record Exam (GRE) score total was 1087 and the mean undergraduate Grade Point Average was 3.74 on a 4-point scale for Cohort One. Two members of the cohort received their first graduate degrees (master's degree) from private institutions, three received the first graduate degrees from a for-profit institution, two received their first graduate degrees from research universities not in Florida, and the remainder received their first graduate degrees from one of the four research universities in Florida (University of Florida, Florida State University, University of South Florida, University of Central Florida).

Other demographic data on this cohort can be reviewed in Table 2.1 and Table 2.2. The cohort began with 26 students, the majority of whom were Caucasian. There were three African Americans, one Asian American, and three Hispanics in the cohort. Students were almost evenly divided between males and females.

The first cohort's professional experiences at the time of enrollment were varied. Eleven out of the 24 who completed this survey item had between 11 to 20 years of education service at the time of enrollment. Seventeen were school or school district administrators and eight were in instructional positions that were classified as non-administrative. Two of the eight were classroom teachers with ambitions of moving into school administration and eventually executive level positions.

Table 2.1 Cohort One demographics (n=26)

Demographic	%	f
Ethnicity		
African American	12	3
Asian American	4	1
Hispanic	12	3
Caucasian	72	19
Gender		
Male	46	12
Female	54	14

Table 2.2 Cohort One employment at time of enrollment in 2010 (n=26)

Enrollment Variable	%	f
Professional experience at enrollment (Yrs.)		
1–10	20	5
11–20	42	11
21–30	23	6
Greater than 30	8	2
Not indicated	8	2
Position at time of enrollment		
Classroom teacher	8	2
Teacher leader, instructional coach	23	6
Assistant principal	35	9
Principal	23	6
School district administrator	8	2
Not indicated	4	1

The role of Critical Friends as advisors, facilitators, and confidants to reflect on questions and challenges that emerged during the redesign, implementation, and refinement processes are explored in this chapter. Critical Friends provide a lens for objective feedback and reflection (Costa & Kallick, 1993) by those not directly involved in a context, but in the case of this college, membership in CPED could have been limiting if the consortium served as the only source of Critical Friends. By extending the role of Critical Friends beyond colleagues in CPED institutions to colleagues in non-CPED institutions across the United States and internationally to colleagues in the UK Council on Graduate Education, and in disciplines other than education (business, nursing, physical therapy), more varied perspectives have been considered. Critical Friends beyond the United States assisted in helping faculty think beyond the parameters of nationalism that might have been limiting (Shahjahan & Kezar, 2013). Educational leadership faculty and doctoral students have been well served by outreach to Critical Friends, especially during program implementation. The local prekindergarten through twelfth grade education community also had influence on program design and implementation, and hence deserve acknowledgment for the program's success. Extending the Critical Friends concept is discussed as a strategy to assure objectivity in input that is appropriate to a specific context. Broadening the Critical Friends concept to the education community that includes school district leaders, EdD in Educational Leadership program graduates, university administrators external to the program, and EdD students may assure protection against input only from a single like-minded group. The broader education community members are long-term stakeholders in this doctoral program's success and related workplace outcomes. The role of Critical Friends in its broadest interpretation in the Executive EdD in Educational Leadership program design, implementation, and refinement are shared, along with challenges that emerged and how they were resolved.

Results of the design and implementation of the Executive EdD in Educational Leadership are provided as support for the identified reform strategies. The Critical Friends concept is a viable innovation strategy for the development and implementation of doctoral programs.

Role of CPED Critical Friends

CPED convenings took place twice yearly and included focused discussions on curriculum, faculty change processes, and particularly what was working well in various institutions related to EdD design and redesign. Through conversations and presentations that related success strategies, organizational components, and potential pitfalls, the redesign lead was assisted in being strategic with redesign and implementation. As in any forum, faculty and administrators represent their institutions and programs in the most positive manner, even when programs have challenges with processes and people. The ability to have authentic conversations and to read between the lines was helpful in determining the best decisions for the unique UCF context.

One of the consistent questions voiced at gatherings of CPED Critical Friends was the question of how to be credible with students who are to be scholar practitioners, when the faculty are scholars with limited or no experience as practitioners (Taylor & Storey,

2013; Storey, Bryant, Fulmer, Hawley, Iceman-Sands, Scheurich, Shakeshaft, & Taylor, 2009). A number of the institutions addressed this challenge with the engagement of adjunct faculty or practitioners in various roles to supplement the scholarly knowledge of full-time faculty. UCF's educational leadership faculty had a long-standing agreement that full-time faculty would have been successful leaders at the principal and school district levels, and faculty agreed that those who joined the unit in the future would meet the same expectation. CPED Critical Friends may not have had a similar practice in the selection of full-time faculty, but in this particular UCF EdD program the doctoral students expect that those who teach the courses, have also been successful in similar professional work.

As the lead for the development of the CPED aligned, EdD created timelines and plans, she chose to consult with CPED Critical Friends on program requirements, curriculum, and the capstone experience possibilities. Critical Friends shared course sequences and delivery models that ranged from traditional-sounding courses to co-taught integrated courses, such as those at Virginia Commonwealth University. Syllabi, relevant readings, and program artifacts from Critical Friends, particularly those at Peabody College at Vanderbilt University, the University of Southern California, and the University of Maryland, were shared with UCF educational leadership faculty to heighten awareness of the diverse curriculum and capstone models being implemented across the United States. Of particular interest were the inquiry and research course syllabi. If the capstone was to change from the traditional dissertation, then it was inherent that the courses leading to the capstone experience had to change first.

In discussion with Critical Friends, it was learned that although the course titles may have remained constant, content and philosophy may have changed. The reality is that universities are bureaucracies with parameters within which program change takes place. An example is the Florida Department of Education Course Code Directory that lists approved course titles that must be used by state affiliated institutions, and therefore traditional-sounding titles may obscure the changes that take place within the context of course delivery. The same holds true of the capstone experience. If a university only recognizes the traditional dissertation, as happened at a CPED colleague institution, then that is what it will be called and the capstone will meet the expectations of the university guide and the designee who monitors acceptance of the final product.

A redesign retreat for UCF educational leadership faculty was planned for August 13–14, 2009, to consider program related data, practices of other institutions, and improvements that might enhance program effectiveness. The UCF redesign lead chose to invite a retreat facilitator from Peabody College at Vanderbilt University, who was not a CPED member but whose EdD program reflected the desired philosophy. The two had engaged in substantive conversation at CPED convenings during which the Vanderbilt EdD model was shared. The facilitator's experience with program design and deep conceptual understanding assisted in thinking of possibilities for redesign among the educational leadership faculty. Although the Critical Friend, who facilitated the planning retreat, was not met with 100 percent acceptance, the strength of the facilitation led to initial agreement on the draft redesign to be renamed the Executive EdD in Educational Leadership (Taylor & Storey, 2011).

The variation in capstone experiences among CPED colleague institutions was extensive. Some were designed as group or collaborative team research while others were conducted by individuals. Some who participated in collaborative team research shared that individual efforts were not up to the expectation of either the other team members or faculty when the research was collaborative. Within a team there may have been resentment since all in the team received the same credit for the final product.

Action research and case studies were included in the range of capstone options of Critical Friends. Research for clients or education organizations was one of the most common capstone models and clearly linked theory to practice, potentially making a research contribution to the education industry. Some CPED Critical Friends shared that they continued to follow the dissertation model for reasons that included university policy.

UCF educational leadership faculty selected the consultation approach or client-based research that would be scholarly and completed on a complex problem of practice identified by an education organization (Taylor & Storey, 2013, 2011). As UK Critical Friends, Costley and Flint (2011), eloquently advocated, the professional doctorate research should take *place in the practice, rather than on the practice* to have great value for graduates as they are in the workplace during the doctoral program and plan to continue for the immediate future. The faculty's belief was that Executive EdD in Educational Leadership graduates would make authentic impact on their work places and be recognized by high-level decision makers for doing so, thus advancing their careers (Lee, Brennan, & Green, 2009).

ROLE OF THE EDUCATION COMMUNITY

While CPED Critical Friends and Critical Friends in other institutions had valuable perspectives, every institution's context is unique as is that of the College of Education at UCF, serving seven diverse school districts representing approximately 750,000 prekindergarten through twelfth grade public school students. School district enrollment ranged from 7,500 to 184,000. During the August 13, 2009, day of planning the faculty decided that the target population for the doctoral program would be educators living within an hour's drive of the university. According to Marsh (2013) 75 percent of the doctoral students lived within a 30-mile radius of UCF's main campus, confirming that the target population was accurate. Therefore, alignment with local school district and education organization needs was essential for the program to have value in the practice.

The redesign lead extends the concept of Critical Friends beyond those in higher education because of the belief that university, college, and program contexts are one of the most important considerations. In this specific context, educational leadership faculty members have reciprocal and ongoing Critical Friends relationships with school and school district leaders that are grounded in their similar professional preparation, career experiences, and commitment to the education profession. Their commonalities lead to mutual respect and trust as Critical Friends (Swaffield, 2005). Educational leadership faculty members are invited by executive leaders to provide input on organizational, political, and curricular issues in the surrounding school districts and at the school level by principals. Formal participation as a committee or task force member is common, informal phone calls or meetings for confidential feedback and to benefit from the other's thinking is a regular occurrence. Three of the seven local school district superintendents earned the EdD in Educational Leadership from the UCF College of Education, as have many of their executive staff (e.g., area superintendents, deputy superintendents, associate superintendents), principals, and assistant principals. When these relationships have been developed over a number of years and through diverse situations, the resulting Critical Friend relationships are an important consideration in program development and implementation.

With this information as background, the school district executive leaders, EdD in Educational Leadership graduates, UCF administrators external to the program, and new doctoral student cohorts were included as Critical Friends, whose input and perceptions were important to consider. Recent graduates were sources of up-to-date perceptions and current doctoral students were sources of ongoing perceptions of curriculum, content, and needs of future executive leaders, as they also served in leadership positions.

Curriculum Decisions

There were important curriculum content decisions to be made. Which content from the EdD in Educational Leadership program should be continued and should new courses be developed? As recommended by Sparks and Waits (2011) input from employers should be sought so that the outcome is aligned with employers' and industry needs. Input from the final two EdD in Educational Leadership cohorts and local school district executive leaders was solicited by asking them to consider a series of curriculum content options from the previous doctoral program and rate each on a Likert scale from 1 extremely important, 2 very important, 3 minimally important, and 4 not important. The ratings' range of very important to extremely important was 43 to 86 percent for content of the core courses (Taylor & Storey, 2011). Respondents were also asked to answer the open ended item "What knowledge and skills will executive leaders of the future need to know and be able to do?"

Using this confidential data, the educational leadership faculty answered the question, "What will future executive leaders need to know and be able to do?" Doctoral program learning outcomes were identified and grouped to form course learning outcomes. The courses were grouped to become content strands: serving students' social, emotional, and educational needs; political governance influences; learning and accountability; human resource development in education organizations; professional leadership in organizations; research; and doctoral field study. As a result of this process, the faculty's decision was to include the courses that were perceived by local executive school district leaders and recent cohorts to be highly applicable to leadership practices of future executive leaders: Organizational Theory, Leadership in Education, Program Planning and Evaluation, Political Governance Influences, and Advanced Legal Studies in Education. Further input from the same Critical Friends resulted in the development of new courses: Community Outreach; Dynamics of Children, Families, and Communities for Education Leaders; Human Resource Development in Education Organizations; Instructional Leadership; and Learning and Accountability. These new courses addressed the needs identified by Critical Friends related to the community's changed demographics and issues affecting learning (urbanization, poverty, family structure, immigration, language, educational equity) and are documented in UCF Curriculum Committee Approval program change documents as well as in prior publications (Taylor & Storey, 2011).

Although the Executive EdD in Educational Leadership was designed to serve the local education community, program learning outcomes reflect national and international prekindergarten through twelfth grade students' learning needs as identified in *For Each and Every Child—A Strategy for Education Equity and Excellence* (Department of Education, 2013) and *Urban Education: A Model for Leadership and Policy* (Gallagher, Goodyear, Brewer, & Rueda, 2012). As executive educational leaders they will be prepared to assume national and international positions with awareness of issues beyond the local context while being well prepared for the local context.

Superintendents and other executive school district leaders were asked to weigh in on the value of the dissertation. Their responses were consistent: the dissertation process was valuable. They wrote that the dissertation's value would be enhanced if the research focus would be on research questions relevant to their school districts' needs (Taylor & Storey, 2011).

After the redesign draft was completed, the same Critical Friends from the school districts were invited to attend an Advocacy Breakfast. The purpose was to show them how their input had been used and to gain their advocacy for the redesigned doctoral program. During this breakfast their input was summarized and the draft program redesign was explained, connecting their input to the program components, including the client-based research. Each was asked for written feedback and if each would be willing to serve as a client for the proposed capstone research, to which they all responded positively.

Research Course Sequence

Most problematic in development of the new courses was the doctoral research sequence. Facility with accessing and using data to inform decisions, policy, and practice was a concept that faculty determined to be essential for enhancing the research curriculum. As noted by Greenburg and Walsh (2012) data-informed decision making as a concept is part of educator preparation curriculums, but generally students do not engage in the application of data-informed decision making for policy development and policy decisions. Mandinach and Gummer (2013) identify that leadership preparation should address data literacy that includes developing the data vision, planning for data structures, and distributed leadership for effective data-informed decision making. The new courses were intended to address these research and data literacy needs of those who practice leadership in education.

The new sequence has courses named Research in Educational Leadership 1, Research in Education 2, and Research in Education Leadership 3. These simple titles distinguish the sequence from other doctoral research courses and identify them as specific to the Executive EdD in Educational Leadership. As the designated research experts in the College of Education, research program faculty voiced that they did not believe that educational leadership faculty should drive the courses' content. Although the research program faculty collaborated with educational leadership faculty and a local school district research designee, there was tension during course development similar to experiences shared by CPED Critical Friends. To ameliorate the tension, it was agreed that research as a program unit would receive productivity credit for the courses. Most important was that the educational leadership faculty would retain control over course content and selection of the program's research course instructors.

Although the educational leadership faculty collaborated with university research faculty and a local school district research expert on content for the new three-semester course syllabi to ensure application to the field while remaining scholarly, the actual delivery by well-qualified university research faculty did not align completely with these intentions. The delivery remained more theoretical than applicable for practicing school leaders. The second research course was taught by a research administrator in a local urban school district who had previously been a middle school principal. Due to her knowledge of research, school level leadership, and school district level leadership the application of research concepts met the faculty's and students' expectations, but did not solve the longer term question of consistent implementation of a scholar practitioner appropriate research sequence by full-time faculty.

Serendipitous to discussion of this issue, the executive administrator of research, accountability, and assessment of a large urban school district announced his retirement, presenting the opportunity to engage him as the full-time instructor whose responsibility would be to refine and deliver the three-semester research course sequence. With a PhD in research from the University of Virginia, tenure early in his career as research faculty at the University of Florida, and school district executive leadership experience the ideal faculty member was found. The engagement of this educational leadership research faculty member met with approval from the research program faculty, alleviating their concerns regarding preparation of the doctoral students in the area of research. He has continued to refine the research curriculum and the delivery of these research courses, exceeding the expectations of both faculty and students.

Client-based Field Study

With options to move away from a dissertation as the capstone research experience, the educational leadership faculty chose a client-based field study model to address research topics that would emanate from executive leaders in the local and state education community. The title "field study" was selected since the EdD in Educational Leadership had used the approved course for dissertation proposal development. Although shortsighted, the faculty thought it would be best to avoid the course design and approval process required at university and state levels for new courses, particularly where the capstone research was concerned. The concept of working toward mutually beneficial outcomes by doctoral students researching complex issues identified by executive leaders and developing recommendations for potential solutions contributes to the improvement of education as well as to the scholar practitioners' contribution to their workplaces (Bryk, Gomez, & Grunow, 2010; Garber, Creech, Epps, Bishop, & Chapman, 2010; Sparks & Waits, 2011). This process aligns with the expectation that professional doctoral graduates develop knowledge, enhance their practice, and enhance the practice of those around them (Lee, Brennan, & Green, 2009). Substantive partnerships during the research component of the Executive EdD in Educational Leadership, naturally, led to the expected outcomes of improved resources, policies, and pedagogy (Morgan-Flemming, Simpson, Curtis, & Hull, 2010). This approach seemed like a win-win solution for doctoral students and the education community, including doctoral students' employers.

In retrospect, during the first decade of the twenty-first century, the UCF Educational Leadership EdD students had encountered increasing difficulty in getting school districts' approvals to gather data, either because the school districts saw the data collection as a distraction for teachers and leaders who were under stringent accountability requirements or that research requests represented time and financial commitment on the part of school and/or school district employees. The faculty had learned to avoid pitfalls (like clients influencing findings) in client-based research from their Critical

Friends, but they encountered other unanticipated challenges that the client-based approach was intended to eliminate.

Theoretically the client-based strategy sounded like it would work, but educational leadership faculty learned that it takes commitment from not only the client, but also those who have access to people and data needed for doctoral students to complete their studies. While the client-based research concept worked well for most students, challenges emerged for some. A few specific ones follow and reflect the dependency on data management systems.

- Data had not been retained or was in hard copy only and data had to be hand entered.
- The school district client wanted to maintain control over the data or access to participants.
- Since researchers were school district employees, access to confidential information required unusually complex coding processes.
- Complex problems that were presented with a sense of urgency for rapid identification of potential solutions, diminished in importance to the clients as new issues emerged.

When data had not been retained, such as achievement data for specific projects or groups, modifications of research questions and methods were necessitated to accommodate the available data or to gather data from knowledgeable others. Restrictions on access to data and people resulted in limited opportunities to invite the target populations to participate and students had difficulty accessing the target populations. The occasional delays in the approvals for studies to be conducted and limited access to data and target populations, limited timeliness of data gathering and most probably negatively impacted response rates. Those who have chaired numerous dissertations know that in any doctoral program these kinds of inconveniences arise and part of the advisement process is working through methodological challenges and documenting the resulting study limitations. The irony is that the client-based approach was intended to eliminate these kinds of detours and redesign experiences.

Education Community: Within UCF, Graduates, and Doctoral Students

Equally as challenging as accessing data and participants was the creation of understanding of the client-based field study by university employees external to the educational leadership faculty, EdD in Educational leadership graduates, and doctoral students. As the name for the capstone changed from dissertation to client-based field study, there was an assumption by various parties that the research would have less rigor and not be of quality as were the dissertations in the EdD in Educational Leadership prior to the redesign. Although the Executive EdD Handbook explained the expectations and process for the research, there were attributions and references made to the redesigned program that the research might be collaborative, might be action research, or might be a project. While these descriptors are not necessarily negative in various university cultures, the implication in the UCF context was that Executive EdD in Educational Leadership students would not follow the protocols of other UCF doctoral students, graduates might not be recognized at the university level, and the program would suffer from the perception that it lacked rigor by the internal UCF education community, as well as the external education community, including alumni of the EdD in Educational Leadership. One of the concerns was that the change in name to client-based field study sounded similar to nonresearch university educational leadership program capstone experiences. That perception was not acceptable to UCF educational leadership faculty, nor to graduates of the EdD in Educational Leadership.

Lack of clarity on expectations by doctoral students and some university faculty and staff came by way of using the field study language instead of the traditional comfortable language of dissertation. Those who did not understand the field study expectations had no experience with research and dissertations; even so they could not conceptualize that doctoral research by a name other than dissertation would be meaningful and rigorous. Rumors abounded and misinformation was shared. EdD in Educational Leadership graduates asked, "How will this change reflect on my degree?" and "Will it have a negative effect on my degree's value?" As a result of lack of respect for the title and negative inferences, the refinement to change the title to dissertation in practice took place by Cohort One's third year in the program and was approved by the UCF Graduate Curriculum Council on October 8, 2012. Cohort One and their research would be afforded the respect deserved within UCF, the College of Education, and in the broader education community. Graduates of EdD in Educational Leadership program responded positively to the new designation and its intent that the research would address complex problems of leadership practice.

Examples of topics identified by executive school district leaders and researched by UCF Cohort One Executive EdD in Educational Leadership students include the following:

- extent equity and access to excellence was achieved 2003–2011,
- value of prekindergarten experience and impact on K-12 achievement,
- alignment of summer intervention reading camp with elementary and middle school students' data based reading needs, and
- an urban school district's Preparing New Principal's Program (PNPP) components value as perceived by program completers, supervisors of completers, and the superintendent's senior staff.

While each individual completed an individual dissertation in practice, there were topics whose scopes were broad enough for different students to investigate a strand of that topic. For instance, the summer reading camp alignment study was actually two studies—one elementary and one middle school. The study on the PNPP of a school district had three individual studies: perceptions of completers, perceptions of supervisors of completers, and perceptions of the senior school district administrators, which yielded important information for the school district decision maker to consider. (School district Level II Principal Certification programs are authorized by Florida School Board Rule 6A-5.081).

Current doctoral students are also part of the education community and have valuable insight into what is working and what needs reconsideration in their program. As Cohort One proceeded through coursework faculty listened to their feedback and made curriculum adjustments accordingly. Critical Friends are in various relationships to those receiving the input and not necessarily in the same type of position. When working with doctoral students, it may be helpful to remember that they are in a subordinate position as a student and at the same time may be in a superior position in their careers, such as a school district superintendent, university administrator, education organization executive, private industry executive, and so on.

Already mentioned was the lack of satisfaction with the initial research curriculum and delivery that was modified during the first cohort's coursework. Two other courses received less than acceptable feedback (Learning and Accountability and, Dynamics of Children, Families, and Communities for Education Leaders). As a result, these were discontinued and essential content related to data-informed decision making and leading urban learning were infused into other courses—Community Outreach and Instructional Leadership. The six credit hours in the deleted courses were added to the dissertation in practice to meet the minimum 15 dissertation hours required for recognition by university policy for a total minimum of 54 credit hours beyond the master's degree. Soliciting, listening to, and acting on current students' feedback to refine the program for cohorts that followed, represents the commitment that the faculty have to students as Critical Friends, to the program meeting their learning needs, and to them as graduates. They are or will be executive educational leaders who will continue to influence recruitment and the program's viability for many cohorts to come.

IMPLEMENTATION OUTCOMES

UCF admitted 26 students in 2010 to the first Executive EdD in Educational Leadership cohort. Data were gathered via surveys from the first cohort and the response rate was 100 percent. The initial survey addressed, "Why did you select this doctoral program?" The survey items identified by the stems in the left column of Table 2.3 were confidentially rated: 1=not important, 2=a little unimportant, 3=neither important nor unimportant, 4=somewhat important, and 5=most important. Interestingly, these students wanted face-to-face instruction although the growing availability of online doctoral program options were available. They liked the guaranteed program structure, assured course sequence, and client-based research. Confirming the value of the clear structure, Byrne, Jorgensen, and Loukkola (2013) suggested that doctoral students should have transparent structures with clarity of expectations in an inclusive research community. Cohort One was drawn to the program by reputations

Table 2.3 Reasons for applying to the program: Cohort One (n=26)

I applied to the program because . . .	M (0–5.0)
Ready to begin doctoral studies	4.0
Like program design	4.7
UCF's reputation	3.9
Wanted face-to-face instruction	4.4
Faculty's reputation	4.0
UCF Ed. Leadership program reputation	3.9
Client-based field study	4.5
Course location	3.9
Expenses compared to other institutions	3.6
Liked cohort model	4.6
Structured sequence program of study	4.7
What I think I'll learn	4.4
To be an effective leader	4.4
Want to be superintendent	2.5
Thought it would be easy	1.4

of UCF, the educational leadership faculty, and the program (EdD in Educational Leadership). Although few identified that they wanted to be a superintendent, there were those who did indicate so and during the program, one of them was appointed as superintendent of an A-rated school district of approximately 60,000 diverse students.

Cohort members were asked if they applied because of the perception that the program would be easy, to which they responded that it was not the case. This item may seem out of place, but it was purposefully included due to the time faculty had spent wrestling with the perception of rigor during program development and early implementation.

Persistence

As mentioned in the chapter's introduction, Cohort One began in August of 2010 with 26 members. Within the first academic year one of the members accepted an international position and discontinued coursework. As of the eighth semester in the program, the 22 of the remaining members were on track to graduate in the ninth semester, which would be an 85 percent graduation rate in three years. Several lagged behind the others in the dissertation in practice progress and may not graduate until the tenth or even eleventh semester, which equates to 96 percent graduation rate in four years. These individuals have had career advancements that are demanding, new additions to their families, and/or while in the program have generally completed their work in less than a timely manner, although acceptable in the final analysis each semester.

To put the graduation rate and timeframe in context, readers should know that UCF measures graduation of doctoral programs at the end of the fourth year. This is why the program was designed for three years with time remaining for those whose studies or other intervening variables presented the need for more time. EdD in Educational Leadership data for 1997–2006 preceding the redesign indicated that at the end of the fourth year, the graduation rate was 40 percent (Poole, 2009). At the seventh year the graduation rate increased to 74 percent, which was high for doctoral programs at UCF (Poole, 2009). UCF allows students seven years from admission to graduate in a doctoral program.

Cohort One's Perceptions

The extent to which the cohort perceived that the redesigned EdD program met their expectations was important to the educational leadership faculty. After completing Milestone One, a whitepaper that required analysis, synthesis, and application of course content and research experienced during the first two semesters of coursework, they completed a confidential survey. The confidential survey asked the cohort to rate each item 1=disagree strongly, 2=disagree somewhat, 3=agree somewhat, and 4=agree strongly. Means for each of the four items was high at 3.70 on the 4-point scale. The response rate was 92 percent and data can be seen in Table 2.4.

A few of the hoped-for student learning outcomes were that doctoral candidates would frame issues differently than before entering the program, that they would understand the value of considering different variables, and that they would impact their workplace more than before the doctoral experience. Related open-ended questions were asked, responses of which were confidential and coded for anonymity. When asked how participation in the doctoral program had impacted their workplace outcomes, overwhelmingly the most common response was related to their decision-making processes. Out of the 24 (92%) who responded to the item, 24 (100%) indicated that they had learned strategies for better decision making and/or that they were more confident in their decision making. Representative examples include: "It [EdD program] has given me a research-based approach to examining our practices" (R1.22) and "I have become a savvy consumer of research and more aware of the impact my decisions make on my school and the students in my school" (R1.15).

> The variety of courses in the EdD has proven to stimulate my thinking in a variety of ways. As an instructional leader I now look at situations a little bit differently, making decisions and knowing the theory and practice behind the decisions. I have become a better communicator, servant leader, and educated student since my enrollment in the program. (R1.18)

Table 2.4 Cohort One end of year 1: extent to which the program met their needs (n=23)

Item	Stem	Mean (0–4.0)
1	The curriculum is relevant to my work.	3.70
2	The quality of the expectations is high.	3.70
3	The course requirements are reasonable.	3.70
4	I feel stimulated and challenged by the curriculum.	3.70

Source: From "A study of the implementation of the Executive EdD in Educational Leadership at the University of Central Florida 2012–2013: A professional practice doctorate" by N. L. Marsh, Unpublished dissertation, University of Central Florida, 2013, Reprinted with permission.

Added also, was that they had learned from course content and from student colleagues to be better leaders and decision makers. "The experiences of my classmates and their perceptions on issues have made a significant impact on how I think about issues and make decisions" (R1.22) and "I approach problems with a greater emphasis on understanding the data and asking the right questions" (R1.15).

No educational leadership doctoral cohort would be successful unless the political environment and education factors beyond the local context were addressed, along with how to maneuver within the political environment and considering other factors. Confidential comments like those that follow reflect doctoral students' learning outcomes. "I have become better prepared to work through the politics I encounter in the field of education" (R1.12) and "It has given me advance information regarding changes from the state and federal government" (R1.22). In conclusion a student expressed, "I am more knowledgeable about the field of education as a whole, not just as it relates to my place of employment" (R1.6). Faculty and students believe that participation in the three-year program was related to the 15 promotions that Cohort One doctoral candidates received as their leadership reflected increased knowledge, skill, and confidence as educational leaders. From the students' responses it appears that the Executive EdD in Educational Leadership program successfully integrated research, theory, and leadership practice as professional doctorate programs should (Scott, Brown, Lunt, & Thorne, 2004). What was learned from Critical Friends in the process assisted in an immediately successful program.

REFINEMENTS AND CONTINUAL IMPROVEMENT

The redesign, implementation, and evaluation process that includes Critical Friends in important roles has been ongoing for almost four years at the time of this writing. In spring 2013, the UCF Educational Leadership faculty hosted the "Executive EdD Research Symposium: A Celebration of Excellence" to honor the success of Cohort One and showcase findings of the dissertations in practice. A formal printed invitation was mailed to the cohort, school district superintendents, executive level school district leaders, and their dissertation in practice clients. The response card included recommended names for recruitment to be in future Executive EdD in Educational Leadership cohorts. These Critical Friends' ongoing engagement is essential for the program to continue to flourish.

The evening celebration began with a reception and research symposium of doctoral candidates sharing their dissertations in practice on interactive boards in an open gallery with school district representatives, the cohorts that are following them, and master's level educational leadership students. After the gallery walk and celebration of research, attendees gathered for the formal portion of the evening to recognize Critical Friends' contributions to the program's development and to Cohort One's success. In addition to recognizing the school district executive leaders, the evening included special recognition of the 14 dissertation in practice clients who represented five public school districts and one private parochial school district. Three diverse and successful educational leadership doctoral alumni were invited to share perspectives on the future of executive leaders and to honor the doctoral candidates: Mr. Walter Griffin, Superintendent of Seminole County Public Schools, Florida; Dr. William Gorden, II, area superintendent of Orange County Public Schools, Florida; Dr. Peter Gorman, executive vice president, Education Services Amplify, Education Division Newscorporation, former superintendent of Charlotte-Mecklenburg Schools, North Carolina (Broad Prize for Urban Education). An attractive keepsake program included each doctoral candidate's name and earned degrees, Dissertation in Practice title, client, and a short Dissertation in Practice abstract. Within this section of the evening's program it was made clear that the Executive EdD in Educational Leadership doctoral candidates were important Critical Friends as one speaker referenced his participation in the development and implementation process. The cohort of 25 doctoral candidates had earned 26 *other* UCF degrees, many of them in educational leadership at the master's or education specialist levels. The value of Critical Friends should be recognized and by doing so with strategic events, like the "EdD Research Symposium: A Celebration of Excellence," the faculty are building a culture through ritual and symbols (Bolman & Deal, 2008) that is important for continued program support by the education community, master's level students as future cohort members, and effectiveness.

Refinement of the program is a continual process regardless of the location in Florida, in another CPED institution, or elsewhere around the globe. Faculty members continue to change and their individual expertise is reflected in the program and in the scholar practitioner focus of each course. Similarly, education as a profession is in a political environment of accountability that has forced close introspection and inspection of program effectiveness on the workplace impact of graduates (Byrne, Jorgensen, & Loukkola, 2013; Sparks & Waits, 2011; Astin & Astin, 2000). These political trends will continue to create a sense of urgency for doctoral programs to respond to needs of the local education community as Critical Friends, while seeking input of Critical Friends in other institutions. The Executive EdD in Educational Leadership design, implementation, and refinement process demonstrates that embracing critical friends in various roles is a strategy for innovation resulting in positive outcomes.

The authors believe that doctoral programs, which are successful and respected by the target population, are responsive to their professional learning needs. As such, recommendations for other program leaders to consider include expansion of Critical Friends to the wide net of professionals who will provide accurate and authentic input, including doctoral students. Context drives who the Critical Friends might be. In large universities, such as UCF, this means other programs within the College of Education and other colleges beyond the College of Education. Perspectives of Critical Friends along with data related to the program's goals can provide a foundation for objective programmatic decision making.

REFERENCES

Astin, A. W., & Astin, H. S. (2000). *Leadership reconsidered: Engaging higher education in real change.* Battle Creek, MI: Kellogg Foundation.
Bolman, L. G., & Deal, T. E. (2008.) Reframing *organizations: Artistry, choice, and leadership* (4th ed.). San Francisco, CA: John Wiley & Sons.
Bryk, A. S., Gomez, L. M., & Grunow, A. (2010). *Getting ideas into action: Building networked improvement communities in education.* Stanford, CA: Carnegie Foundation for the Advancement of Teaching.
Byrne, J., Jorgensen, T., & Loukkola, T. (2013). *Quality assurance in doctoral education—results of the ARDE project.* Brussels, Belgium: European University Association.
Carnegie Project on the Education Doctorate. (2008) www.cpedinitiative.org
Costa, A. L., & Kallick, B. (1993). Through the lens of a critical friend. *Educational Leadership, 51*(2), 49–51.
Costley, C., & Flint, K. (April 21, 2011). Experience of being in-the-world of practice for doctoral researchers and their research. Paper presented at the International Conference on the Professional Doctorate: Edinburgh, Scotland.
Department of Education. (2013). *For each and every child—A strategy for education equity and excellence.* Washington, DC: US Department of Education.
Gallagher, K. S., Goodyear, D., Brewer, R. J., & Rueda, R. (2010). *Urban education: A model for leadership and policy.* New York: Routledge.

Garber, M., Creech, B., Epps, W., Bishop, M., & Chapman, S. (2010). The archway partnership: A higher education outreach platform for community engagement. *Journal of Higher Education Outreach and Engagement, 14*(3): 69–81. Retrieved from ERIC database. (EJ905564)

Greenburg, J., & Walsh, K. (May 2012) *What teacher preparation programs teach about K-12 assessment: A review.* Washington, DC: National Council on Teacher Quality.

Lee, M., Brennan, L., & Green, B. (2009). Re-imagining doctoral education: Professional practice doctorates and beyond. *Higher Education Research and Development, 28*(3): 275–287.

Mandinach, E. B., & Gummer, E. S. (2013). A systematic view of implementing data literacy in educator preparation. *Educational Researcher, 42*(1): 30–37.

Marsh, N. L. (2013). A study of the implementation of the Executive EdD in Educational Leadership at the University of Central Florida 2012–2013: A professional practice doctorate. Orlando, FL: University of Central Florida. Unpublished dissertation.

Morgan-Flemming, B., Simpson, D. J., Curtis, K. B., & Hull, W. (2010). Learning through partnership: Four narratives. *Teacher Education Quarterly, 37*(3): 63–79. Retrieved from ERIC database (EJ902709).

Poole, M. (2009). *UCF progress to degree study.* Orlando, FL: University of Central Florida.

Scott, D., Brown, A., Lunt, I., & Thorne, L. (2004). *Professional doctorates: Integrating professional and academic knowledge.* Berkshire, UK: Open University Press.

Sparks, E., & Waits, M. J. (March 2011). *Degrees for what jobs? Raising expectations for universities and colleges in a global economy.* Washington, DC: National Governors Association (NGA) Center for Best Practices.

Storey, V. A., Bryant, M., Fulmer, C., Hawley, W., Iceman-Sands, D., Scheurich, J., Shakeshaft, C., & Taylor, R. T. (2009). Finding voice among critical friends: Staying faithful to Shulman's vision of the scholar practitioner EdD. Paper presented at the annual meeting of the University Council for Educational Administration Convention 2009: Anaheim, CA.

Swaffield, S. (2005). No sleeping partners: Relationships between head teachers and critical friends. *School Leadership and Management, 25*(1), 43–57.

Taylor, R. T., & Storey, V. A. (July–September 2011). Designing and implementing the professional doctorate in education: Comparing experiences of a small independent university and a large public university. *International Journal of Educational Leadership Preparation, 6*(3) http://www.ncpea-publications.org

Taylor, R. T., & Storey, V. A. (2013). Leaders, critical friends, and the education community: Enhancing effectiveness of the professional practice doctorate. *Journal of Applied Research in Higher Education, 5*(1), 84–94.

Shahjahan, R. A., & Kezar, A. J. (Jan/Feb 2013). Beyond the "national container": Addressing methodological nationalism in higher education research. *Educational Researcher, 42*(1), 20–29.

CHAPTER 3

Critical Friends Groups from Afar: Can Long Distance Relationships Work?

Alisa Belzer

Critical Friends Groups (CFGs) are intended to promote learning through feedback and critique in collaborative groups of trusted colleagues (Bambino, 2002; Costa & Kallick, 1993). Much of the literature on CFGs in education assumes school-based interactions that occur on a regular basis among dyads or groups of up to 12 that are aimed at improving instructional practice. While specific definitions, formats, and activities vary, CFGs tend to be data driven and discussions are structured systematically through the use of protocols (National School Reform Faculty, 2012). A key element of successful CFGs, emphasized repeatedly in the literature, is the establishment of trust among participants (Bambino, 2002; Costa & Kallick, 1993; Swaffield, 2005), which develops when members take the time to understand each other's work contexts, problems and challenges, data presented, and when nonjudgmental, supportive, and yet honest feedback and critique are offered; (Costa & Kallick, 1993; Swaffield, 2005).

In this chapter, I suggest that CFGs have the flexibility to meet the needs of groups who do not meet under the typical conditions. However, simply adopting the language and activities typically associated with CFGs without fully considering the implications of atypical CFG work contexts may limit the benefits associated with them. In the context of The Carnegie Project on the Education Doctorate (CPED) (a consortium of universities who have committed to working together to reenvision and redesign the education doctorate (EdD), CPED website, 2013) the participants are loosely bound together by a common goal of redesigning their doctoral programs, meeting infrequently with inconsistent participation, and working on many different kinds of tasks using varied formats when they are together. CFG has potential among CPED members, but requires rethinking the format and procedures of a CFG in the context of the long distance relationships that define the nature of CPED member interaction.

While long distance CFGs present additional challenges to all parties involved, they are not necessarily ill-fated. Long distance CFGs have been successfully implemented to achieve positive outcomes. Knowles (2002) proposed that an e-learning environment coupled with innovative pedagogical practices could provide support for the relational and contextual learning association with CFGs, even without face-to-face interaction. Bozalek and Matthews (2009) provide qualitative support for the assertion that e-learning can be an effective medium for students to operate as Critical Friends. In these examples of e-learning, however, the primary area of concern isn't the frequency, consistency of membership, or diversity of tasks found in CPED, but only the method of communication across distances.

Faculty and students from CPED member universities have face-to-face convenings just two times a year, defining the relationship among members as primarily long distance. The structure of the convenings provides a context for CPED member institutions to engage in many key tasks relevant to reenvisioning and redesigning their doctoral programs and sustaining the consortium. There are many opportunities for learning and collaboration within CPED, particularly at convenings. However, these opportunities are not often built around giving and receiving informed critique based on the kind of deep familiarity and understanding of the challenges and problems of participants' program and university contexts associated with CFGs (Swaffield, 2005), even though the language of CFGs is sometimes invoked. By describing three kinds of activities that CPED has asked its members to engage in, I point to the challenges of creating CFGs when the community functions mostly through long distance relationships. These examples can raise questions about ways to stretch the form and function of CFGs to make them more effective even in long distance relationships.

Convenings as Gatherings of Critical Friends

The two-day CPED convenings, held fall and spring each year at locations that rotate among CPED university members, are the primary context for Critical Friends potentially to form working relationships;

much of the time together is spent in small groups working on a range of tasks across institutions. Smaller meetings also take place at the annual meetings of AERA and UCEA. Generally, one to three faculty and graduate students from each university in the consortium attend. However, the individuals that attend from each institution often vary from one meeting to the next. The specific tasks of convenings have shifted over the years of CPED's existence. At first they focused on developing understandings of design elements and establishing guiding principles. More recently, they have focused on deepening the work of redesign. Fundamentally, they are opportunities to develop common understandings of what it means to be a CPED-influenced EdD program and share and learn from other. These can be an important support in the process of reenvisioning, implementing, and engaging in continuous improvement of redesigned or new EdD programs.

Convening activities vary from meeting to meeting but have some common features. There are generally a few presentational sessions that are designed to transmit information and stimulate new thinking related generally to the EdD and current "hot topics" in the relevant fields. There are also interactive sessions in which faculty and graduate students facilitate discussion and sharing on topics relevant to the design of CPED-influenced EdD programs. There is at least one activity at every convening that collaboratively generates new knowledge about what it means to be a CPED-influenced EdD program. Much of this generative work is done in small groups, shared in the large group, synthesized by volunteers subsequent to the meetings, sent back to the group for feedback, and then posted to the CPED website. Topics at the most recent convening included the host university's dean discussing "key levers for change," how undergraduate engineering programs have addressed a problem of practice in the preparation of professional, student dissertation topics and experiences, balancing the EdD with the PhD, managing an accelerated degree process, program evaluation and continuous improvement, research preparation of "scholarly practitioners," and an assessment rubric for "dissertations in practice." The convening generally closes with a planning session that looks ahead to upcoming meetings and the future of the consortium.

The convening agendas have varied and evolved over the years primarily for two reasons: first, due to the recent addition of about 25 "Phase 2" institutions joining the original "Phase 1" institutions in the consortium; and second due to the developing maturity of CPED. As some issues and challenges are addressed, others emerge as programs implement new and diverse doctoral programs. The challenge in designing the convening agendas is to try to ensure that the needs of all member institutions are met while understanding that institutional needs may be very different depending on where they are in the design process and whether they are Phase 1 or Phase 2 institutions.

In an effort to meet these diverse needs, a "Critical Friend Session" was introduced at a recent convening focused on "signature pedagogy," one of the CPED design concepts. Participants were given a modified CFG protocol and two focusing questions to frame the discussion. In my small group, the process quickly broke down, perhaps due to a lack of training and experience among the participants. Time allocations were not adhered to, focusing questions were not the focus, substantive challenges were not addressed, and critique and feedback were not given. Instead, we heard in considerable detail about how one university has implemented signature pedagogy and the challenges they have experienced there. Participants asked many questions. A CFG protocol is designed to ensure that each Critical Friend has an equitable amount of time to interact with the group and to benefit from their support and advice. But on this occasion, the breakdown of CFG protocol meant that one member dominated the group and that Critical Friends did not have the opportunity to both give and receive critical feedback. In addition, the domination of the CFG by one institution meant that the conversation was neither substantive nor generative. What started out as a CFG quickly devolved into a sharing session. While the conversation had some value even if only as an example and a reminder of the importance and challenge of designing signature pedagogy, it seems unlikely to have yielded significant learning and change among group members.

Mentoring New Members as Critical Friends

CPED has recently expanded the consortium and doubled its membership. In an effort to effectively utilize the CPED network and speed-up the learning curve of new member universities, new members were matched with original CPED universities. After a "speed dating" type encounter at a convening (potential matches were narrowed down by CPED staff so that participants met each other from 3 to 4 universities), matches were made based on first, second, and third choices of mentors and mentees.

> The mentor-mentee relationship can function as a starting point for thoughts, questions and feedback as we continue to go through this

process. We envision mentors as those able to provide helpful suggestions to questions and concerns of their partner institution rooted in the experience of change within the mentor institution. As mentees go through unique changes within their own institutions, we expect the mentors will also learn much and continue to be challenged by this transformation. Finally, this relationship will allow for a smooth adjustment for new members to the notion of Critical Friends and sharing (remember how hesitant Phase I members were at first about sharing program information). Email correspondence from CPED staff, 2011.

Pairs were asked to interact with each other around specific tasks and topics on a monthly basis until the next convening (five months). This mentoring relationship, established as a Critical Friendship, had the potential to be the enactment of another CFG within the CPED consortium. However, this hope was not realized for me and my mentee.

Underpinning both CFGs and mentoring relationships is trust; at least as important is the time to establish it. However, our mentee university did not contact me and I did not contact them. I found that the demands of qualifying papers to read, a student admissions process to complete, transfer credits to review, a spring program retreat to design and facilitate, and a new student orientation to lead, as well as teaching and committee work, in spite of good intentions to do so, simply did not allow the time to develop a mentoring relationship through the assigned activities. Although they were meant to lead up to a face-to-face meeting at the next convening, the interaction there was not based on ongoing Critical Friends activities, and the fact that another faculty member attended the next convening (for the first and only time) meant that the mentoring relationship was temporarily transferred to her. She reported a productive conversation during which she responded to specific questions about how we are addressing challenges in our professional practice doctorate redesign; but this encounter did not contribute to the development of a long-term relationship built on trust needed for CFs to function well together.

Following this convening, there were no formal structures put in place for mentoring pairs to continue their work together, although there was time to meet again at a subsequent convening. Some pairs may be more conscientious and more proactive in providing and seeking guidance. Without proximity, with little time to spare, and without a task that could be mutually beneficial, however, I did not feel motivated to establish the type of relationship that could have led to a Critical Friendship with someone I barely know who works in a context I am almost completely unfamiliar with.

CRITICAL FRIENDS REPORTS

As a result of funding from the Fund for the Improvement of Post-Secondary Education (FIPSE), CPED engaged in a study of its influence on the EdD change process in CPED institutions. It utilized faculty and graduate students from the 21 original consortium members as field workers who conducted site visits at each other's universities. Faculty and student interviews and observations were completed, and relevant documentation about programs and the change process were collected. In addition to analyzing the site visit data and then writing a case report of the institution for the study, researchers were required to write a "Critical Friend report" for the institution they visited.

As a researcher on this project, I was both the author and receiver of a Critical Friend report. As an author, my major concern was whether my report would be useful to the university I visited. It was important to me that the report was one of support and challenge and was not viewed as a program evaluation. Secondarily, as with any report it was important to ensure that the content was factually correct and that the feedback was beneficial to faculty, the program, and the institution. However, I had no direct communication with the university I visited following the writing of the report. I did learn at a later convening that there had been several rapid changes following the CPED/FIPSE visit, which suggested to me that the report had quickly become dated, regardless of whether it had been initially apt. However, building upon what I felt to be a burgeoning relationship, I offered to provide further feedback and act as a sounding board if it would be helpful. My offer was never acted on.

Given the effort I had put in to writing what I hoped would be a helpful report to the university I visited, I eagerly anticipated receiving our Critical Friend repot. Feedback was built into this process as would be expected in a Critical Friend relationship, but the descriptive material did not seem to fully capture the features of the program and feedback was not directed at a problem faculty had identified as key; the feedback was not particularly helpful or insightful, and there was no structure for ongoing conversation about it. With limited familiarity with each other's programs and no structure for ongoing conversation about the feedback, the opportunity for learning was short-circuited. The site visits were a learning experience, but primarily because of the time we spent together hearing about each other's programs.

LEARNING ABOUT PROFESSIONAL DOCTORAL EDUCATION IN CPED AND THE CHALLENGE OF LONG DISTANCE CRITICAL FRIENDSHIPS

CPED has worked hard to create meaningful opportunities to learn from and with colleagues in a number of ways. These opportunities can be understood through the lens of Cochran-Smith and Lytle's (Cochran-Smith & Lytle, 1999) typology that identifies sources and the nature of knowledge with regard to teacher learning in professional development settings. Although their focus on professional development is not completely parallel to the CPED higher education context, their idea that sources of learning come from knowledge *for* practice, knowledge *in* practice, and knowledge *of* practice is relevant.

Knowledge *for* practice is generated through formal, and traditional, empirical research carried out by university researchers and communicated to teachers. Knowledge *in* practice is generated through on-the-ground teaching experience, and the development of practical expertise is communicated through teacher-to-teacher sharing. Knowledge *of* practice is generated through critical inquiry and reflection by practitioners connecting their work to larger issues while taking a critical stance on research and theory. Although not completely parallel to opportunities for learning in teacher professional development settings, convenings and other CPED activities are designed to promote learning as well as the generation of new knowledge. For example, when we had a presentation on the report of the blue ribbon panel on the clinical preparation of teachers as we did at one convening or on innovations in undergraduate engineering education; we are presented with knowledge *for* practice. When we participate in sessions during which we share our particular solutions to various design challenges, we are gaining knowledge *in* practice. When we collaborate to develop new ways of conceptualizing and enacting the professional practice EdD we are gaining knowledge *of* practice.

The assumptions about teachers as knowers and generators of knowledge that undergird the concept of CFGs are most congruent with a knowledge *of* type conception of teacher learning. However, the examples of higher education CFG activities described here seem to fall short of the mark in creating a context for this type of learning, most especially in the area of providing feedback that has the potential to improve practice and promote constructive change.

The three examples described here of CPED applying a CFG approach (or at least using the language of CFGs) point to several challenges and suggest that the traditional CFG structures and expectations do not work among a group of colleagues that mostly work at a distance and lack deep familiarity with each other's challenges within their particular contexts of practice. The challenges of CFGs seem related to several overlapping issues: length of time and frequency of CFG interactions, familiarity, and consistency. These are fundamentally caused by the fact that we are trying to nurture our Critical Friendship essentially as a long distance relationship. Most people acknowledge that long distance relationships of any kind are challenging at best; if they are to survive thrive, they need special care and handling that is distinct from face-to-face relationships.

CFGs in any context may often be challenged by a lack of time, but I believe that CPED CGFs face more daunting challenges than school-based or other onsite groups do. This belief is based on the assumption that when Critical Friends gather, it is generally for the sole purpose of engaging in CFG activities. At CPED convenings, however, there are a variety of tasks and activities to complete. Activities designated specifically as Critical Friend–type interactions are only one of many activities and tasks to be completed in a busy agenda. Participants at convenings have many goals and objectives for participating, as does CPED for bringing members together. By the end of the convening, attendees tend to be overwhelmed. They are often focused on the many new ideas and information they have encountered and a daunting "to do" list to address once they return to their home institutions. Therefore, when we get back to work, convening activities and relationships can feel very distant and disconnected from our day-to-day lives. Without purposefully creating them or taking individual initiative, it may feel like there are few incentives to build and sustain the kinds of relationships that are needed for CFGs. Although relationships are easily rekindled at convenings, they quickly cool when we are apart; they do not build over time in a way that could promote the deep knowledge necessary for the effective functioning of a CFG. Similarly, the FIPSE/CPED site visits and subsequent Critical Friend reports suggested the development of closer relationships, but without follow up the distance can quickly reestablish itself despite the intensity of the site visit. In the case of the mentoring relationship an initial structure was put in place, but like the best laid plans for staying in touch after being together in a long distance relationship, they were hard to sustain once we returned to the intense demands of our professional lives.

In addition to a short time frame with many distractions that are allotted for CFG-type activities at convenings, institutions only meet biannually, giving almost no continuity to build understanding of each other's contexts, challenges, and resources. Further adding to this challenge, participation at the convenings is inconsistent. While most consortium members try to send faculty and students to every convening, the same people are not always available to attend each time. So while familiarity with an institutional program may slowly grow over time, actual collegial relationships are made more disjointed by shifting attendance at convenings. In addition, when substitutes are sent, they may have less engagement with their doctoral programs or less familiarity with CPED, creating even greater challenges to building the community needed for CFGs. To extend the metaphor, this constantly changing participation is almost like sending a sibling to the next reunion in a long distance relationship. The sibling is from the same family, has some similarities, and knows a lot of the same things, but his or her presence is still a different relationship that requires building a new foundation. Due to CPED's size, convening participants tend to mix in different combinations for almost every task with fewer opportunities to learn deeply about each other's work as would be typical in an ongoing CFG group in which everyone either works in the same context or comes together regularly and becomes deeply familiar with and knowledgeable about each other's work sites. Because we are not consistently working with the same people each time we are together, we tend to spend a lot of time just trying to get to know each other by explaining and asking about each other's programs. We do this for our own information at least as much as to be able to give sensible and meaningful feedback when asked. Therefore, what are set aside as CFG activities may function more often as sharing opportunities. By the time participants meet again, understanding of conditions gained about a colleague's program at the last convening may have already changed. Because of these discontinuities, feedback may often fail to address the root cause of issues and challenges. While the literature may suggest that failure to go deep into the issues presented in a CFG may be due to a lack of trust (Bambino, 2002; Costa & Kallick, 1993; Swaffield, 2005), the condition of long distance relationships seems to greatly complicate the challenge of giving critical feedback. It seems likely that a lack of time, infrequent contact, and inconsistent relationships may also impede the building of trust. Swaffield (2005) asserts that Critical Friends demonstrate positive regard for each other while also offering informed critique. When CPED members come together at convenings, it is easy to show positive regard for each other because we are all working on the same challenges and assume the best of our colleagues who have all made the same choice to blaze a new path in doctoral education. However, the informed critique part of the relationship is far harder to achieve given that involvement with each other tends to be transient and brief.

Critical Friends are not born; they are made through training, time, practice, and experience. Some convening attendees may be conceptually guided by Critical Friends in their interactions with colleagues from other universities, but because CFG protocols have not been a consistent element of CPED others may hear the language of Critical Friends activities with little awareness of what this means in practice and few skills to enact the attributes of a Critical Friends. Storey and Richard (2013) suggest that CFGs can succeed only when the participants are aware of the benefits of using the method, are motivated to take part in the process, and are provided with the necessary time and resources. I would argue that even with training, evolving membership and long distance relationships have made this ideal difficult to enact.

As noted earlier, despite the inherent challenges of trying to be long distance CFGs, CPED has created a context for substantive learning. I would argue, however, that this happens less because we are Critical Friends than through a general willingness among members to share their experiences, which we are asked to do in many ways. For example, members receive preconvening assignments to compile and report program information that is shared with others. Doing so is a double opportunity to learn; doing the assignment is sometimes as eye opening as seeing the preconvening work completed by other universities and has helped to push our thinking and our actions along in areas that we might have been neglecting. In addition to sharing, we also learn through collaborative knowledge generation when we do conceptual work contributing to reenvisioning doctoral education. We did this, for example, when we worked on developing CPED principles or the dissertation award rubric revision. These are highly generative activities that have had an impact on both CPED as an organization and consortium members' programs. Presumably, CPED members have an interest in collaborating and learning from others because it can be mutually beneficial to their goal of redesigning their doctoral programs.

However, the multiple opportunities to share and generate new knowledge at convenings and through other CPED organized activities leave it up to individuals and university teams to take away what they feel they can use and what they need. While there is a great deal of dialogue among convening participants, it generally stays in the realm of clarifying questions (e.g., how do you …? Why do you …? What have you found when you …?), and comments that compare and contrast our programs (e.g., It seems like you do this, but we do that because …). These are highly generative activities that have had an impact on both CPED as an organization and consortium members' programs, but they fall outside of the realm of CFGs.

Rethinking Critical Friends Groups as Long Distance Relationships

In order to maximize the benefits of CFGs in the long distance relationship of CPED members, there is a need to stretch members thinking on how to relate to each other and do the work of redesigning the EdD, not just at convenings and other events, but also between face-to-face interactions.

In order to address some of the challenges identified in this chapter, there needs to be a two-pronged approach: ongoing and explicit training and self-conscious reflection on the processes and outcomes of CFGs activities at every convening, and more purposeful building of relationships among colleagues engaged in ongoing and continuous work projects. Taking action in each of these areas can deepen familiarity with what it means to be Critical Friends and will strengthen the likelihood that CPED members can provide substantive feedback and critique rather than constantly just getting to know each other.

If Critical Friends need to learn how to participate in CFGs, there is a need to acknowledge that in a community with evolving membership and infrequent interactions, learning has to be sustained and ongoing. Every convening could not only include a CFG activity that is facilitated by an experienced Critical Friend, but also explicit learning opportunities for becoming effective Critical Friends should be planned. For example, a fishbowl activity in which experienced Critical Friends follow a CFG protocol could consist of a group member presenting the problem followed by a probing session. The next two steps, warm (positive) feedback and cool (negative) feedback, would be completed with the presenter silent. Finally, a challenge to the presenter ends the protocol. This process is then repeated for each group member to ensure that each Critical Friend in the group has their voice heard. This requires each group member to keep to the established time frame. Following the fishbowl, small groups could discuss what they saw in terms of opportunities for learning, strategies for interaction, and impressions of the overall process. Subsequently participants would have an opportunity to participate in a CFG around the same problem of practice. In this way awareness of CFGs as a strategy to improve practice is continually renewed and skills are continually improved. Given the busy agenda of convenings, embedding this kind of training in work that is of timely importance to the community is imperative. Otherwise, it becomes nothing more than an exercise focused on process without substantive benefit.

Explicit work on building relationships in the community is also an important element to the successful implementation of CFGs where participants meet infrequently. In this way, participants can gain familiarity with each other's program and get past the clarifying questions that are so common at convenings. At least some time at every convening could engage participants in an activity with colleagues from the same universities as a way to build up knowledge of each other's programs. CFGs could be formed that are stable from convening to convening. While some individuals may vary within these groups, the group as a whole would develop deeper knowledge of each other's programs and work contexts. This familiarity could clear the way for more effective CFGs. They could work on an ongoing theme or issue that carries over from convening to convening or identify areas of focus relevant to the meeting agenda or the timely needs of group members. If this work is truly relevant and helpful to its members, they may find ways and reasons to stay connected between convenings.

I have experienced, first hand, how and why this ongoing connection can occur. I have been working with three CPED colleagues from other universities between and during CPED events on a problem of practice that is of mutual interest. We use a structure we learned about through CPED to impel our work forward and we use video conferencing to meet. After initially spending significant time getting to know each other's programs and concerns about the issue we are working on (supporting the development of graduate student writing), we have shared course materials and ideas, and in doing so have provided feedback and critique. Our familiarity with each and our shared interests and understanding of the problem have enabled us to focus on the work we need and want to do and have gradually enabled us to generate knowledge *of* practice through Critical Friend–type interactions. This experience demonstrates that when colleagues in long distance relationships have the opportunity to get to know each other through ongoing work, join together around a common interest, and work over time, they can engage in CFGs in spite of the distance. This experience suggests that with modifications CFGs can be enacted to produce substantive learning through collaborative feedback and critique, but to do so means rethinking what it means to be Critical Friends, from afar.

References

Bambino, D. (2002). Critical friends. *Educational Leadership, 59*(6), 25–27.

Bozalek, V. and Matthews, N. (2009). E-Learning: A cross-institutional forum for sharing socio-cultural influences on personal and professional identity. *International Social Work, 52*(2), 235–246.

Cochran-Smith, M., & Lytle, S. L. (1999). Relationships of knowledge and practice: Teacher learning in communities. *Review of Research in Education, 24*(1), 249–305.

Costa, A. L., & Kallick, B. (1993). Through the lens of a critical friend. *Educational Leadership, 51*(2), 49–51.

CPED website. (2013). http://cpedinitiative.org. Retrieved April 26, 2013, from http://cpedinitiative.org/about.

Knowles, A. J. (2002). E-learning in Social Work Education: Emerging Pedagogical and Policy Issues. *Currents: New Scholarship in the Human Services, 1*(1), 1–17.

National School Reform Faculty. (2012). Retrieved April 11, 2013, from http://www.nsrfharmony.org/faq.html#1.

Storey, V. A., & Richard, B. (In press). Carnegie Project for the Educational Doctorate: The role of critical friends in diffusing doctoral program innovation. In C. A. Mullen & K. E. Lane (Eds.), *Becoming a Global Voice—the 2013 Yearbook of the National Council of Professors of Educational Administration*. Ypsilanti, MI: NCPEA Publications.

Swaffield, S. (2005). No sleeping partners: Relationships between head teachers and critical friends. *School Leadership and Management, 25*(1), 43.

Role of Critical Friends Groups on EdD Program (Re)design

CHAPTER 4

Critical Friends' Perspectives on Problems of Practice and Inquiry in an EdD Program

Deanna Iceman Sands, Connie L. Fulmer, Alan Davis, Shelley Zion, Nancy Shanklin, Rodney L. Blunck, Nancy L. Leech, Ron Tzur, and Maria Araceli Ruiz-Primo

> *A critical friend ... is a trusted person who asks provocative questions, provides data to be examined through another lens, and offers critique of work as a friend ... Critical friends are clear about the nature of the relationship ... listen well ... offer value judgments only upon the request of the learner ... respond to the learner's work with integrity, and ... advocate for the success of the work*
>
> —*Costa & Kallick, 1993, pp. 49–50*

Conversations continue to evolve within the Carnegie Project on the Education Doctorate (CPED) regarding the nature of the dissertation in practice and the associated inquiry skills/coursework (Carnegie Project on the Education Doctorate, 2012). Questions abound, for example, regarding the nature, scope, impact, and format of the dissertation in practice. Because the approach to this culminating project diverges across institutions of higher education involved in the CPED consortium and because there is a commitment to allow flexibility to institutions to address their unique contexts, it is unclear what research/inquiry experiences and coursework are needed to support

Doctor of Education (EdD) students to carry out the dissertation in practice with rigor and in a manner that truly develops scholarly practitioners who contribute to advancing problems of practice in contexts such as schools, districts, and community-based organizations. This chapter will report on the efforts of doctoral faculty from the School of Education and Human Development (SEHD) at the University of Colorado Denver to seek input from our partners in those contexts to better understand the nature of the work and how inquiry does, can, and should support their work as well as the nature of authentic means and formats for communicating inquiry results in a manner that would be constructive within their organizations. Interviews were conducted to ascertain the views of our Critical Friends, including superintendents; leaders from nonprofit and community-based organizations; executive leaders from higher education contexts; and district-based leaders such as directors, coordinators, and mentors, on those questions. The results from these conversations will be used to modify the nature of our EdD program dissertation in practice as well as the experiences and courses required to develop students' knowledge and skills to carry out the respective inquiry.

Overview of the CPED Initiative

The basis for the work of the CPED stems from the notion that the fundamental goals of the PhD in education differ from those of the EdD (Levine, 2007; Shulman, Golde, Bueschel, & Garabedian, 2006). Freeman (1931), almost 80 years ago, identified three major differences between the two degrees: unlike PhD students, EdD students were (a) not required to learn a foreign language, (b) required to have a professional experience, and (c) writing dissertations that synthesized information, but did not discover new information. More recently, the differences between the degrees have been delineated more clearly. According to Shulman et al. (2006) "the EdD [is] intended as preparation for managerial and administrative leadership in education, focuses on preparing practitioners—from principals to curriculum specialists, to teacher-educators, to evaluators—who can solve educational problems" (p. 26). In contrast, these authors believe the PhD in education to be a traditional research degree wherein students go on to teach in faculty roles. Yet, "in reality, the distinctions between the programs are minimal" (Shulman et al., 2006, p. 26).

Based on these discussions, the CPED was developed (Carnegie Project on the Education Doctorate, 2012d). At its core, the work of the CPED consortium is to distinguish between the doctorates in education, especially the roles and work of research scholars as opposed to scholarly practitioners (Carnegie Project on the Education Doctorate, 2012b). The guiding principles for research capture the notions that the PhD and EdD should be different; with the EdD focusing on developing professional knowledge by integrating practical and research knowledge (Carnegie Project on the Education Doctorate, 2009).

The Role of Research/Inquiry and the Dissertation in Practice in the EdD

As programs consider the nature and scope of research/inquiry and the capstone dissertation process in the EdD, three of the six CPED working principles (Carnegie Project on the Education Doctorate, 2012d) have particular relevance: scholarly practitioner, inquiry as practice, and dissertation in practice. Each of these principles will be delineated. First, according to the CPED (2012c), scholarly practitioners blend practical wisdom with professional skills and knowledge to name, frame, and solve problems of practice. They use *practical* research and applied theories as tools for change because they understand the importance of equity and social justice. They disseminate their work in multiple ways, and they have an obligation to resolve problems of practice by collaborating with key stakeholders, including the university, the educational institution, the community, and individuals. The second CPED principle is inquiry as practice, which is the process of posing significant questions that focus on complex problems of practice (Carnegie Project on the Education Doctorate, 2012c). By using various research, theories, and professional wisdom, scholarly practitioners design innovative solutions to address the problems of practice.

At the center of Inquiry of Practice is the ability to use data to understand the effects of innovation. As such, Inquiry of Practice requires the ability to gather, organize, judge, aggregate, and analyze situations, literature, and data with a critical lens. The final CPED principle that is relevant is the dissertation in practice (Carnegie Project on the Education Doctorate, 2012d). As the culminating experience that demonstrates the scholarly practitioner's ability to solve problems of practice, the dissertation in practice exhibits the doctoral candidate's ability "to think, to perform, and to act with integrity" (Shulman, 2005).

Given that CPED consortia members collectively prescribed these as working principles, not as strict guidelines, the extant literature on the EdD (e.g., Hyatt & Williams, 2011) and information from the CPED website (Carnegie Project on the Education Doctorate, 2012a) indicate great variety in the manner in which these principles are enacted by the various CPED-affiliated institutions with regard to the number and nature of research/inquiry courses and the nature and format of the dissertation in practice. For example, upon reviewing several profiles of institutions belonging to CPED (Carnegie Project on the Education Doctorate, 2012a) the numbers of research/inquiry courses were found to vary from 6 to 22 credits; and the nature of the research courses varied from a sole focus on mixed methods to courses on basic descriptive and inferential statistics, literature reviews and professional writing, action research, evaluation research, and advanced qualitative and quantitative methods.

The nature and format of the dissertation in practice diverge as well (Archbald, 2008; Carnegie Project on the Education Doctorate, 2012). For example, at the 2008 convening, hosted by the University of Southern California, various speakers and a panel of the USC Inquiry Committee members described their faculty's conversations, debates, and programmatic deliberations on these topics (Carnegie Project on the Education Doctorate, 2008). As a prelude to the panel discussion, Dr. Myron Dembo from the University of Southern California stressed that these exchanges began with a focus of *what are we doing* and needed to move to considering *why are we doing this* and for reasons other than "this is the way it has always been done, this is what I learned in my graduate studies and this is what we are going to give to our students" (Carnegie Project on the Education Doctorate, 2008).

Throughout this session and subsequent CPED convenings debate on inquiry courses, the following questions continued to be discussed: How many courses? What should be the content of courses? What is the best format and approach of courses (e.g., online, intensive, and so on)? Should EdD and PhD courses be the same or different? Is it inquiry or research—are these the same or different and if so, how? Deliberation of questions having to do with the dissertation in practice approach and format included: Is it the five-chapter dissertation? Should it be a group or individual effort? What are the parameters of a "Problem of Practice?" What is the role of constituents or members of other organizations in the content and process? Should students be given a set of narrow choices of methods to approach their inquiry? If so, which ones? Should we be uploading to ProQuest or other outlets in order to share what we have learned? Based on these discussions, few solutions were identified.

Debates regarding the dissertation in practice continue as well. Again, review of consortia members' profiles reveal vast differences in what is required to fulfill this capstone experience (Carnegie Project on the Education Doctorate, 2013). The nature of the research or inquiry conducted can include empirical or nonempirical work; apply designs that are qualitative, quantitative, or mixed methods; and employ specific designs such as ethnographies, program evaluation, action research, or quasi-experimental. Candidates in programs can be involved in generating novel work or extending existing data sets, and be expected to work individually or in more collaborative teams. Depending on the institution, EdD students are expected to generate culminating projects that range from a white paper, article, or monograph, to a more traditional five-chapter dissertation document. During the fall 2012 convening, as consortium members tackled the development of a set of standards and criteria that could be used to judge the dissertation in practice, questions regarding the requirements of this element continued. For example, in response to a proposed standard that the dissertation in practice "is expected to have generative impact on the future work and agendas of the scholar practitioner," (Carnegie Project on the Educational Doctorate, 2012) members asked, "What is meant by generative impact? Is this doable in a dissertation capstone?" Feedback ranged between more traditional questions, again seeking to differentiate the traditional PhD dissertation to the dissertation in practice (i.e., How do we define and evaluate rigor for the two "dissertations?"), wondering if APA was the appropriate stylistic guide for the formatting of final products, to musings that a product meant to have impact might be better represented by blogs, websites, graphic novel, or U-Tube video. As is the case with the CPED principle of Inquiry of Practice, great variety existed and conversations as to whether delimiting the form for what is being called the dissertation in practice continue. What is agreed upon is that both are focused on practice and that local context matters; thus faculty in EdD programs must be have a clear sense of the nature of problems in practice among their constituent base, the types of inquiry utilized or sought after to address those issues, and the manner in which results can be conveyed in authentic, productive ways.

History of the EdD at CU Denver

Previous iterations of the SEHD's EdD curriculum included three and then four inquiry courses. These courses have included introductory research, measurement for educators, intermediate statistics, and program evaluation. While taught with the EdD audience in mind, the syllabi were not modified significantly from those used in courses with students in a research methods masters' program or the PhD program. For reasons beyond the scope of this chapter, the entire EdD curriculum underwent a significant change in the fourth year of the program, during which no students were admitted. As a result, the revised program plan of study now allows for only three inquiry courses. The fluctuation in the number and nature of the inquiry courses is symptomatic of the uncertainty faculty have as to what inquiry courses are most appropriate to achieve the ideals of the EdD as conceptualized by work within CPED. Faculty in the school plan to use the results of the Critical Friends' inquiry described herein to inform the nature and content of those courses as well as to consider changes to the current approach to the dissertation in practice.

Beginning with the first cohort of students and prior to the collective decision among CPED-affiliated institutions to adopt the dissertation in practice nomenclature, the SEHD's EdD capstone involved a Thematic Dissertation Group (TDG) experience. Our approach drew heavily from work done at the University of Southern California (Dembo & Marsh, 2007; Marsh & Dembo, 2009) and was consistent with recommendations of the Carnegie Foundation and the Council of Academic Deans in Research Education Institutions (CADREI). In short, through a thematic dissertation unifying theme, a small group of EdD students joined together such that they could be collectively mentored and learn collaboratively from one another's dissertation. Group themes were organized by faculty to address and advance solutions that would resolve problems of practice drawn from schools, districts, colleges, or other learning organizations. In some cases faculty had direct relationships with district personnel and used the TDG process to continue or expand existing inquiry projects. In other groups, faculty and students created relationships with outside entities based on the overarching question and individual projects planned. Within each TDG, individual students worked either on closely related topics and collected empirical data or with the same database but asking different questions in order to produce their own, unique dissertations. Students were required to assist each other in developing their proposals and to critique each others' work.

Typically, TDG projects focused on innovation in educational practice and involved written products that comprehensively addressed, generated, and/or interpreted knowledge applicable to educational practice. Products were not intended to broaden (but may, nevertheless) the literature base or contribute new knowledge to the field of study. Individual students were required to generate a series of capstone documents containing the following four elements: (a) a statement of the problem explored by the student including a brief description of the theoretical approach and conceptual framework that informed the inquiry; (b) a review of the literature substantiating the research problem as well as the theoretical approach and conceptual framework used; (c) a technical/research report; and (d) a formal presentation to representatives of the organization in which the study was conducted that reported the inquiry results and implications. Formats for these elements varied by individual and thematic dissertation group but maintained the function or purpose of each element listed above.

For example, in one TDG there was a single faculty member and all five of the students were working under the umbrella of one topic with common conceptual frameworks, methods, and research questions that yielded five individual cross-case questions. These students investigated the leadership practices of principals of successful schools serving English Language Acquisition (ELA) learners. A review of literature produced a working definition of leadership practice, which students then used to identify actual leadership practices occurring in these five schools. Cross-case questions focused on (a) how do the mean scores of the principals' on a common survey relate to student achievement scores of each of these schools, (b) what common themes emerge from the stories of five principals, (c) how did critical events (work and life) uncovered in principals' stories influence the motivation behind the leadership practices of the principals, (d) what are the common elements of leadership practices of these principals, and (e), which of the essential supports and key indicators in evidence-based frameworks relate to the relative success or failure in mathematics are evident in the leadership practices of these principals. Findings from these thematic dissertations contributed new elements to the literature-derived definition of a leadership practice (e.g., a specific work focus, tools, activities, and proximal/ distal goals). This framework can be used by principals to improve their professional practice, by school employees as a structure for peer coaching and professional development of principals, and by faculty of principal preparation programs to prepare future leaders with the capacity and working knowledge of how a leadership practice produces results in schools. The products of this work included five individual monographs that were contributions to the leadership literature, but more importantly, this applied definition of a leadership practice promises to produce future leaders with the capacity to lead other successful schools.

Another example was a TDG focused on STEM education and professional learning, where one student in the group focused on the impact of a professional intervention to promote teachers' content knowledge and fidelity of implementation of a new science curriculum. This dissertation culminated with a 1-page summary, a 3-page Executive Report, and a 70-page monograph consisting of the research problem/questions, literature, methods, key findings, and implications substantiated by empirical data. Another student conducted a study of how adaptive teaching methods can resume mathematics learning of failure-experienced elementary students. She presented the results to the principal and teachers at that school, and prepared a manuscript for publication in a teacher journal in mathematics education.

Within the context of the revisions to the EdD curriculum, the SEHD doctoral faculty had multiple conversations about the nature of both the types of inquiry needed as well as the nature and format of our capstone dissertation. Some faculty voiced the opinion that our constituents don't know what they don't know and they need inquiry. Conversely, other faculty felt that based on the general lack of experience that IHE faculty have in the roles for which the EdD is meant to prepare graduates, SEHD doctoral faculty did not have the basis by which to know what individuals advancing to leadership roles do or need with regard to inquiry. Faculty also considered the notion that while leaders across practice-based settings may not be required to engage in inquiry, having gone through the experience of conducting research they will better understand inquiry and have a sense of the types of inquiry they may need to help approach their problems of practice, determine if resources exist in their organizations to carry out that examination, or if they need to seek individuals external to their context to examine the problem at hand. in addition, the content, format, and utility of the final TDG projects remained debatable. Faculty simply did not know if the executive summary, monograph, and presentations combination or manuscript and presentation formats were of benefit to the organizations in which the inquiry was conducted. Overall, the CU Denver faculty remained unconvinced that the program expectations for our approach to inquiry courses and capstone experience were the best experiences for preparing our graduates for the leadership roles they would have after completing the program.

Using Critical Friends Perspectives to Identify Innovations for Inquiry and the Dissertation of Practice

Given continued conversations and debates regarding the nature and role of inquiry in EdD programs and the corresponding relationship to the dissertation in practice, this study focused on the thoughts and opinions of Critical Friends who currently held executive leadership positions in school districts, institutions of higher education, and education-related community-based organizations. The intent was to connect the SEHD's EdD inquiry courses and scope and format of the dissertation in practice to the authentic roles of these Critical Friends and the problems of practice they face daily in their professional lives. As such, it was hoped that the process would help to define and advance program innovation (Rogers, 2003).

Separate, role-alike focus group interviews or conversations (Merton, Fiske, & Kendall, 1990; Onwuegbuzie, Dickinson, Leech, & Zoran, 2009; Vaughn, Schumm, & Sinagub, 1996) were hosted with five superintendents, three executive leaders from institutions of higher education, and seven community-based partners. These Critical Friends were not selected randomly; indeed, they had long-term connections to the school or faculty and had participated in program development or evaluation initiatives, served as co-instructors or adjunct faculty, or participated in advisory board roles. At the beginning of each conversation, the context for the exchange was presented to participants. Two central research questions guided our work: (a) What do educational leaders consider as problems of practice and does, and how does, inquiry or research contribute to advancing solutions to those problems? and, (b) In what ways do leaders communicate results of their inquiry on problems of practice? What are the implications of these uses for preparing educational leaders? Audio tapes of these conversations were transcribed and a thematic analysis was conducted to discern commonalities and differences between the three constituent groups.

Critical Friends' Perspectives

In the sections below the perspectives of three focus groups of Critical Friends provide current examples of what researchers (Greenfield, 1979; Immegart & Boyd, 1979; Ravetz, 1995; Willower, 1979) have reported regarding the nature of scientific knowledge and resolution in fields that deal with complex social problems and seek to address them in uncontrollable contexts where "facts are few and political passions are many" (Ravetz, p. 366). According to Willower (1979), "Anyone who hopes to improve an organization needs first to understand it, and understanding is the chief legacy of inquiry, whether its object be the stars, the functioning of the brain, or school organizations" (p. 79). The following Critical Friends' perspectives provide fertile starting places in regard to three main areas: (a) problems of practice, (b) whether it is research or inquiry, and (c) how to best communicate the results of studies.

Problems of Practice

According to our Critical Friends Groups, problems of practice emerge when organizational efforts collide with internal and external constraints. An organizational problem of practice "is any situation in which work efforts are not being actualized" or evidenced by "evaluation and formative assessment systems in our schools." Signs of core problems emerge from both formal and informal feedback and state data. According to one of the Critical Friends, "It's the small things and the big things—curriculum, student achievement, facilities, transportation, technology—and all are related to money." Problems become salient when "angry phone calls and emails bring attention to them," or "when expected outcomes are not achieved," or when something "that should be relatively easy becomes a major complication taking longer than it should." These problems of practice happen when the assumptions of operations or models in use "are only achieving partial outcomes." These problems arise from a variety of reasons related to having insufficient staff, time, or money to do the job or to reach goals and objectives and from the fact that student aspirations, resources, and participation involve social systems beyond the reach of schools. Compounding these problems is the loss of "good people who are worn out [and] try to seek a job that's more fulfilling or where they have greater support for the work that they do—not just financial support but moral support" as well.

Across institutional types, these critical-friend leaders distinguished between short-term problems, which required short-term responses and could then be set aside, and long-term problems, which required organizational attention year after year. Examples of short-term problems identified through our Critical Friend conversations were changes in state rules and regulations (e.g., new regulations governing teacher certification), the departure of key personnel in leadership positions, and fine-tuning or automating standard operating procedures. Chief among their long-term problems were institutional outcomes that were judged to be inadequate in the broader political environment (e.g., low test scores, low graduation rates, attainment gaps associated with ethnicity and resources), significant changes in the policy environment (e.g., new mandated content standards and state-level teacher evaluation policies), demographic changes (e.g., more underprepared students entering higher education than ever before), multiyear declines in resources (e.g., reduced state funding of education), and persistent internal problems of leadership (e.g., low staff morale, a "revolving door" of top leaders).

Our Critical Friend leaders acknowledged that addressing such problems require solutions that (a) are systemic and coordinated rather than piecemeal, (b) reflect an understanding of the processes within the control of the institution that could influence key outcomes (e.g., theories linking learning, instruction, and perseverance), (c) take into account the political and organizational realities inside and outside the institution (e.g., finding the right people to lead the change effort and achieving buy-in and support from various constituencies), and (d) are informed by valid data with systems for collecting, analyzing, interpreting, and reporting at multiple levels in the organization. One participant expanded on this last point, arguing for cultivating an organizational culture of inquiry, in which data were used at all levels to identify what is working well and not working well, and to monitor changes to determine how they were proceeding and how outcomes might be changing as a result.

Most of the approaches to long-term problems described by our Critical Friend leaders could be classified under three broad types: (a) ongoing processes aimed at gradual and continuous improvement, (b) management of targeted change efforts, and (c) efforts to expand revenue (emphasized by leaders of community organizations). Ongoing processes to bring about gradual and continuous improvement included (a) institutionalized feedback and evaluation systems providing cycles of collecting outcome and perception data, data analysis, and reporting at different levels of the organization to inform decision making and strategic planning, (b) ongoing professional development, including efforts to identify and disseminate "best" practices, and (c) attention to communication and relationship-building through both formal and informal channels.

It Is Research or Inquiry?

Musings about possible differences between "research" and "inquiry" have occurred both among CPED consortium members and faculty in the SEHD at CU Denver. Our Critical Friend participants offered several opinions. Some Critical Friends described research as formal, emphasizing controlled comparisons, and aimed at generalizable knowledge. Inquiry was described as less formal and included both procedures (asking questions, collecting evidence, interpreting evidence, and using evidence in decision making and to inform practice), and dispositions (a "culture of inquiry," an openness to question and seek new information and approaches). Many of these leaders commented on the importance of inquiry, but none argued for the importance of conducting formal research within their organizations. One participant said, "I think inquiry is probably more about being reflective and asking the right questions, and research is the structured process for answering some of those questions. They are not the same." Another shared that "the best research in my opinion would be things that can be applied to the school setting. The research has to be practical."

Some of our Critical Friends argued that in their experience, research-based knowledge of practice defied generalization and transfer from setting to setting because contexts varied so much from school to school and over time. At the same time, several were interested in identifying and implementing "best practices." One superintendent offered that "in my role, I find meta analyses most useful" as evidence in support of best practices, while another complained that efforts to implement best practices gleaned from previous research often failed to yield the anticipated results.

Other participants described the use of less formal inquiry to inform their understanding of what practices would work best in their settings to address current problems. For example, several higher education Critical Friend leaders described useful experiences, such as site visits to other institutions and meetings or conference sessions in which participants from other institutions described practices or changes in practice they had implemented and how those had worked. One Critical Friend stated, "Because we are part of a system, our research includes looking at other sites because we want the best practices. We are branching out, looking at other institution's websites, making phone calls, and site visits."

None of our district or higher education Critical Friends advocated conducting controlled experiments or causal modeling within their own organizations to inform practice. Leaders of nonprofit and community programs and agencies did speak of the importance of outcome evaluation, in part because funders insisted upon it.

The types of inquiry that our Critical Friends engaged in were mainly of two types: (a) systems of data collection and analysis, usually on an annual cycle, to provide the basis for formal reports, judging performance, setting improvement goals, and identifying emerging problems; and (b) focused inquiry in respect to a particular problem or anticipated change. The latter varied a great deal in respect to scale and methodology, and was not labeled "research" by leaders. At the large and formal end of the spectrum, one leader described school improvement efforts led by outside consulting firms such as McRel (formerly Mid-Continent Regional Educational Laboratory), sometimes costing more than $100,000, and involving various types of data collection and feedback. On the small and informal end of the scale were projects described by leaders such as collecting information regarding quality of service from higher education students making use of the Student Services Office through surveys, phone logs, and focus groups. Finally, Critical Friends across all categories spoke of the need to have access to new information as it unfolded, through channels of formal and informal communication within the organization and, to a lesser extent, across institutions.

Communicating Inquiry Results

All three types of Critical Friends—superintendents, higher education/state department of education personnel, and community/nonprofit directors—reported needing to communicate achievement data, progress toward organizational goals, and meeting of grant targets. Across all three groups, face-to-face meetings for the purpose of communicating informative data was seen as most important. One community/nonprofit director stated the importance of communicating in a manner that is transparent and addresses what works and what doesn't work: "We share it. Our approach is experimental learning, so we share how foolish we were to do X, Y, and Z openly with partners and with other folks in our trainings. We tell it because we want to help them avoid things. Then, the learning was worth it. But, if it is kind of a secret then, you know, we're all at a loss." A community/nonprofit director stressed the need when "giving out data to be really aware of who you're giving it [to] and what is your purpose in giving it to them," and "the ability to communicate and not use the jargon of a particular field." In the end, "You need to be able to think complexly, but know how to communicate in ways that can help move forward." The superintendents discussed these points with emphasis on the ability to "lead dialogue that solves problems. Communication [is defined as] bringing the right groups together at the right time and also [understanding] communication as talking points and personal conversation."

The need for one-on-one meetings or informal sharing over beverages was seen to be very important by all three Critical Friend groups. Often these communications occurred to prepare news to be released at larger face-to-face meetings. One community/non-profit director explained, "If there is a change or something that we're going to communicate to all our regions, most of the time, I've already connected with people individually to get their feedback." Different from the other two groups, community/nonprofit directors emphasized that sometimes they need to be seen "as neutral territory and welcoming to everybody and every group." Neutrality was also seen as a communication strategy, "If I'm having difficulty connecting with other folks, is there a neutral party that I can connect to that can connect me in a different way?"

In terms of written communications, the three Critical Friend groups prepared newsletters, executive summaries, short brochures, annual reports with bulleted points, and short white papers. Higher education and state department of education personnel stressed the need to find "different ways to communicate with people—with our outside community—our website, our letters that go out to them, posters, electronic media throughout the campus." They also indicated that communications needed to be succinct and able to be read within five minutes.

IMPLICATIONS AND FUTURE DIRECTIONS

This chapter centered on three issues arising from analysis of information provided by Critical Friends who serve in roles as superintendents, higher education leaders, and community-based partners, namely, identifying problems of practice, leaders' thinking about how inquiry differs from research, and ways in which inquiry findings (and methods) can be communicated to inform their educational efforts. This section elaborates on three key implications of our study.

The first implication is how we need to work more closely with organizational personnel when identifying problems of practice for TDG. Currently, a typical way of narrowing down such problems consists of faculty members proposing umbrella themes to the EdD students. In some cases those themes arise from existing partnerships faculty have with external organizations and in others the faculty propose work that has yet to be vetted or connected to a practice-based organization. Students then rank their choices for a TDG and once assigned, conduct an inquiry project. The information reported in this chapter challenges us to figure out ways in which problems can be recognized and specified via a more genuine partnership that brings together inquiry issues essential for leaders in the learning organization. Our data indicated that leaders' major foci would address such questions or issues as (a) what constitutes best practices, (b) how, or the extent to which, organizational goals are accomplished via efforts set to this end (e.g., data and analysis of practices that improve student outcomes), and (c) how to resolve inherent tensions (or "collisions") between organizational goals/efforts and constraints—both internal and external. Because these issues vary by organization (e.g., short term or long term), the need to partner in articulating the inquiry questions is paramount.

The second implication pertains to the Critical Friends' clear articulation of how research and inquiry differ. Most leaders seem to prefer the nomenclature of inquiry to research, as they related inquiry to more informal, reflective, practical, and most responsive to the nuances of local contexts. As our Critical Friends went on to describe approaches to inquiry that were most useful, data-driven decision making, program evaluation, surveys, focus groups, and syntheses of existing literature emerged. On the surface, while these descriptions seem familiar with what may be found in research courses within a doctoral program—the challenge for faculty in EdD programs becomes how to contextualize and situate the development of these skills in a manner that is consistent to the nomenclature conveyed by our Critical Friends.

The third implication pertains to our participants' emphasis on what and how inquiry findings are communicated. Our Critical Friends outlined a number of methods by which inquiry can be communicated to help their causes, including (a) face-to-face discussions including leading structured, problem-solving dialogues; (b) short, succinct summaries that can be captured through executive summaries or white papers; and (c) nontraditional and more innovative formats that would include technology-based approaches. Currently, our program does not include a structured way (e.g., a course or an assignment) that focuses on EdD students' competence and confidence in interpreting data and communicating findings in ways highly accessible to educational leaders in their organization(s). Furthermore, the current, primary manner in which findings from their dissertations in practice are shared does not meet our Critical Friends' descriptions of effective or efficient modes of communication.

As a participating consortium institution and one committed to CPED's design principles, this work provides our doctoral faculty valuable information as they consider next steps in the revisioning of our EdD inquiry courses and dissertation in practice process. We are committed to building on the lessons learned from our Critical Friends to advance and strengthen our EdD program. Clearly, if we are to actualize the overarching goals of the CPED consortium as well as their working principles, understanding our local context through the eyes of our Critical Friends is foundational.

References

Archbald, D. (2008). Research versus problem solving for the education leadership doctoral thesis: Implications fro form and function. *Educational Administration Quarterly, 44*, 704–739.

Carnegie Project on the Education Doctorate. (2008). *Inquiry issues.* Retrieved from http://www.cpedinitiative.org/convenings/october2008/inquiry_issues.

Carnegie Project on the Education Doctorate. (2009). *Working principles for the professional practice doctorate in education.* College Park, MD: Author.

Carnegie Project on the Education Doctorate. (2012). *Notes from DIP posters 10–14–12.* October Convening.

Carnegie Project on the Education Doctorate. (2012a). *Consortium members.* Retrieved from http://cpedinitiative.org/consortium-members.

Carnegie Project on the Education Doctorate. (2012b). *Consortium work. Retrieved from* http://cpedinitiative.org/consortium-work.

Carnegie Project on the Education Doctorate. (2012c). *Design concept definitions.* Retrieved from http://cpedinitiative.org/design-concept-definitions.

Carnegie Project on the Education Doctorate. (2012d). *The Carnegie Project on the Education Doctorate is a national effort aimed at strengthening the education doctorate Ed.D.* Retrieved from http://cpedinitiative.org/.

Carnegie Project on the Education Doctorate. (2013). *Consortia members.* Retrieved from http://www.cpedinitiative.org/consortium-members.

Costa, A. L., & Kallick, B. (1993). Through the lens of a critical friend. *Educational Leadership, 51*, 49–51.

Dembo, M. H., & Marsh, D. D. (2007). *Developing a new Ed. D. program in the Rossier school of education at the university of southern California.* Los Angeles, CA: University of Southern California.

Freeman F. N. (1931). *Practices of American universities in granting higher degrees in education: A series of official statements* (Vol. 19). Chicago, IL: University of Chicago Press.

Greenfield, T. B. (1979). Idea versus data: How can data speak for themselves. In G. L. Immegart and W. L. Boyd (Eds.), *Problem finding in educational administration: Trends in research and theory* (pp. 167–190). Lexington, MA: Heath.

Hyatt, L., & Williams, P. E. (2011). 21st century competencies for doctoral leadership faculty. *Innovative Higher Education, 36*, 53–66.

Immegart, G. L., & Boyd, W. L. (1979). *Problem finding in educational administration: Trends in research and theory.* Lexington, MA: Heath.

Levine, A. (2007). *Educating researchers.* New York, NY: The Education Schools Project.

Marsh, D. D., & Dembo, M. H. (2009). Rethinking school leadership programs: The USC EdD program in perspective. *Peabody Journal of Education, 84*, 69–85.

Merton, R. K., Fiske, M., & Kendall, P. L. (1990). *The focused interview: A manual of problems and procedures* (2nd ed.). New York, NY: Free Press.

Onwuegbuzie, A. J., Dickinson, W. B., Leech, N. L., & Zoran, A. G. (2009). A qualitative framework for collecting and analyzing data in focus group research. *International Journal of Qualitative Methods, 8*(3), 1–21.

Ravetz, J. R. (1995). *Scientific knowledge and its social problems.* Piscataway, NJ: Transaction.

Rogers, E. M. (2003). *Diffusion of innovation* (5th ed.). New York, NY: Free Press.

Shulman, L. S. (2005). Signature pedagogies in the professions. *Daedalus, 134*(3), 52–59.

Shulman, L. S., Golde, C. M., Bueschel, A. C., & Garabedian, K. J. (2006). Reclaiming education's doctorates: A critique and a proposal. *Educational Researcher, 35*(3), 25–32.

Vaughn, S., Schumm, J. S., & Sinagub, J. (1996). *Focus group interviews in education and psychology.* Thousand Oaks, CA: Sage.

Willower, D. J. (1979). Some issues in research on school organizations. In G. L. Immegart and W. L. Boyd (Eds.), *Problem finding in educational administration: Trends in research and theory* (pp. 63–85). Lexington, MA: Heath.

CHAPTER 5

CPED as an Incubator for a Clinical Practice Approach to Professional Teacher Preparation at Washington State University: Finding and Promoting Mutual Contexts of Change

Richard D. Sawyer

To challenge the inherent isolation, narcissism, and individualism that schools (and universities) foster within their faculty (Lortie, 1975), the Carnegie Foundation and the 25 initial member universities of the Carnegie Project on the Education Doctorate (CPED) intentionally structured CPED as a tightly charged site of innovation and envisioned institutional change. The twice-yearly three-day meetings convened an eclectic mix of graduate students, college deans, clinical faculty, K-12 teachers, college professors, and school administrators. These convenings operated as retreats to stimulate imaginative thinking and scaffold institutional change. Each convening mixed a wealth of engaged speakers and thinkers (e.g., Lee Shulman scaffolding thought), complex educational concepts ("laboratories of practice"), concrete examples of university change (e.g., the University of Southern California's work with site-based partnerships), presentations of doctoral students (e.g., student research posters at Fresno State University), and educators working to change their institutions. At the convenings, singular ideas evolved into frameworks, frameworks changed into practice, and practice reshaped conceptual frameworks.

CPED has spawned change and itself has become a story of change. As part of this story, I examine in this chapter my personal evolution of a conceptual framework—the Tripartite Model of Practitioner Preparation (Sawyer & Imig, 2011).

The clinical practice model (see Figure 5.1) provides ways to link a professional practice doctoral program with both a teacher preparation program and K-12 school-based partnerships. This model for practitioner education first emerged in CPED and then, helix like, benefited from repeated dialogic transactions between CPED and my workplace practice. The focus of this specific case study then is the evolution of the clinical practice framework from the standpoint of a particular individual in a specific setting. The setting is both CPED convenings as well as aspects of my work at Washington State University (WSU) where I have collaboratively started, designed, and continue to chair a 14 year-old graduate-level Masters in Teaching Secondary Teacher Preparation Program (the MIT S Program), as well as a new Teacher Leadership EdD Program (TL EdD Program). I examine this framework through the dual lens of Complexity

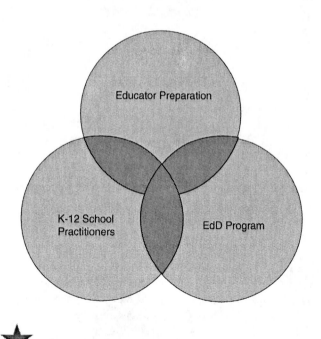

New form of practice.

Figure 5.1 A Tripartite Model of Educator Preparation.

theory (CT) and Critical Friends theory. This chapter first presents an illustrative case study of the impact of a Critical Friends framework at CPED both to my own perception of clinical practice as well as to specific changes I have attempted to make to the MIT S and the TL EdD Programs. Following this description, I draw from Critical Friends theory and Complexity theory to analyze the role that CPED has played in this change process.

COMPLEXITY THEORY AND CRITICAL FRIENDS THEORY

Complexity theory posits a framework for the examination of change processes within complex systems (e.g., those found in schools). Complex systems involve a large number of elements (e.g., actors, environments, and media) that interact dynamically and environmentally (Cilliers, 1998). These collective contexts are considered parts of constantly unfolding and historically situated individual, structural, and environmental narratives. As open systems, complex environments are dynamic, constantly changing, and responsive to interactions, but operate with disequilibrium in relatively unpredictable and often hidden ways (Byrne, 1998; Morrison, 2008). These complex environmental networks challenge the change process. While participants may seek meaningful and at times rational change, their attempts to produce change are often mediated by unpredictable interactions within the system (Bloch, 2005). As such, complexity theory rejects linear models of cause and effect in which "changes of equal size produce equal effects" (Bloch, 2005, p. 197). Such positivistic and technical rational approaches are considered inadequate as a framework for understanding how seemingly rational actors actually engage in the change process within messy and irrational systems.

The holistic and nonlinear nature of complex systems challenge their investigation. In terms of their research, cases studies offer a means by which to describe and identify complex processes at play within a particular change process. Opfer and Pedder (2011) suggested that research of complex cases focus on the delineation of "emergent patterns of interaction within and between levels of activity that would constitute an explanatory theory" (p. 379) of learning. In complexity theory, change is examined not as discrete variables, but as holistic interactions involving rich and multidimensional relationships (Davis & Sumara, 2006). Davis and Sumara (2012) suggest that research on complex phenomena "is on occasioning the emergence of complex phenomena—that is, not just identifying them, not just better understanding what makes them go, but more deliberate efforts to trigger them into being, to support their development, and to sustain their existence" (p. 31). Critical Friends theory offers one means by which to analyze what supports and sustains complex change. As Critical Friends theory has been described at length in this volume, I will focus on how CPED structured Critical Friends Groups to promote change in individual perspective and action. Specifically, I examine the Critical Friends theoretical conception of reflection as an opportunity to gain perspective and in-depth new understandings. Storey and Richard (2013) summarize this process:

> Implementation of CF of theory protocol (grounded in the charette process) starts with a presentation followed by a probing session. The next two steps, warm (positive) feedback and cool (negative) feedback, are done with the presenter silent. Finally, a challenge to the presenter ends the protocol. Challenge in this process has a constructivist interpretation and is not meant to be adversarial but rather a stimulation to reflect or act, and a questioning that prompts reasoning and explanation or the consideration of different viewpoints. (p.58)

This process can engender new understandings and support the innovative thinking necessary for program development. Key to this process is a dialogue context that is supportive yet critical, grounded in personal meaning making and offering new perspective. The collaborative and public nature of this process is important. By presenting current perspectives, listening to new ones, and then responding yet again in a public forum, critical friends are positioned to imagine how others are listening to their thoughts, thus further reinforcing the dialogic imagination (Bakhtin, 1981).

CPED as a Scaffold of New Ideas and Change

CPED is not an isolated, "stand alone" institution. From the start it has been structured as a platform for meaningful Critical Friends dialogue. When I first attended CPED in 2007 as a representative of WSU, a founding CPED member, I immediately found a stimulating and generative intellectual home for my work in teacher preparation. Throughout this time, CPED has always exerted a strong influence in my thinking about the design, implementation, evaluation, and eventual redesign of an EdD program in teacher leadership.

The following examples of convenings show the intentional interactive nature of CPED and the meaningful, contextualized work of its members. The convenings have been designed to help CPED participants make connections between new participant-generated ideas and grounded workplaces practice. These two contexts—CPED and the institutional workplace—are here presented in tandem as a context of analysis.

Stage One: Palo Alto and the Genesis and Nurturing of a Clinical Practice Approach

In order to promote constructive change at the convenings, CPED asked participants to complete a short preconvening assignment as a frame for their shared work at the convenings. The assignment for the Palo Alto convening asked members to delineate their program principles as well as their evaluation approach for those principles. This task in turn helped participants to scaffold their discussion in relation to one of the keynote presentations of the convening: Marsha Levine's (2011) overview of the NCATE Blue Ribbon Panel on Clinical Preparation and Partnerships for Improved Student Learning (BRP), commissioned by the National Council for Accreditation of Teacher Education.

Levine situated the report within three core problems currently facing public education in the United States: (a) The gap in student achievement; (b) the gap between teacher preparation and both well-established as well as emergent challenges P-12 schools face on a daily basis (e.g., changing demographics, technology challenges, and notions of subject matter); and (c) the gap between helpful knowledge and meaningful action/change—the difference between what educators know to make a difference and what they actually do. She described these high leverage problems as a basis for a meaningful and truly collaborate partnerships between K-12 schools and teacher preparation and teacher leadership doctorates in colleges of education. Her words came to dominate much of my program planning from that morning in Palo Alto to this day.

At the end of Levine's presentation, we had a chance for initial whole-group discussion. A number of people immediately problematized her words: How could clinical practice with its multiple partners be financially supported? Who would coordinate, value check, and sustain it? The criticism notwithstanding, I started thinking about what an intriguing idea it was at least for my school and—given how each of us at CPED was positioned to impact educational programs, how achievable: At my institution I personally wore two hats, the chair of both a high school teacher preparation program and a Teacher Leadership EdD program, both with their own strengths and challenges and both basically disconnected from each other.

Working in field/university partnerships, it occurred to me that I could use the questions Levine posed as a large, institutional problem of practice—to combine these two separate programs. Rearranging a few quality pieces at our institutions—our teacher/administrator preparation programs, our Teacher/Administrator Leadership doctoral programs, and our work with expert and usually overlooked practitioners in the field—we could create a new way of preparing educators. As Levine put it: It's not a quantitative combination: It's an entirely new qualitative way of working. It's education in a new key. David Imig at that session called it the negative space between words. For me to begin to understand this change, I had to engage in aesthetic and metaphoric thinking. At the conference table, I sketched a diagram (Figure 5.2).

I then shared some initial thoughts about the diagram (Figure 5.2) with the whole group. It suggests that with a little fine-tuning, three separate teacher preparation structures (teacher preparation, teacher development in an EdD program, and field partnerships) could overlap to delineate a new, dynamic form. This overlap, to reference Levine's words, would create a new space, a new lens. Her view of teacher preparation was grounded in the experience of K-12 students as understood by clinical practitioners who work with those students. This clinical view of student learning is then blended into all levels and aspects of teacher/practitioner preparation. What I found

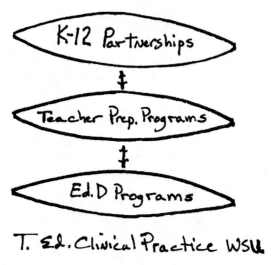

Figure 5.2 Teacher preparation structures.

stimulating was that Levine was elaborating on a larger notion of practitioner preparation for schools (teachers, administrators, and scholarly practitioners), while we were more narrowly focused on just one aspect of it.

Following this discussion we were asked at our tables to think first individually and then collectively about how our institutions are engaged or can engage in clinical practice to close the three gaps that the BRP reported. Each table had a mix of institutions presenting a range of views. This process gave each of us a chance to apply the BRP's report to our own work in a critical yet supportive way. Each of us had a chance to present, explore, and receive feedback on the efficacy of our principles in practice. Coming back to the whole group, there was considerable talk about how as an organization CPED could begin to disseminate our ideas. We decided to create a couple of key discussion blogs, with one of it being on clinical practice.

Later in the convening, Levine, Imig, and I talked and we decided to pursue the idea of clinical practice together before the next convening in Vermont a few months later. I was asked to write a short piece about clinical practice and post it to the blog before the Vermont convening, as a way to begin to scaffold discussion there about clinical practice.

Fieldwork at Washington State University

Back at WSU, I wrote a CPED blog entry. In this short discussion I built on the format given to us in Palo Alto, in which I compared the principles from the BRP to those of both CPED and my institution in a three-column format. I thought that it would be helpful to show the similarities between these principles. I considered the three gaps that the BRP raised as a problem-solving basis to show the inherent usefulness in aligning the principles from the three contexts (i.e., the BRP, CPED, and my institution). I highlighted how the BRP report underscored the key importance of complex and situated clinical knowledge (of practitioners learning within the context of actual student experience) to teacher preparation, held by practitioners (both teachers and administrators). I further mentioned that the BRP report supported colleges of education as central players in teacher preparation and inservice teacher professional development in a partnership approach. Furthermore, in recognizing practitioners as generators of knowledge and active participants in the educational change process, the report was consistent with the mission of professional practice doctoral programs, especially those at land grant institutions. Such programs often seek that its graduates return to schools to engage in collaborative, often partnership-based, inquiry and action for improved student learning. I also mentioned that the engagement of a shared problem-solving approach could add coherence for partners with similar yet slightly different missions and goals.

After posting these comments on the CPED blog, a lively conversation ensued, with an additional 25 comments. Jill Perry, one of the founders of CPED, facilitated a Critical Friends discussion by framing it with the following question (Perry, 2011):

> Rick offer[ed] suggestions for what might constitute a program of studies and research. Taking [his] concept, what would you add? How would you redirect it or strengthen it? Could the proposed strand of work encompass some of the ideas that Bryk and Gomez have articulated?

All of the responses were thoughtful and moved my own thinking forward. I have summarized the feedback discussed in bullet form (Table 5.1).

True to a Critical Friends impact, the comments in Table 5.1 have expanded the conception of clinical practice not just for me, but for all CPED members. For me, the questions about respecting practitioner time, creating systemic policy, involving the community more fully, and understanding implementation issues continue to resonate for me.

Stage Two: Vermont and a Public Stance

Shortly before returning to the next convening at the University of Vermont in fall 2011, I had the opportunity to plan with Marsha

Table 5.1 CPED blog entry online discussion

Feedback
- Involve the community more broadly.
- Expand the view of a clinical practitioner.
- Engage in group problem solving.
- Engage graduates as cultural bridges between the three partners.
- Include a policy stance involving state departments of education.
- Expand the nature and role of capstones/dissertations to promote clinical practice.
- Consider the increased demands on already overworked full-time practitioners.
- Foreground democratic processes in the clinical practice model.
- Include practitioners in inquiry.

Levine the next steps for a strategy to move the clinical practice agenda forward among the CPED participants. Specifically, we considered how to facilitate the different institutions' use of clinical practice to address the gaps outlined by the BRP. Our goal was to leverage the collective energy and educational reach of our respective schools to bring about meaningful change.

By this time, my tentative ideas about clinical practice had evolved into a loose model, the Tripartite Model of Clinical Practice Educator Preparation, which Imig and I named during the presentation. Although there is considerable literature in terms of professional development schools as well as clinical practice more generally, our approach—involving clinical practice as a means to link a teacher preparation program to a Teacher Leadership EdD program—was new. And, more importantly to my own situation, this particular approach now offered new possibilities and ways to approach previously encountered problems with teacher preparation.

At this convening my position changed from participant to facilitator, a change in role which also changed my relationship to the topic. Imig and I made a short presentation and then led a whole group discussion on the topic. While at this point I was gaining considerable commitment to this topic, there was perhaps a greater range to the other participants' views. Some CPED participants began to consider new possibilities in relation to clinical practice, while others articulated seminal dilemmas found in partnership work.

Following the convening, Michael Neel, a University of Maryland graduate student and CPED coordinator, and I drew up characteristics of clinical practice as a framework for program redesign (Table 5.2).

I then used these principles with the MIT S Program Committee to implement a clinical practice approach into the program. Given funding and partnership challenges that we have faced, we sought a multistep change process and initially focused on a few feasible goals:

- The introduction of a new philosophical framing to the program (in support of clinical practice),
- A new intertwining of theory (coursework) and fieldwork in the program,
- A restructuring of student work to highlight the role of Washington State school reform, and especially the Teacher Performance Assessment (TPA) that had become a defining feature of the program and students' performance,
- And, in support of the above goals, a revision to program course sequence.

Table 5.2   Clinical practice

Characteristics:
- Field-contextualized practitioner knowledge, decision making, and activity integrated into the planning, implementation, evaluation, and improvement of all program characteristics.
- Preparation as theory and practice "helix."
- Redesigned partnership model between P-12 schools, community, and higher education.
- Changes in curriculum to reflect new design.
- University reward system structured around clinical practice and service.
- Research on system patterns of practice that promote and sustain clinical practice transformations.

Clinical faculty:
- Bridge theory/practice and university/field fault lines.
- Are certified and accountable for its candidates' performance and student outcomes.
- Work transcends traditional role of cooperating teacher preservice supervisor.
- Are rewarded for work and carry university title.

Introducing a new philosophical focus to the program meant changing the program course sequence to support a different kind of program, with a different beginning, middle, and end to it. Table 5.3 characterizes the MIT S program both before and after the initial program revision.

The initial changes to the program were primarily structural and involved rearranging existing program pieces. For example, two EdD students were teaching courses in the program, but more as adjuncts than core faculty. After the initial change, they were part of a collaborative group that began to plan the initial student classroom visits. Another change to the program was the interweaving of inquiry more centrally into it. Instead of having a capstone action research course, the program was revised to ideally have inquiry frame students' work within it. Students engaged in the CPED concept of "problems of practice" as a means by which to critique and open their practice. And the third change to the program was the introduction of the "helix" in the theory/practice connection. It is important to note, that each of these changes were dependent in some part on the EdD Program and the expertise of its students and faculty as contributing to the MIT S Program.

Thus the changes in the MIT S Program were done in tandem with changes to the MIT Secondary Program. Table 5.4 characterizes

Table 5.3 MIT S Program before and after program revision

Initial MIT S Program	MIT S after convenings
• 4 semester program • Initial coursework semester not connected to field • University supervisor as conduit to field and planning • TPA integrated into program • Mentor Teachers not EdD Students • Inquiry course at end of program • Action research project at end of program	• 4 semester program • Initial coursework threaded with field work, coordinated by clinical practice group • Systemic practitioner/university planning for field and course work • TPA integrated into program • Some Mentor Teachers EdD Students • Inquiry course at beginning of program • Inquiry as lens woven throughout the program

Table 5.4 TL EdD Program before and after program revision

Initial TL EdD	TL EdD after convenings
• On Multiple Campuses • No Teacher Preparation Internship Option. • EdD Students not Mentor Teachers. • No clinical practice planning group. • No clinical practice laboratory of practice inquiry group.	• On Multiple Campuses • Teacher Preparation Internship Option. • Some EdD Students now Mentor Teachers. • Clinical practice planning group for MIT S "helix." • Clinical practice laboratory of practice inquiry group.

the TL EdD Program both before and after the initial program revision.

Part of the changes to the TL EdD Program were informed by an evaluation we did of the initial aspects of clinical practice that linked the MIT S and the TL EdD Programs, before a revision. Last year, for example, we asked two of our EdD students, one who is a high school social studies teacher and the other an English teacher, to also start teaching in our secondary certification evening program. The social studies teacher taught the classroom management course and the English teacher an academic content area reading course. Both of them created strong ties between the theory that they are teaching and their actual practice, thus intertwining (to some extent) theory and practice for their MIT students. A couple of the MIT students were also able to visit the EdD students in their own high school classrooms in order to apply the theories they were learning to classroom practice. For formative feedback, we conducted a survey of the leading participants in this emerging clinical practice project (the MIT students, the EdD students, and the high school students) and found a strong awareness and appreciation of how this approach was promoting not only strong theory-practice connections, but also a certain teacher agency among the MIT students.

However, most of the participants also mentioned that direct and more prolonged exposure to the EdD students' high school classrooms as a laboratory of practice (my words, not theirs) for their exploration of theory-practice connections would have been helpful. This finding prompted our initial program changes. We have now decided to offer a specific two- or three-semester course-based internship to our EdD students on clinical practice. This option allows those students who were interested in pursuing teacher education as the focus of their work, to do so in a clinical practice model—that is, in a "cutting edge" model of teacher preparation. It also reduces the university's expenses, at a time when it is impossible to incur additional program costs. This internship would be for our EdD students who wish to prepare for a career in teacher/educator preparation or professional development. We are now considering these additional changes to the program:

- Placing the EdD student with a mentor/collaborator who is a teacher preparation professor in the MIT Program,
- Providing opportunities for EdD students to teach/co-teach MIT courses,
- Integrating a range of EdD students' K-12 classrooms into the MIT program as strategic and collaborative labs of practice,
- Organizing collaborative research projects among all participants,
- Integrating on-site teacher professional development into the model.

All of these changes were scaffolded and in many ways supported by the Critical Friends network found in CPED.

Complexity theory suggests that change evolves along multiple pathways at different structural and individual levels. The changes that we made to the two programs at this time lay somewhat at a surface level, more at the periphery than the heart of the two programs. For example, the planning for the initial threaded observations involved both classroom teachers and university faculty members. Given work schedules, I met with members of these two groups separately, so they did not actually come together. In the discussions, we all selected ways that the teaching interns could examine theory within authentic, classroom situations (e.g., in relation to teacher curriculum planning), but the flow of suggested activities went from the university to the school, not mutually back and forth. The work of the classroom teachers change as they accommodated the university's requests, and the work of the university faculty changed as they linked theory more closely to practice in their classes, but the university faculty did change to accommodate curricular requests from the classroom teachers. In a true partnership, the work and contribution of each partner changes the core curriculum of the others, and that was not the case here. However, complexity theory also suggests that changes in practice develop in organic ways and the basis for deeper personal and curricular change was introduced at this time.

The following section of the chapter analyzes the contribution of a Critical Friends approach to the program changes.

Discussion: Dynamics of the Critical Friends Approach as a Platform for Critique and Change at CPED

The boundaries of this illustrative case study included aspects of both CPED convenings and the MIT S and TL EdD Programs and their field components at my university. The analysis examined the CPED Critical Friends' process from the specific vantage point of one concept for one person. It drew from complexity theory to highlight the layered, holistic, and multifaceted interaction between CPED and university activity. The intention of this interaction has been to promote participant thinking leading to individual and institutional change. The following is a two-level matrix borrowed from developmental teacher supervision (Glickman & Gordon, 1987; Glickman, Gordon, & Ross-Gordon, 2001) examining levels of conceptual thinking in relation to the engagement of action, thus differentiating four different levels in a change process. Table 5.5 illustrates this matrix.

The horizontal axis illustrates both more superficial and deeper levels of conceptual thinking about clinical practice; while the vertical matrix illustrates both more superficial and deeper levels of institutional change, resulting in a total of four cells. The most desirable category, of course, is found in the fourth cell in the upper right corner: a deep conceptual understanding of clinical practice coupled with institutional ownership of the implementation of a clinical practice

Table 5.5　Levels of conceptual thinking in relation to the engagement of action

Thinking about CP	Lower Action Level	Deeper Action Level
Deeper Conceptual	2. Conceptual capacity for change, but frustration over its lack.	4. Deeper connectional thinking put into action. Institutional change and buy-in from participants.
Lower Conceptual	1. Safe, static, and traditional: Routine thinking, lack of action.	3. Incoherent action not grounded conceptually, historically, or environmentally. Institutional buy-in for contrived change.

approach. The least desirable but possibly safest category is found in cell one, a definitive lack of understanding of clinical practice along with a lack of an attempt at change. Cell three is the most frustrating for the actor, involving a deeper conceptual level but a lack of action—in essence, the rapid spinning of a disengaged gear. And, cell two is potentially the most damaging, illustrating the production of action (here in teacher preparation) without personal and institutional conceptual awareness.

As a complex system, a tension has existed between the openness of CPED and its structure, which scaffolds change and the established and structurally lodged interaction patterns at the university setting. CPED provides a platform for participants to critique, develop, and evaluate new ideas about their programs. While CPED has fairly consistently triggered an intention of change, my university has created a complex environment supporting certain aspects of change while challenging others.

On the university level, degree programs represent exceptionally complex organizations. In some ways, they resemble little solar systems, each with its own history, culture, and ways of operating. From their inception, before becoming available to students, programs go through an approval process involving a range of organizations (e.g., a department, college, university faculty, curriculum committee, the graduate school), which require new programs to define, codify, and establish predetermined curriculum. This process by its very nature limits program creativity and interdisciplinary engagement. Once programs are approved, they are difficult to change. The university reward structure supports faculty research but not service or program development work. (This university limitation to collaboration is underscored in this particular situation by the K-12 reward structure, which is currently focused on standards and student test scores, not school-university partnership efforts). The understandable university faculty goal is to routinize a new program (both for their sake and for that of students). Program boundaries are often set to guide the successful functioning of a program, in essence operating as an operational road map. This map shows the known landscape, not the new. These boundaries, the result of considerable debate and work, can be formidable. Even program accountability mechanisms can hinder change efforts, as they tend to focus on measurable and defined outcomes and products, not learning processes. Collaboration as a goal embraces change, not stability, challenging accountability structures. As can be seen from this description, individual programs can be complex. With this particular change to implement a clinical practice approach, however, two programs needed to first work together and then with a K-12 community.

A further level of complexity in a situation involving collaborative change is not structural, but individual. A complex structure focuses faculty thinking on the structure—its problems and interactions. In this particular situation, it was a Critical Friends dynamism within the CPED space that provided the catalyst for a new way of thinking about how these programs could work together. For me personally, the Critical Friends framework operated in a particular way at CEPD. CPED participants, consistent with Critical Friends theory, engage each other in meaningful and direct conversation. As pedagogical tools, CPED uses a range of interaction approaches. In general, each convening has focused on specific theory-practice themes (e.g., clinical practice), around which the event is structured to provide participants multiple forms of engagement with the topic. The general pattern has been preconvening homework, followed by a convening presentation (sometimes by an expert in the field and other times by a CPED member) on a similar topic, then individual reflection on the topic. This individual thinking is then followed by table-group conversation often framed by the preconvening assignment. These conversations, which are thus grounded in participants' specific contexts, are then followed by whole group discussion. Much of the interaction structure then of CPED draws from a Critical Friends framework intended to promote the reconceptualization of participant views about specific topics.

While the structure supports a change in thinking, there is usually a catalyst speaker or introduction of a new idea that sparks the imagination. Levine's presentation had such an effect on me. I had been involved in a range of clinical-practice based partnerships and professional development efforts before hearing her speak. However, when she called for "turn[ing] teacher preparation upside down," she sparked my imagination. Although I had initiated two school-university partnerships before, her words turned my thinking upside down. It was then that clinical practice, a relatively well-known approach in teacher preparation, emerged for me in a new way and moved into the forefront of my program planning. Before hearing Levine speak, my attention was focused on program maintenance at WSU. After hearing her speak, I realized that these program challenges related to curriculum and student development could be reconceptualized. Again, Levin did not speak in a vacuum: Her words contributed to a Critical Friends situation that scaffolded a reconceptualization of thinking about existing programs. The specific breakthrough came when I realized that combining programs would have the potential to create mutually reinforcing and shared learning outcomes (e.g., preservice teacher preparation with inservice teacher professional development), not separate student outcomes, thus leading to more work. It is not surprising that such a realization could arise in a generative Critical Friends situation involving dialogue and collaboration focused on problems of practice.

Specifically, the Critical Friends discussions contributed to the examination and the attempted solution of a number of individual program challenges. On the one hand, the MIT Secondary Program faced a number of seminal challenges in teacher preparation. On a relatively superficial level, these challenges were about the separation of theory and practice. Having coursework separate from fieldwork made difficult for teacher candidates to see the immediate value of theory to promote authentic learning and of theory and practice together to solve classroom-based problems and dilemmas. On a more meaningful level, however, these were challenges about collaborating with schools to prepare new teachers to solve twenty-first century problems (e.g., closing the achievement gap). And on the other hand, the TL EdD Program faced a number of challenges in providing and modeling new approaches to prepare teacher leaders. These were challenges about how to prepare teacher leaders to mutually engage a rich and complex set of skills and habits of mind. The challenge we faced at WSU was not about teaching about these skills and habits of mind, rather, it was about modeling and engaging doctoral students in authentic problems of practice related to them. As we distributed and shared our knowledge in Critical Friends discussions at CPED, we articulated ways that would allow doctoral students to gain leadership and professional development skills through their collaborative work with new teacher candidates. In this complex process, we erased some boundaries between these two programs, providing the teacher candidates with the classrooms and authentic knowledge of the doctoral students, and the doctoral students with the messy, real-world challenge of engaging in teacher preparation and partnership work.

Levine's provocative words added a highly resonate quality that animated the existing CPED Critical Friends scaffolding. It was partly the clarity of her vision that reenergized my own vision in terms of partnerships in teacher preparation. And from there, the CPED procedure let me explore and personally move the clinical practice concept forward. First, CPED asked its participants to do "homework" before the convening in order to promote constructive change and to frame the work we do in person. The assignment for Palo Alto asked members to first consider their program principles and then their evaluation system for those principles. We then worked first individually and then as a group, examining our program (framed by their principles) in relation to the three gaps that Levine had discussed.

A Critical Friends approach was at play here. We arrived at Palo Alto already having considered our programs as homework. What was interesting about doing this assignment was that we completed it where we worked. Subsequently discussing it at CPED, we placed our programs in a new environment, basically destabilizing them and disrupting—in a minor way—their narratives. We then talked about our programs in relation to the three gaps and heard—and importantly imagined—new responses to them. This process allowed us to begin to view our programs in a new way. Later that day, when I was asked to write some of my ideas for the CPED blog, I began to explore my ideas in a new medium for a slightly different type of audience (although the same people). It was in this format that I began to move my ideas forward in relation to changing my own programs.

The next structural step was the engagement of the CPED discussion and new ideas into the actual university arena. This step was basically orchestrated by Perry of CPED and Levine and again, was very consistent with a Critical Friends approach. I now moved from the realm of theory to that of messy practice in considering how to change the program. This step in the process began to illustrate a key consideration for me: theories and beliefs work in tandem with practice to scaffold change.

Initially, the changes that we made to the two programs were primarily university based. This start toward creating a clinical theory-practice helix has primarily involved university people with the teachers who were also EdD students. Part of this first step involved rearranging the program's course structure to promote MIT student inquiry. We are doing this by moving the capstone action research course to the beginning of the program, now focusing on teacher inquiry as a conceptual program lens for the interns. A second part of the initial program change was to intertwine course work with field work in the first semester of the program with strategic one-week field placements embedded within the coursework. The goal here was to promote interns' deeper understanding of the meaning of theory in the practice of student interaction and learning. The intention was not just to examine how theory plays out in practice, but rather how theory and practice combine in unpredictable and situated ways for students to form new meanings. School-university shared planning has partly organized this effort, an organization explicitly informed by the BRP's report. The second step in this process will be the restructuring of the actual MIT student internship. This plan, as yet unrealized, will be to place the interns with either EdD students who are teaching in secondary classrooms or mentor teachers who partner with the program.

At this point, our conceptualization of clinical practice is ahead of its implementation. Still, the clinical practice model of practitioner preparation is "under construction": It is developing and emerging. Many if not most of these program changes can be linked to the CPED Critical Friends approach. Without the charged and engaged nature of this approach in CPED, these changes would not have happened. The professional literature is much more theoretical than operationalized in this particular area, so it would have been difficult for it to frame the change. And the MIT program itself and its history did not provide a catalyst for change, although it has provided its partial foundation. The conceptual trigger for change came from CPED. However, the change process itself as it unfolded in practice has been complex and involved on a larger level the interaction of two different programs and their relationship to the field. On more of a micro-level, the change process has involved structural, conceptual, and participant meaning-making levels within those programs and the field.

Examining the institutional change through Complexity theory suggests that the nature of the open system itself both simultaneously promoted certain aspects of the change, while hindering others. In my own case, the culture of the institution has acted to absorb both innovation as well as its interpretation (Sarason, 1982, 1995), even when individuals have rhetorically embraced it. Furthermore, the course curriculum context has also tended to limit the extent of this change. Again, complexity stresses the importance of the analysis of levels of change. In terms of CPED's impact on the change of our institution, I have been the one to benefit from attending CPED. I have been exposed to its ideas in an immediate, dynamic, and interactive way. However, although I have been fortunate enough to attend CPED convenings, my immediate work colleagues have not. Therefore there has been one large step of separation between my colleagues and CPED, my colleagues being informed about CPED by me in less than ideal settings (e.g., as one item among many on a meeting agenda, or by the water-cooler in a hall). Thus workplace interpretations of new ideas tend to norm those ideas into existing ways of thinking and acting. I have been fortunate to work with people who have embraced CPED ideas, but as complexity theory shows, once those new ideas enter into an open system, the definitions of those ideas change in unpredictable ways. The second aspect to this open system is that it does have narrative boundaries. As I have found, new ideas are still subject to interpretations that are deeply nested within existing interpersonal, intellectual, and institutional narratives. Clearly, we need to move a Critical Friends approach to the university.

RECOMMENDATIONS

Traditionally, the mission of universities has been to contribute slowly and methodically to a field of scholarship, not to the world of practice. University scholarship that provides perspective, critique, and theory has contributed greatly to humanity and the improvement of society for all its members. What CPED and its university partners are attempting to do is to shift the light of that scholarship and place it not just above practice (even slightly), but actually within it. By underscoring the relationship of theory to practice found within the concept of the scholarship of practice (Hutchings & Schulman, 1999), CPED seeks to support professional practice doctorates focused on research tied to practice, to create cycles of continuous improvement.

My recommendations for my own practice as well as for that of others involved in similar endeavors is to use the concept of the scholarship of practice as an organizing frame throughout the different stages of program design, implementation, improvement, and continuation. For a partnership to operate in a new key, then its creation must also be done in a new key: in a collaborative, dialogic way that promotes new perspectives and builds shared understandings. Engaging in work that attempts to partner K-12 schools with universities by its very nature needs to be collaborative, distributed, and equitable, and for it to be equitable, the collaboration needs to begin from the start with the initial planning. As with any meaningful endeavor, an active problem-solving stance provides focus and motivation to the planning. I would suggest that the most meaningful and high-leverage problems to use in this process are those that schools are facing daily in the United States. If the goal is to create a doctoral program to improve practice (and habits of minding leading to that improvement), then those problems need to be grounded in the complexities found in the field that require collaboration and distributed expertise from multiple partners to solve. Schools and universities provide different perspectives, yet together they can create a new shared perspective that combines their expertise. As suggestions for high-traction problems of practice, Levine summarized three at CPED (2011): (a) The gap in student achievement; (b) the gap between teacher preparation and both well-established as well as emergent challenges K-12 schools face on a daily basis (e.g., changing demographics, technology challenges, and notions of subject matter); and (c) and the gap between helpful knowledge and meaningful action/change—the difference between what educators know to make a difference and what they actually do. But regardless of the focus, which should be decided collaboratively by all the partners, a central and changing focus can guide the partnership throughout its various stages. The difficult part is designing a program around thematic concepts rather than traditional coursework, but it is much easier to do this at the program's formation, rather than after its establishment.

My second recommendation is to actually establish the working procedure among the partners as a Critical Friends Group, or a similar process. Meaningful and uncontrived clinical practice is not only complex, but must be open to—and actually generated from—multiple voices and perspectives. Critical Friends theory gives an organizing framework for this process. It is important to note that as a semiformalized process, a Critical Friends framework can be organized to provide all members with equal time and opportunity—within a safe space. A number of years ago Dan Lortie (1975) discussed schools as sites that promoted individualism, narcissism, and conservatism of thought. Critical Friends Groups can combat this form of retrenched thinking by not only allowing participants to hear new perspectives, but by also imagining new responses to their perspectives.

CONCLUSION

Our efforts to restructure both an MIT Secondary Program and a TL EdD program at WSU around a tripartite model of practitioner preparation are now entering their second year. We have reorganized the course structure and begun to intertwine theory and practice in students' coursework and field experiences to create a more meaningful internship experience for our teacher candidates and to prepare our TL EdD students to work in teacher preparation and professional development as an authentic and combined effort.

One thing that the use of complexity theory has shown is how CPED, through the promotion of a Critical Friends approach, has scaffolded new conceptions about clinical practice. There has been interplay of CPED-generated theory about clinical practice with specific program demands and realities in teacher preparation and professional development at WSU. It is probably simplistic to say that the new conceptualization has lead the changes in the programs at WSU, but I think that it is safe to say that CPED did trigger new ideas that led to our reconceptualizing program possibilities. The actual program realities created fertile ground for these new ideas and gave life to them.

REFERENCES

Bakhtin, N. (1981). *The dialogic imagination.* Austin: The University of Texas Press.

Bloch, D. P. (2005). Complexity, chaos, and non-linear dynamics: A new perspective on career development theory. *The Career Development Quarterly, 53*(3), 194–207.

Byrne, D. (1998). *Complexity theory and the social sciences.* London and New York: Routledge.

Cilliers, P. (1998). *Complexity and postmodernism: Understanding complex systems.* London and New York: Routledge.

Davis, B., & Sumara, D. (2006). *Complexity and education: Inquiries in learning, teaching, and research.* New York: Routledge.

Davis, B., & Sumara, D. (2012). Fitting teacher education in/to/for an increasingly complex world. *Complicity: An International Journal of Complexity and Education, 9*(1), 30–40.

Glickman, C. D., & Gordon, S. P. (1987). Clarifying developmental supervision. *Educational Leadership, 44*(8), 64–68.

Glickman, C., Gordon, S. P., & Ross-Gordon, J. M. (2001). *SuperVision and instructional leadership: A developmental approach* (6th ed.). Needham Heights, MA: Allyn & Bacon/Longman Publishing.

Hutchings, P., & Schulman, L. S. (1999). The Scholarship of Teaching: New Elaborations, New Developments. *Change*, September/October, 10–15.

Levine, M. (2011, June 7). Report by the Blue Ribbon Panel on Clinical Preparation and Partnerships for Improved Student Learning [PowerPoint slides]. Paper presented at the convening of the Carnegie Project on the Education Doctorate, Palo Alto, CA.

Lortie, D. (1975). *Schoolteacher: A sociological study.* Chicago: University of Chicago Press.

Morrison, K. (2008). Educational philosophy and the challenge of complexity theory. In M. Mason (Ed.), *Complexity theory and the philosophy of education* (pp. 16–31). West Sussex: Wiley Blackwell.

Opfer, V. D., & Pedder, D. (2011). Conceptualizing teacher professional learning. *Review of Educational Research, 81*(3), 376–407.

Perry, J. (2011, September, 27). Restructuring EdD programs to include clinical knowledge & preparation. [Web log entry]. Retrieved from http://cpedinitiative.org/forum-topic/restructuring-edd-programs-include-clinical-knowledge-preparation.

Sarason, S. B. (1982). *The culture of the school and the problem of change.* Needham Heights, MA: Allyn & Bacon/Longman Publishing.

Sarason, S. B. (1995). *School Change: The personal development of a point of view.* New York, NY: Teachers College Press.

Sawyer, R. D., & Imig, D. (2011, October). The tripartite model of educator preparation. Paper presented at the meeting of Carnegie Project on the Education Doctorate, Burlingame, VT.

Storey, V. A., & Richard, B. (2013). Carnegie Project for the Educational Doctorate: The role of critical friends in diffusing doctoral program innovation. In C. A. Mullen & K. E. Lane (Eds.), *Becoming a Global Voice— the 2013 Yearbook of the National Council of Professors of Educational Administration.* Ypsilanti, MI: NCPEA Publications.

CHAPTER 6

Growing Organically: Building on Strengths for Vermont Doctoral Education

Colleen T. MacKinnon

The landscape is a complex weave of tightly woven environmental, economic, social and demographic threads. You cannot define or preserve a landscape by focusing on only one thread. We can not realize our own visions of landscape and community by talking among ourselves within our own professional enclaves, within our own, like-minded social networks. (Sanford, 2002)

ROLE OF RURAL CONTEXT FOR PROGRAM EVOLUTION

Sheep farming, and an insatiable hunger for timber depleted Vermont's once virgin forests in the late 1800s, leaving behind a hardscrabble landscape dotted with struggling hillside farms. When soils no longer yielded sustainable crops, a vast exodus of discouraged Vermonters left for more fertile soils in western states (Albers, 2002). Italian marble workers and French Canadian immigrants brought new energy to the state, and Vermont's marble-works, textile mills, and dairy farms replaced sheep, along with an emerging tourism industry as Vermont's population grew slowly throughout the 1900s, not surpassing 500,000 until the 1970s (US Bureau of the Census, 1995). As noted in an overview of Vermont's agricultural heritage, "although the often-repeated saying that Vermont 'has more cows than people' was never exactly true, the Green Mountain State is correctly considered a place where agriculture long defined the lifestyle, values, and the hopes and dreams of its citizens" (Harvest, 2013, p. 1).

Depressed milk prices and overproduction of milk forced a new generation of farmers to make decisions in the 1980s to abandon farming traditions as whole-heard buy-outs (also known as the *dairy termination program*) again changed Vermont's landscape from quintessential black and white Holsteins grazing across vast fields of alfalfa to slowly sprouting housing developments (Wadsworth & Bravo-Ureta, 1992). Vermonters with proud traditions developed a reputation for resisting influences of the outside world, with a common refrain directed toward incoming "flatlanders" from the lowlands of Connecticut, Massachusetts, New York, and New Jersey, advised that a cat can have kittens in the oven but they'll never be biscuits. In other words, one is welcome to come and settle, but be mindful of local culture. Rural traditions remain strong in the small towns of Vermont, which offer an incongruous contrast with the city of Burlington, the home of the flagship university of the state. Burlington, ironically known as a great small city that happens to be near Vermont, is now a refugee resettlement community and the Burlington School District reports that more than 50 native languages other than English are spoken by their students, expanding Burlington's global connectedness (Burlington School District, 2013, p. 3).

Traditions of participatory democracy prevailed throughout Vermont's history and provides cultural cues for how the Doctor of Education (EdD) program evolved to become an interdisciplinary program. A small state population of far less than 1 million enables neighbors to get to know each other and become colleagues; it is not usual to bump into the governor or one of the congressional leaders at a local hockey game or farmers' market, and Vermont has become a place where individuals expect to affect decisions, partly due to the historical precedence set by past decades of community-building from the ground up.

It is amidst this culture of fierce independence, self-reliance, interdependency, and capacity for reinventing oneself that the UVM's EdD program emerged in the early 1980s to address the need for a new kind of educational leadership in Vermont, and the program quickly established itself as an essential program for collaborating across agencies for change strategies that would make a difference in the lives of children and their communities. Building on strengths (Cooperrider, Whitney, & Stavros, 2003), faculty established the program's foothold in helping shape the future of Vermont, further solidified by being situated at the state's only research university (Carnegie-classified as a High Research-Activity institution). The EdD program continues to evolve, and it is poised to shoulder major responsibility for leadership development for decades to come. Changes in curriculum, structure, and focus will additionally be amended as faculty refines the EdD in relation to a newly instituted educational leadership PhD program.

This chapter describes the UVM's pathway from offering a single doctoral degree for educational leadership to the adoption of a PhD running parallel to the EdD, a process advanced at time when many other institutions participating in Phase I of the Carnegie Project on the Education Doctorate (CPED) were in a converse process of eliminating PhD programs. Faculty within UVM's Educational Leadership and Policy Studies Program believed CPED-like characteristics were already well-established in their applied research EdD program. Resistance to CPED influences was not an issue. They instead, had a different problem. Faculty charged with developing a PhD needed to untangle the complexities of a high-functioning EdD program that produced both scholarly practitioners and scholarly researchers in order to reconstruct the EdD as a singular degree for field-based scholarly practitioners distinct from a PhD for researchers. In the process, faculty affirmed CPED-like practices already in existence more than they resisted new ones. In addition, this chapter elaborates on the EdD and PhD dichotomy, which addresses critique presented by Critical Friendship Groups' processes: With the establishment of a PhD degree in 2012, the UVM program is further challenged to differentiate the EdD from the PhD within the institution and to articulate ways that the EdD degree is particularly suited for scholarly practitioners focused on addressing the immediate demands of contemporary social problems within a rural and increasingly international context.

LEARNING FROM CRITICAL FRIENDS IN THE CPED NETWORK: NEW LEXICON AND OLD HABITS OF HEART, MIND, AND HAND

Currently, the College of Education and Social Services (CESS) is home to the Department of Education; the Department of Educational Leadership and Developmental Sciences; and the Department of Social Work. With programs accredited by the National Council for the Accreditation of Teacher Education, the Council for Accreditation of Counseling and Related Educational Programs, and the Council for Social Work Education, faculty of the college adeptly bridge local context with national conversations about standards of best practice. Housed in the Department of Leadership and Developmental Sciences, faculty of the Educational Leadership and Policy Studies program engage with colleagues across disciplines to address a range of social problems.

Supported by a grant from the Fund for Improvement of Post-Secondary Education (FIPSE), a CPED-FIPSE research team visited the UVM in spring 2012 to collect data about CPED-influenced changes made in the doctoral program for inclusion in a larger analysis of CPED Phase I impact. Researchers also assumed the mantle of "Critical Friends" (Costa & Kallick, 1993; Storey & Richard, 2013) to provide valuable outside perspectives of program strengths and challenges. The team's report, which outlined their data collection and findings, spoke as much to a newly established PhD program as it did to the EdD program. Well into its second decade, the EdD program had long been serving both practitioner and research communities. Particularly due to the close working relationships between higher education faculty and field partners, with graduates of the EdD program working in either vector, sorting out the two degree objectives tested long-held assumptions about doctoral education in general.

Noting that UVM's EdD program design includes many CPED characteristics, and that clarifying EdD and PhD differences was a challenge for faculty, researchers essentially shone a light on that very issue that proved to be most vexing. Reflecting on observations of the CPED-FIPSE researchers, faculty agreed for the most part with the analysis and aimed to continue with their work to more clearly differentiate the EdD from the PhD, which will be discussed further after first providing more contexts for current challenges.

To understand how an EdD program came to look much like a PhD program, it might be instructive to review the path of the program's changes during another period of intentional analysis and transformation during the 1990s. Following the EdD program's establishment in 1982, program faculty oversaw the evolution of the program from one that had initially been established for educational administrators to a highly desirable program for professional leaders from a variety of backgrounds who were intent on furthering their leadership proficiency. In 1995, the core faculty of the then-named Educational Leadership Program committed to an analysis and redesign of the existing program to support an interprofessional cohort, which would ultimately "sustain stronger interagency development among professionals from schools, institutions of higher education, and human service agencies" in order to better address "the complexity of problems" that demand the attentions of each domain (Aiken, Prue, & Hasazi, 1999, p. 70). They began with a statement of their core beliefs as articulated in their then newly created mission statement.

> Graduates of the doctoral program in educational leadership and policy studies should possess the knowledge, dispositions, principles, and skills to be humane, imaginative, and competent leaders who can make a difference in the lives of youth, adults, families, and communities. (p. 71)

Faculty committed to building a program that would support candidates in bridging typical territorial boundaries imposed by budgets and traditions of working in silos. By immersing a cohort of students from multiple disciplines into an intensely shared experience of core academics and scholarly inquiry, faculty could help forge those relationships that might persist beyond the conference of a degree. As Aiken, Prue, and Hasazi noted, a well-designed program cognizant of the necessary interdependencies inherent in a small state can "build foundations for enduring partnerships among all leaders from our communities, institutions of higher learning, health care organizations, and public schools" (p. 81). In addition, these relationships would certainly have implications beyond state borders, particularly as our graduates take what they learn to a new location. Dewey (1937) asserted that "no social change is more than external unless it is attended by and rooted in the attitudes of those who bring it about and of those who are affected by it" (p. 4). Establishing meaningful transformation could begin with leaders versed in the knowledge, skills, and dispositions required to engage stakeholders in the hard work of social change, and faculty have continued to hone curricula and structural elements to ensure that leaders in a variety of social institutions are prepared to establish enduring partnerships for these efforts. Reflective analysis of program efficacy and attention to broader social constructs has continued to prod faculty to examine intent, practices, and outcomes. In the context of a culture of continuous improvement, and openness to external forces, faculty were once again faced with an opportunity to consider shifts in program direction with both the advent of CPED discussions and an internal push for a PhD program.

Although faculty of the college began the conversation to review its doctoral offerings in the fall of 2005, including a charge to develop a PhD, confusion about the role of the EdD in academe continued to reign as a challenge, particularly because faculty of UVM's program were comprised of both PhD and EdD degree recipients. Discussions about introducing a PhD program therefore created an explicit need to differentiate the curricular objectives and experiences for the EdD program (The University of Vermont, Progress Report, May 31, 2008, p. 1).

The program at the time was "organized according to four domains"—Organizational Theory, Inquiry/Applied Research, Critical Perspectives, Learning and Development—, which remain intact today, with the addition of a fifth domain, Policy Study and Analysis, thereby making the thematic study of policy more explicit.

In 2007, when UVM joined the CPED, UVM offered only the EdD in Educational Leadership and Policy Studies, which was described as an applied research and education degree for professionals serving in leadership and management positions in elementary and secondary schools, colleges, and universities, health care, law enforcement, and social service organizations.

> The program has been designed to respond to the expanding demands placed on leaders in educational and human service organizations where leaders are increasingly expected to design and supervise local research and varied evaluative studies; interpret and apply recent national research findings; analyze and apply governmental regulations and court decisions; develop organizational responses to emerging social expectations; organize and lead staff development programs; understand and apply broad-based economic principles and social and fiscal policy; develop and manage budgets; assess and respond to the psychological needs of educational consumers; employ effective interpersonal management and decision-making skills. (The University of Vermont, 2008)

Its mission, "to produce leaders who can construct and apply knowledge to make a positive difference in the lives of individuals, families, and communities" (The University of Vermont, Doctoral Program in Educational Leadership and Policy Studies Handbook, 2012, p. 5), guided program design and curricula. Taking full advantage of UVM's small size, the EdD program has benefited from the relatively easy access to state government officials, agency leaders, and other university and school stakeholders. Many College of Education and Social Services faculty members and doctoral students engaged in research that has direct value for the citizens of Vermont, and dissertations often looked very much like capstone projects suggested by CPED partners' dialogue. And many dissertations also looked very much like a traditional PhD dissertation. Discussions about introducing a PhD program therefore created an explicit need to differentiate the curricular objectives and experiences for the EdD program, while at the same time holding onto an essential focus on social justice and human rights for both programs. The CPED-FIPSE research team in their 2012 report noted this confusion about the two degrees among stakeholder groups.

UVM's Signature Pedagogy: Building Networked Communities for Problem Solving

Shulman (2005) defined signature pedagogies as a focusing construct for program design that in practice could help graduates of programs internalize characteristics and skills that would be most useful for sustaining and strengthening a field of practice.

> [Signature pedagogies] implicitly define what counts as knowledge in a field and how things become known. They define how knowledge is analyzed, criticized, accepted, or discarded. They define the functions of expertise in a field, the locus of authority, and the privileges of rank and standing. As we have seen, these pedagogies even determine the architectural design of educational institutions, which in turn serves to perpetuate these approaches. (p. 54)

Borrowing from Noddings's (1984) promotion of an "ethic of care," faculty had built over a couple of decades a curriculum and structural elements that would both explicitly teach and model practices that advanced personal growth and developed capacity for ethical leadership (Gerstl-Pepin, Hasazi, & Killeen, 2006). For example, faculty revised curriculum around a core sequence and instituted an intentionally diverse cohort model that "included students who focus on K-12, higher education, social services, and community leadership" (p. 252), which might allow students to better collaborate across fields of professional practice with a shared commitment to social justice, informing problem-solving strategies.

Students are accepted into the program based partly on a demonstrated commitment to social justice and personal aspirations for using the doctoral program to further goals. Connections to social justice issues, as well as the cultural and geographic landscape of Vermont, can be seen in the topics of dissertations.

- Initiation of field services in the Agency of Human Services
- Exploring sustainability of school improvements in Vermont schools

- Effects of policy on gender equity in Vermont technical education
- Vermont welfare practices
- Vermont refugee experiences
- Public school teacher hiring practices in secondary schools
- Aspirations of rural youth living in poverty
- Analyzing statewide youth risk surveys
- Organizational restructuring of a Vermont agency
- Communities of practice and school reform
- Organizational leadership in higher education
- Democratic schooling in Vermont communities
- Vermont foster youth aging out of state custody
- African-American communities in rural Vermont
- Full-service schools through integrated partnerships

To use Shulman's framework of a signature pedagogy that facilitates the establishment of the habits of heart, mind, and hand that can propel a discipline into the next generation, it could be said that the UVM program had established this framework long before faculty became involved in the CPED initiative where faculty learned to name these activities as such. Faculty commitment to reflective inquiry was foundational to program design and ensured that by "using pedagogy that emphasizes human affect as well as thought and action, lifelong learning becomes a disposition and pattern of behavior" (Su, 2011, p. 407).

An ethic of care infused throughout the program and a focus on human rights ensured candidates were developing the necessary habits of heart that would serve to improve ethical decision making in one's day-to-day practices. Maintaining a cohesive and rigorous curriculum with clear expectations for scholarly inquiry promoted habits of mind that candidates could readily access to work collaboratively across disciplines to address significant problems in the state and beyond. And by making the program an applied research program, faculty could mentor candidates in developing habits of hand as candidates used their field-based work settings as a laboratory of practice, addressing significant issues in conjunction with teams of faculty and field partners.

In one laboratory of practice, EdD program faculty led a cross-disciplinary research team in a project referred to as the Incarcerated Women's Initiative (IWI). Comprised of graduate students, State Agency of Human Services Department of Corrections staff members, and prisoner advocates, the IWI aimed to inform policy and strategies that could support incarcerated women with their transitions out of prison and thereby reduce recidivism (Meyers et al., 2007). Because of the caretaking role of women and the effects of parental incarceration on children, this initiative was perceived as a priority that crossed typical agency boundaries, and, therefore, provided a worthwhile and instructive focus for doctoral program faculty and candidates.

The IWI offers an example of ways that UVM doctoral studies aligned with CPED principles and built on established relationships already existing in the state to provide authentic learning opportunities that make a difference in the lives of youth, families, and communities. Vermont's relatively small size compared to other states and the interdependency of professional relationships ensure frequent interactions, and continuous informal feedback loops drive program improvement on a regular basis. It might be for this reason, perhaps, that program faculty may have reluctantly approached CPED-driven changes to the EdD program because many CPED characteristics were already in place. Relationships like those provided by CPED Critical Friendship Groups had, in effect, been long-used by UVM faculty throughout the development, growth, and reenvisioning of the program though a Critical Friendship protocol had not been formally applied.

As the example of the incarcerated women's initiative illustrates, the EdD program was designed to build interprofessional networks for solving some of Vermont's thorniest problems. No social problem operates in isolation and strategies to address elements of most problems rely on multiple disciplines for collaborative problem solving, which "suggest a communal or constructivist stance toward leadership" (Furman & Gruenewald, 2004, p. 66). Social problems that affect schooling require individuals in leadership roles to have the skills and dispositions to work with community members and other professionals for identifying root causes and potential strategies for transformation (Jean-Marie, Normore, & Brooks, 2009).

Vermont's traditions of building a network of community members to focus on problem solving can also be illustrated with the implementation of special education practices, with Vermont taking on an early leadership role nationally, particularly related to special education inclusion (Lipsky & Gartner, 1996).

Following the legislative adoption of a new school funding formula for the state, faculty and graduate students of the EdD program conducted research to examine the impact of finance reform coupled with requirements for more equitable learning opportunities for all students (Furney, Hasazi, & Clark/Keefe 2005). With a more centralized state role in funding, there logically followed greater state oversight of schooling. Furney, Hasazi, and Clark/Keefe found that integration of "newly developed programs and approaches" resulted in "increased opportunities for educators to learn together, share ideas, create a more common language, and improve the alignment of general and special education programs" (p. 173). Their research showed that school district leadership combined with a state policy focus with greater accountability practices resulted in a higher level of collaboration in problem solving. Problem solving built on collaborative approaches, combined with policy that ensures adequate resources for targeted professional development and greater accountability measures, led to practices that benefited *all* students. Their research particularly emphasized the need to prepare leaders ready to take on the challenges posed by an integrated professional development system tied to standards and accountability measures, often relying on interagency coordination. Baker and Stahl (2004) observed that in the context of publicly funded provisions, "service is inherently selective" due to the need to categorize individuals to define services at the level of an "individual—as opposed to the diagnosis—as the unit of analysis" (p. 175). To maintain humanity in services, building capacity for effective collaboration in organizations, means learning to share roles in ways that may be unfamiliar. In the instance of special education, those in leadership roles must adeptly help an organization balance discrete accountability practices with inclusive educational practices. Drawing on principles of building on strengths, faculty of UVM's doctoral program created opportunities to practice collaborative leadership and partnered with candidates in research that further informed this field of knowledge.

Pushing Geographic Boundaries for New Learning and Leading

Leadership in the college and program has been integral for pushing dialogue about the reach and scope of doctoral education. Throughout her 13-year tenure beginning in the early 1990s, the former dean of the college of Education and Social Services, Dr. Jill Tarule, helped expand the growth of graduate education and empowered faculty to reach across boundaries through their scholarship and teaching, forging partnerships with state agencies, nonprofit foundations, and state colleges in the interest of better serving Vermont's children, youth, families, and communities (The University of Vermont, 2013a). And many initiatives within the college had a national focus as well, perhaps most notably in the field of special education. EdD graduates and their collaborative program thrived amidst this well-organized confluence of interdisciplinary scholarship, particularly due to the applied research focus.

Dr. Fayneese Miller arrived in 2005 and brought with her a vision for continuing to expand the reach of graduate programs beyond Vermont borders. Becoming part of a national conversation on the EdD through the CPED initiative became one strategy among others for national and international research foci. At the same time the dean charged faculty to "[begin] a conversation to review [the college's] doctoral offerings and to rethink the teacher and doctoral education program" (The University of Vermont, 2006, p. 1). As noted in the proposal to the CPED leadership, the opportunity for CPED participation came at a time when the faculty would "benefit from conversation about planning and program development as part of a national team" (p. 5) as they were looking to reenvision doctoral programming in the college. The dean and faculty members presumed that joining CPED in a national conversation about the EdD would "allow us to partner with other institutions that are attempting to rethink its programs, identify problems with doctoral education, and develop programs that are of high quality and meet the needs of professionals in education" (pp. 5–6). The dialogue would be particularly valuable as faculty formulated a vision for a PhD program that was clearly distinct from a redesigned EdD.

DEVELOPMENT OF THE PHD PROGRAM: PRESENTING A CONTRAST FOR THE EDD

With a charge to develop a PhD program, faculty members took on the challenge of contrasting the EdD and PhD degrees so that each could further expand on the mission of the Educational Leadership and Policy Studies Program commitment to developing a cadre of leaders equipped with the knowledge, skills, and dispositions to advance social justice. Golde and Walker's (2006) examination of traditional PhD models demonstrated the importance of building a continuum of stewardship for a profession that clearly acknowledges the outcome of one who embarks on that path. Wrestling with entrenched perceptions about PhD and EdD characteristics and accompanying virtues, faculty had to deconstruct entrenched biases that considered the EdD as something lesser than the PhD, and reengage students and faculty in the process of rebuilding an understanding of the EdD as a program that stands on equal footing with the PhD. Using the medical model analogy that describes the difference between the EdD and the PhD as being like the difference between an MD and a PhD, one would expect the degree of choice for those intent on becoming a scholarly practitioner to be the EdD and for those intent on becoming a scholarly researcher, the degree of choice would be the PhD.

In defining the goals and characteristics of a doctorate in the field of education, Richardson (2006) highlighted that for those specifically intending to pursue a PhD in the interest of perhaps working in higher education, program faculty have an obligation to ensure PhD candidates gain practical knowledge so as to appropriately challenge one's own beliefs and misconceptions about education. In the UVM doctoral program reconceived as a dual track where PhD and EdD degree candidates come together, program faculty envision that these intentional pairings will promote collegial relationships between PreK-12 systems and higher education that will persist long after candidates graduate from the programs (Aiken & Gerstl-Pepin, 2013, p. 13).

Drawing on leadership research that emerged during the 1980s, Lipman-Blumen (1996) underscored the changing demands for leadership due to changing social conditions and knowledge and understanding of individual agency.

> As the leadership paradigm shifts from independence to *interdependence*, from control to *connection*, from competition to *collaboration*, from individual to *group*, and from tightly linked geopolitical alliances to loosely coupled global *networks*, we need to encourage a new breed of leaders who can respond effectively to such conditions. (p. 226)

As this paradigm takes hold, which supports a human rights framework, faculty can use what could be perceived as a program limitation—that of a limited enrollment for PhD candidates due to resource capacity—as a program strength. Feasibility analyses that suggested program capacity would require PhD and EdD doctoral students to work in parallel may in the end promote positive working relationships between PreK-12 systems and higher education.

One of the next major challenges for the Educational Leadership faculty is to "[create] opportunities for new dissertation formats that engage a wide range of research methodologies, alternative timeframes for completion, and expanded committees" (Aiken & Gerstl-Pepin, 2013, p. 20). As Archbald (2008) noted, "the dissertation is an intense experience in socialization and training for the candidate" (p. 4). By supporting dissertations that intentionally guide PhD and EdD candidates on a path that helps socialize them for their future roles, the program will help clarify the two degrees and also support interprofessional collaboration. The dissertation not only goes beyond merely demonstrating knowledge, skills, and dispositions expected of graduate study, but also has the potential to create a meaningful impact on an organizational leader, the organization, policy, or setting at the center of study.

For example, whereas an EdD graduate will most likely require skills-sets that allow for moving quickly toward context-specific problem solving to immediately address a localized problem, a PhD graduate's application of research skills may not hinge on the same sense of urgency, but, instead, knowledge gained from that research may have applications that inform a broader arena. An EdD graduate in the field may turn to PhD colleagues in research settings for developing collaborative approaches to tackling a specific issue that interferes with some element of student success. Conversely, a PhD candidate may turn to EdD colleagues in the field when they are looking for field-based settings and field partners for their research.

In Stokols's (2006) review of collaborative research literature, he found that "certain factors such as *spatial proximity* among team members, *a shared history of* collaboration on prior projects, *clear and equitable communications about collective goals and outcomes,* and the *presence of leaders who are able to foster a climate of cooperation,* all enhance participants' readiness for collaboration and prospects for success" (p. 73). In the field of educational leadership, one degree cannot do without the other, and forming those symbiotic relationships in graduate school may have lasting benefits. Shared resources and coursework will ensure that those who intend to remain in higher education as scholarly researchers will develop close collaborative relationships with field-based scholarly practitioners.

CONTINUING TO DEFINE THE EdD AND THE PhD

One of Vermont's own, Senator Justin Morrill, was instrumental in the adoption of The Morrill Act of 1862. Building on earlier agricultural education movements, the Morrill Act solidified a connection between higher education and agricultural economies, "shaped by society and interwoven with it in a complex manner" (Duemer, 2007, p. 144), and Vermont's flagship university continues to shape and be shaped by its environment. The evolving trajectories of doctoral education, with a refocused EdD and a new PhD, occurs at time when the university has committed to transdisciplinary research, in a continuation of Morrill's advocacy for higher education institutions to build strong connections among stakeholders (The University of Vermont, 2013b). Increasingly, UVM faculties seek to work across disciplines and across schools and colleges, furthering interprofessional scholarship for a new era.

Shulman (2005) noted that "signature pedagogies simplify the dauntingly complex challenges of professional education because once they are learned and internalized, we don't have to think about them; we can think with out them" (p. 56). A recent report on opportunities to learn for Vermont students indicates that in Vermont, given the rural context with limited resources, "without the integration of health, human services and education in such a way as to make the best use of limited resources of the state and its communities the potential impact of on-going attempts to improve services and outcomes will fall short" (Meyers & Rogers, 2012, p. 52).

The EdD is well-situated to meet challenges noted by Meyers and Rogers with its long-standing practices of working across disciplines through interprofessional cohort models and collaboration. Whereas the PhD is still in its infancy, the capacity for building a shared history of collaboration between EdD and PhD candidates promises to further drive the next generation of interprofessional research and problem solving in Vermont and internationally. Celebrating 30 years of an applied research program with new visions for the future, and with such a dominant role in a little state, UVM's Educational Leadership Program can provide significant leadership in professional capacity building for effective change that can make a difference for children, youth, families, and communities, and this work can only be strengthened through ongoing dialogue with CPED partners in the process of helping to clarify best practices for EdD and communicating program impacts to a larger audience.

References

Aiken, J. A., & Gerstl-Pepin, C. (2013). Designing the Ed.D. and Ph.D. as a partnership for change. Manuscript submitted for publication.

Aiken, J. A., Prue, J., & Hasazi, S. B. (1999). Leadership preparation: Designing and planning for interprofessional doctoral education and practice. *The Journal of Leadership Studies, 6*(3/4), 67–83.

Albers, J. (2002). *Hands on the land: A history of the Vermont landscape.* Cambridge, MA: MIT Press.

Archbald, D. (2008). Research versus problem solving for the education leadership doctoral thesis: Implications for form and function. *Educational Administration Quarterly, 44*(5), 704–739.

Baker, D. L., & Stahl, E. M. (2004). Case study of interagency coordinating councils: Examining collaboration in services for children with disabilities. *Journal of Disability Policy Studies, 15*(3), 168–177.

Burlington School District. (2013). Burlington School District 2011–2012 annual report. Burlington, VT. Retrieved March 28, 2013, from http://bsdweb.bsdvt.org/Board/annualreports/Feb2013.pdf.

Cooperrider, D. L., Whitney, D., & Stavros, J. M. (2003). *Appreciative inquiry handbook.* Bedford Heights, OH: Lakeshore Publishers.

Costa, A. L., & Kallick, B. (1993). Through the lens of a critical friend. *Educational Leadership, 51*(2), 49–51.

Dewey, J. (1937). Education and social change. *Social Frontier, 3*(26), 235–238. Retrieved March 28, 2013, from http://www.tcrecord.org/frontiers/Content.asp?ContentId=13522.

Duemer, L. S. (2007). The agricultural education origins of the Morrill Land Grant Act of 1862. *American Educational History Journal, 34*(1), 135–146.

Furman, G. C., & Gruenewald, D. A. (2004). Expanding the landscape of social justice: A critical ecological analysis. *Educational Administration Quarterly, 40*(1), 47–76.

Furney, K. S., Hasazi, S. B., & Clark/Keefe, K. (2005, Winter). Multiple dimensions of reform: The impact of state policies on special education and supports for all students. *Journal of Disability Policy Studies, 16*(3), 169–176.

Gerstl-Pepin, C., Haszai, S., & Killeen, K. (2006). Utilizing an "ethic of care" in leadership preparation: Uncovering the complexity of colorblind social justice. *Journal of Educational Administration, 44*(3), 250–263.

Golde, C. M., & Walker, G. E. (Eds.). (2006). *Envisioning the future of doctoral education: Preparing stewards of the discipline.* San Francisco: Jossy-Bass.

Harvest. (2013). Vermont history of agriculture. Retrieved March 28, 2013, from http://harvest.mannlib.cornell.edu/node/50.

Jean-Marie, G., Normore, A. H., & Brooks, J. S. (2009). Leadership for social justice: Preparing 21st century school leaders for a new social order. *Journal of Research on Leadership Education, 4*(1), 1–31.

Lipman-Blumen, J. (1996). *Connective edge: Leading in an interdependent world.* San Francisco: Jossey-Bass.

Lipsky, D. K., & Garnter, A. (1996). Inclusion, school restructuring, and the remaking of American society. *Harvard Educational Review, 66*(4), 762–796.

Meyers, H. B., Hasazi, S., Baege, M., Gerstl-Pepin, C., Gordon, R., MacKinnon, C., et al. (2007). Vermont Agency of Human Services Incarcerated Women's Initiative complete report. Burlington: Vermont Research Partnership at the University of Vermont. Retrieved March 28, 2013 from http://www. uvm.edu/~vrp/IWICompleteReport_June_07.pdf.

Meyers, H. B., & Rogers, J. D. (2012). Full report: Educational opportunities working group on aligning funding, opportunities to learn and outcomes of the educational system. Retrieved March 28, 2013, from http://www.leg.state.vt.us/reports/2013ExternalReports/286246.pdf.

Noddings, N. (1984). *Caring: A feminine approach to ethics and moral education.* Berkeley: University of California Press.

Richardson, V. (2006). Stewards of a field, stewards of an enterprise. The doctorate in education. In C. M. Golde & G. E. Walker (Eds.), *Envisioning the future of doctoral education: Preparing stewards of the discipline* (pp. 251–267). San Francisco: Jossey-Bass.

Sanford, G. (2002). The bleat of the sheep, the bark of the tree: Vermonters and their landscape, a view from the archives. *Vermont History, 70,* 10–18.

Shulman, L. S. (2005). Signature pedagogies in the professions. *Daedalus, 134*(3), 52–59. Retrieved March 28, 2013, from http://www.mitpress-journals.org/doi/abs/10.1162/0011526054622015.

Stokols, D. (2006). Toward a science of transdisciplinary action research. *American Journal of Community Psychology, 38*(1–2), 63–77.

Storey, V. A., & Richard, B. (2013). Carnegie Project for the Educational Doctorate: The role of critical friends in diffusing doctoral program innovation. In C. A. Mullen & K. E. Lane (Eds.), *Becoming a Global Voice— the 2013 Yearbook of the National Council of Professors of Educational Administration.* Ypsilanti, MI: NCPEA Publications.

Su, Ya-hui. (2011). The constitution of agency in developing lifelong learning ability: The "being" mode. *Higher Education, 62*(4), 399–412.

The University of Vermont. (2006). Strengthening doctoral education in CADREI institutions: Carnegie Network on the Professional Practice Doctorate. Unpublished manuscript, College of Education and Social Services.

The University of Vermont. (2008). The University of Vermont 2009–09 online catalog. Retrieved March 28, 2013, from http://www.uvm.edu/academics/catalogue2008-09/?Page=read.php&SM=offeringmenu.html&p=/Academic_Offerings/Educational_Leadership_and_Policy_Studies_%28Ed.D.%29.

The University of Vermont. (2012). *Doctoral Program in Educational Leadership and Policy Studies, Ed.D. handbook 2012.* Retrieved March 28, 2013, from http://www.uvm.edu/~cess/doctoral/CESS_EdD _Doctoral_Handbook.pdf.

The University of Vermont. (2013a). *Higher Education and Student Affairs Program faculty.* Retrieved March 28, 2013, from http://www.uvm .edu/~uvmhesa/?Page=facultybio.html&SM=faculty_menu.html.

The University of Vermont. (2013b). *Transdisciplinary research initiative.* Retrieved March 28, 2013, from http://www.uvm.edu/~tri/.

upon successful program completion. The new policy stipulated that award of provisional administrator certification required applicants to hold a valid Kentucky teacher certificate, provide evidence of at least three years full-time teaching experience, achieve passing scores on the two required professional examinations (i.e., School Leaders Licensure Assessment, Kentucky Specialty Test of Instructional and Administrative Practices), and submit a completed curriculum contract signed by a designated university professor. The new provisions thus allowed teachers to begin their preparation as school administrators after successfully completing their teacher induction program, a state-mandated requirement for all first-year teachers.

In response to these new requirements, faculty representatives from the 11 institutions with then-approved preparation programs met regularly to develop guidelines for program redesign. One recommendation that was adopted required all programs to include a set of six courses utilizing common course numbers (i.e., introduction to school administration, school law, school finance, human resources management, school-community engagement, school improvement). These redesigned programs changed previous curricula significantly through the focus on knowledge and disposition indicators within the ISLLC *Standards* and the integration of field-based projects and information technology use. All professors involved with the redesigned preparation programs thereafter meet annually during a full-day seminar to discuss program concerns, share course materials, present research findings, and conduct related business.

Unanticipated Impact of Policy Change

In 2001, shortly after graduates of redesigned programs began to seek placements as principals, the Kentucky Department of Education (KDE) received a State Action Education Leadership Project (SAELP) grant from The Wallace Foundation. KDE officials wanted to determine the current status of P-12 leadership and thus hired professors to conduct survey research. Data gathered through those surveys indicated that 1,285 teachers had been awarded provisional administrator certification since new programs had been approved (Björk, 2002). According to superintendent survey respondents, however, the statewide principal applicant pool at that time included only 630 potential candidates (Björk, Keedy, Rinehart, & Winter, 2002), suggesting that in 2001 over half of the graduates from recently redesigned programs were not perceived by superintendents to be qualified to assume a principalship.

Soon after the 2002 release of those survey results, the EPSB began tracking career paths of program graduates against its active principal candidate pool. The number of teachers holding provisional certification but not seeking principal placement mushroomed to over 3,000 by 2004. The EPSB executive director became concerned that too many teachers were completing principal preparation programs rather than advanced teacher development programs to satisfy the KERA-introduced requirement to earn a master's degree within the first ten years of full-time teaching. He began actively advocating for redesign of all graduate programs for P-12 educators. As a result of diverse actions and activities sponsored by EPSB and supported by Wallace Foundation grants across three years, the Kentucky General Assembly passed legislation in 2008 requiring significant changes.

Second Mandated Program Redesign

The 2008 revision of the Kentucky Administrative Regulation related to standards for accreditation of educator preparation units introduced Teacher Leader Master's Programs. All master-degree programs for teachers approved by EPSB prior to May 31, 2008, were closed to admission of new candidates after December 31, 2010. Likewise, the Kentucky Administrative Regulation concerning professional certification of school leaders stipulated that all principal preparation programs approved prior to May 31, 2009, could not admit new candidates after December 31, 2011. Kentucky universities wishing to provide principal preparation were required to submit their program proposals to EPSB no later than December 31, 2012.

The most significant change with regard to the preparation of principals was the elimination of the MEd in school administration. Henceforth, all candidates admitted to approved principal preparation programs must hold a graduate degree upon admission, which was a requirement prior to the 1998 policy revision. Applicants to principal preparation programs must also (a) present evidence of three years of documented full-time teaching experience, (b) submit a written statement attesting to their skills and understanding in three areas (i.e., ability to improve student achievement; leadership; advanced knowledge of curriculum, instruction, and assessment), and (c) provide an agreement signed by a superintendent pledging support for the candidate to participate in high quality practicum experiences. The purpose for these more demanding admission requirements is to assure that those admitted are ready and willing to assume administrative positions after completing their initial principal preparation.

A significant change with regard to preparing teacher leaders and school principals is the required engagement of P-12 practitioners in the design and delivery of redesigned programs. All program proposals submitted to EPSB for review had to include evidence of (a) collaboration with academic disciplines and programs outside the field of education, (b) collaboration with districts in providing appropriate field experiences for candidates, and (c) requirement for candidates to defend a capstone project based on action research before a panel composed of program faculty and educational practitioners at program conclusion. Proposals for redesigned principal preparation programs also had to include signed collaborative agreements with districts that specify joint screening of principal candidates as well as codesign and codelivery of courses.

Program Redesign: Informed by Critical Friends and Graduate Data

When EDL faculty began initial discussions about principal program redesign, only two professors had taught in the previously approved program for several years. Four senior faculty members had recently retired or assumed positions at other universities, and the three new assistant professors hired to replace them had relocated from other states. A decision was made to postpone principal program redesign to allow the assistant professors to engage in constructed conversations with educational practitioners. Thus, a principal program codesign team was formed that included five professors (i.e., author, three assistant professors, lecturer) and nine educational practitioners (i.e., school and district administrators, directors of state AdvancED agency, executive director of a regional education cooperative). The team met five times during 2009 to review together the revised educational leadership standards (CCSSO, 2008) and performance expectations (Sanders & Kearney, 2008), recently enacted state policy and related program redesign documents, test-preparation questions in the revised certification examinations, and proposed curricular changes in the school law and finance courses. Meetings were held at district offices and local schools. Although the team disbanded after six months due to scheduling challenges, the Critical Friend discussions about principal preparation and school leadership expectations in Kentucky provided foundational information that new faculty needed.

During that same time period, the dean of the College of Education appointed a Masters Redesign Steering Committee comprised of (a) faculty and professional staff from the College of Education;

(b) faculty representatives from the College of Arts and Sciences, College of Fine Arts, and College of Agriculture; (c) practitioners and administrators from the local school district; and (d) representatives from two regional educational cooperatives that provide professional development for P-12 certified personnel. The EDL chair and the director of graduate studies (author) were invited to participate because the revised state policy required a teacher leadership course in all redesigned, advanced teacher preparation programs. The steering committee met monthly over a two-year period to review professional literature, plan curricular frameworks, and discuss field experiences for the revised programs. As program proposals were being developed, the committee chairs designated specific time on meeting agendas for members to conduct Critical Friend reviews. Throughout the process, representatives from the EPSB were also consulted to gain critical feedback on possible design features.

Analysis of Candidate Data

During that same time period and working within my responsibilities as the EDL director of graduate studies, I conducted a comprehensive review of files for students admitted between June 2000 and June 2008. I then determined their postprogram career paths using the online, open-access database maintained by the EPSB, which archives P-12 educators' work positions. With approval from the Institutional Review Board at the University of Kentucky, I invited program graduates to complete the *School Leadership Preparation and Practice Survey* administered by the National Center for Evaluation of Educational Leadership Preparation and Practice (n.d.).

The diverse data sources revealed important information about EDL's program graduates. First, within two years of program completion, almost all teachers holding a graduate degree upon admission to the previous preparation program were serving as principals, assistant principals, or other positions requiring administrator certification. Further, most indicated on their admission materials (e.g., resume, professional statement) that they had served in teacher leadership positions prior to beginning principal preparation. These data suggested that experience as a teacher leader prior to entry into a preparation program may be a predictor of future placement as a principal (Muth, Browne-Ferrigno, Bellamy, Fulmer, & Silver, in press). Second, data revealed that almost all program graduates awarded a MEd degree (i.e., their first graduate degree) were still serving as teachers. While diverse factors influence a teacher's decision to become a principal, one explanation could be that the only option for leadership development in Kentucky at that time was through participation in principal preparation programs.

Program Development Activities

Data gathered from the survey and graduate files, review of the admission requirements for redesigned principal preparation programs, and engagement in activities about redesign of graduate programs for teachers clearly indicated that EDL needed to develop a teacher leadership program that prepared graduates to assume both formal and informal leadership positions with emphasis on working with principals and colleagues on schoolwide matters. As the director of graduate studies for our department at the time, I assumed responsibility for coordinating the program development activities, drafting the program application and proposal documents, editing all course syllabi to assure consistency in format and content placement to expedite review processes, and shepherding the proposal through the University of Kentucky and the EPSB approval processes. Faculty assumed responsibility for course syllabi development and critical reviews of proposal drafts.

Program development required multiple brainstorming sessions, comprehensive reviews of literature, conversations with and feedback from diverse P-12 leadership practitioners and university colleagues, and development of new course syllabi. Following critical reviews of the new course syllabi and program application by multiple faculty advisory and governance bodies at the University of Kentucky, the courses and program were approved by the Faculty Senate in May 2010. A formal program proposal (i.e., a 70-page single spaced document excluding course syllabi) was then prepared and submitted to EPSB for review. After four revisions to address critical feedback by an external review committee composed of teachers, EDL received approval from EPSB in May 2011 to deliver the Teacher Leadership Program and to recommend the addition of the Teacher Leader Endorsement to graduates' teaching certificates. However, EDL faculty decided to postpone launch of the new program in order to complete redesign of the principal preparation program.

Lessons learned during the development and approval processes required for the Teacher Leadership Program, the hiring of two new associate professors from other states, and explicit design requirements in the EPSB review rubric expedited development of the new Principalship Program. Although the previous principal preparation program was approved to award the EdS degree, the EDL faculty elected to embed principal certification within its EdD program to give applicants two degree options. In 2009, the faculty had converted the EdD program into an executive, hybrid model similar to the CPED-affiliated program for community college leaders at the University of Kentucky. Adding another specialization option (i.e., principal certification courses) to the EdD program was an appropriate decision.

Five courses from the old principal preparation program (i.e., school safety, school finance, school law, human resources management, school-community engagement) required only minor revisions. Three new courses (i.e., supervision of curriculum and instruction, supervision of assessment and accountability, organizational learning and school culture) were developed. The new courses had to be approved through the University of Kentucky system, which was done simultaneously with program approval through EPSB to assure that the program could be launched as soon as possible. The new director of graduate studies and the chair for the new principal preparation program assumed responsibilities for proposal development and program approval. Faculty assisted them by writing portions of the proposal, editing course syllabi to assure consistency in layout and inclusion of required information, and gathering written support for the program from superintendents. The Principalship Program proposal was submitted to EPSB in November 2011. After three revisions to address issues raised by the EPSB review committee, it was approved to recommend principal certification in May 2012.

The following sections present overviews of the two programs. In Kentucky, the word *candidate* is used to designate an adult engaged in professional preparation at a postsecondary institution, while *student* refers to children and youth enrolled in P-12 schools. The terms *doctoral student* and *doctoral candidate* are used where appropriate.

Teacher Leadership Program

The Teacher Leadership Program offered by EDL was designed to address expanded leadership expectations for educators. Developed through collaboration with P-12 school partners, the program provides candidates with individualized coursework, professional development opportunities, and job-embedded experiences. Candidates complete an individualized program of studies that consists of 30 credit hours of approved graduate-level coursework, which includes

15 credit hours of core coursework and 15 credit hours of electives. Candidates successfully completing the program are awarded the MEd degree or the EdS degree (if holding graduate degree upon program admission) from the University of Kentucky and are recommended to EPSB for the addition of the Teacher Leader Endorsement to their teaching certificate.

The overarching program goal of the Teacher Leadership Program is to prepare teachers to assume leadership roles and responsibilities that "support school and student success" (Harrison & Killion, 2007, p. 74). The theory of action for the program is the "Framework for School Leadership Accomplishments" (Bellamy, Fulmer, Murphy, & Muth, 2007, p. 34) in which student learning is the central focus accomplished through conditions that create a learning-centered school environment (i.e., learning goals, instruction, student climate, related services, family and community partnerships) and support the learning environment (i.e., family and community partnerships, resources, school operations, staff support, renewal).

Standards-based curriculum and continuous learning assessment. The program is framed by the advanced level *Kentucky Teacher Standards* (EPSB, 2008), *Educational Leadership Policy Standards: ISLLC 2008* (CCSSO, 2008), and *National Educational Technology Standards for Administrators* (International Society for Technology in Education [ISTE], 2009). Candidates are required to complete self-assessments of their understanding and use of these standards at three points during the program (i.e., admission, retention, completion). Those self-assessments as well as other documents created throughout the program (e.g., leadership platform, professional growth plan, observations of diverse classrooms, practicum log) are uploaded to candidates' individual electronic portfolios, which are reviewed by program faculty. The summative assessment for the program is defense of candidate's action research report (i.e., capstone project) before a committee composed of program faculty and P-12 educational practitioners.

Individualized professional development. To address candidates' individual professional learning needs, the program provides considerable flexibility. All candidates must successfully complete the 15 credit hours of core coursework (i.e., ELS 600, ELS 604, ELS 620, ELS 621, ELS 624). Teachers holding a graduate degree upon program admission can earn the Teacher Leader Endorsement by completing the 15 credit hours of core coursework and all components of the continuous assessment plan. Candidates seeking the MEd degree or EdS degree must successfully complete an additional 15 credit hours of elective courses selected from options inside or outside the program to meet their unique learning needs as well as all components of the continuous assessment plan. Table 7.1 displays the scope of curriculum and sequence of courses in the program.

Outcomes. The goal of the Teacher Leadership Program is to prepares teachers to assume schoolwide leadership roles, both formal (e.g., school-governance committee member, department chair, grade-level team leader) and informal (e.g., instructional model, peer mentor, school-community collaborator, curriculum team member). Thus, throughout the program candidates work with principals and other educators to complete learning-focused assignments that expand their knowledge about curriculum, instruction, and assessment and that develop their leadership skills, particularly within professional learning communities. If graduates of this program determine in the future that becoming a principal is an appropriate career choice for them, they will have the required graduate degree, leadership experience, and advanced knowledge of a schoolwide instructional program to apply for admission to one of Kentucky's redesigned principal preparation programs.

Principalship Program

The new principal preparation program offered by EDL provides candidates with knowledge and skills required for effective instructional leadership, school management, and change agency. Candidates may

Table 7.1 Teacher Leadership Program scope and sequence

Fall Semester	Spring Semester	Summer Semester
Year 1		
ELS 600, Leadership in Learner-Centered Schools Elective	ELS 604, Leadership in Professional Learning Communities	ELS 620, Action Research for School Renewal 1
	ELS 612, Leadership for Technology and Innovation or Other Elective	ELS 616, Leadership for Inclusive Community or Other Elective
Year 2		
ELS 621, Action Research for School Renewal II	ELS 624, Leadership Practicum	
ELS 608, School Law & Governance for Teachers or Other Elective	Elective	

select from the EdS degree or EdD degree options. The program of studies consists of 45 credit hours of approved graduate-level coursework, including the 36 credit hours of coursework required for principal certification (EdS degree) and an additional 9 hours of research courses to support scholar-practitioner research to address key issues in their respective schools and districts (EdD degree). Clinical experiences and action research are embedded within the certification courses and designed to support candidates development as transformational leaders who can successfully facilitate the implementation of high quality practices in diverse school settings. EdD candidates complete additional research courses and produce a three-chapter dissertation based on action research about an authentic issue or problem of practice and evaluation of implementation to address the issue or problem.

Conceptual framework and admission requirements. Because the University of Kentucky is both a research extensive and a land-grant institution, the Principalship Program was designed to prepare premier educators across the commonwealth to be transformational leaders who facilitate the use of evidence-based practices in P-12 settings. The conceptual framework for the program combines three literature-based themes: (a) learning-centered leadership, (b) transformational leadership, and (c) implementation science. The program was designed to enable aspiring principals to become transformational leaders through opportunities to build their knowledge base, practice skills, implement skills in work-embedded experiences, and debrief using a framework specifically created for the program that utilizes transformational leadership and implementation science knowledge bases. A Principal's Toolbox, a set of online modules designed to provide just-in-time learning experiences to improve on-the-job performance (e.g., delivering effective presentations, writing effective memos, managing an online personal learning network), is currently under development for use by program candidates and graduates.

Because the Principalship Program is an adaptation of the department's executive, hybrid EdD program, all applicants including those selecting the EdS degree option must meet requirements for admission to the regular EdD program (e.g., GRE scores, graduate GPAs, writing ability, successfully completed graduate-level basic statistics course, recommendations). They must also meet requirements specified in state policy for admission to redesigned principal preparation programs (e.g., three years of full-time teaching experience, leadership experience, knowledge of academic program). Admission decisions are based on holistic reviews of applicants' application files, performance during interviews with faculty, and dispositions about school leadership and the principalship.

Guaranteed support for high quality field experiences. A significant change in state policies related to graduate programs for P-12 certified personnel was the requirement for job-embedded field work. To assure aspiring principals engage in high quality field experiences, one recommendation for admission to the new Principalship Program must be from the applicant's superintendent. If admitted, the candidate's superintendent must sign a memorandum of agreement that

- describes how the district will assure that candidate has opportunities to observe and participate in school and district leadership activities,
- confirms that candidate will have access to school and district data to use when completing program assignments, and
- specifies the number of days that candidate will be released from work responsibilities to engage in practicum.

Standards-based curriculum and embedded field experiences. The differences between the old principal preparation program and the recently approved new one are evident by entries in Table 7.2. The left column displays the scope of curriculum and sequence of courses in the previous MEd/EdS program, whereas the right column displays the scope and sequence of the new EdS/EdD program. Candidates seeking the EdS degree must complete 36 credit hours of coursework (Level I), successfully defend their capstone project during a formal oral examination, and pass the two state-required examinations to be recommended to EPSB for provisional certification as school leader. They must complete an additional six credit hours (Level II) and assume a principalship to be recommended for professional certification.

Candidates seeing the EdD degree must complete 49 credit hours of coursework that includes the Level I and Level II courses described above plus an additional 9 credit hours of research courses and at least 4 credit hours of dissertation residency courses after passing their qualifying examination. Although EdD candidates defend their capstone project (i.e., certification requirement) at the same time as the EdS candidates, they are advised to complete the doctoral program before assuming a principalship. The University of Kentucky recently shortened time to degree completion in order to assure doctoral candidates graduate.

Table 7.2 Comparison of University of Kentucky Principal Preparation Programs

Semester	Scope and Sequence of Previous	Scope and Sequence of New
	MEd/EdS in School Administration	EdS/EdD with Principal Certification
Year 1 Fall	EDL 601, Introduction to School Leadership and Administration EDL 628, School Law and Ethics EDL 610, Leadership Practicum I (1 credit hour)	EDL 706, Leadership for Learning-Centered Schools I EDL 751, Foundations of Inquiry
Year 1 Spring	EDL 625, School Safety and Discipline Leadership EDL 627, School Finance and Support Services EDL 611, Leadership Practicum II (1 credit hour)	EDL 661, School Technology Leadership EDL 707, Leadership for Learning-Centered Schools II
Year 1 Summer	EDL 634, Leadership for Human Resource Development in Schools EDS 613, Legal & Parental Issues in Special Education EDL 612, Leadership Practicum III (1 credit hour) *Level I Coursework Complete*	EDL 627, School Finance and Support Services EDL 628, School Law and Ethics
Year 2 Fall	EDL 669, Leadership for School Problem Solving (action research) Elective	EDL 634, Securing and Developing Staff EDL 646, Leadership for School-Family-Community Engagement EDL 625, School Safety and Discipline Leadership EDL 708, Organizational Learning in P-12 Schools *Level I Coursework Complete*
Year 2 Spring	EDL 646, Leadership for School-Community Relations EDL 650, Leadership for School Program Improvement *Level II Coursework Complete* *Defense of Portfolio (MEd or EdS oral examination)*	*Defense of Capstone Project (EdS oral examination, Chapter 1 of EdD dissertation)*
Semester	Scope and Sequence of Previous	Scope and Sequence of New
	MEd/EdS in School Administration	EdS/EdD with Principal Certification
Year 3 Fall		EDL 771, Action Research I
Year 3 Spring		EDL 771, Action Research II
Year 3 Summer		EDL 792, Research in Educational Leadership *Qualifying Examination (defense of Chapter 2 and proposal for Chapter 3 of dissertation)*
Year 4 Fall		EDL 767, Dissertation Residency (2 credit hours)
Year 4 Spring		EDL 767, Dissertation Residency (2 credit hours) *Oral Examination (defense of three-chapter dissertation)*

With the exception of EDL 751 Foundations of Inquiry, a required methodology course in the EdD program, each of the 10 courses in Level I of the Principalship Program includes approximately 60 clock hours of required fieldwork during which candidates observe, participate in, or lead school leadership activities. Certification courses include readings, assignments, and activities linked to one or more of the ISLLC standards (CCSSO, 2008) and technology standards (ISTE, 2009). Before exiting the program, candidates thus complete approximately 600 clock hours of field experiences related to school leadership. The field-based experiences within the ten courses in the new program replace the three-course practicum series (EDL 610, EDL 611, EDL 612) in the old program. Although field-based assignments were often embedded within other courses in the old program, state policy at that time did not require them. Thus, five courses constitute the principalship specialization area (15 credit hours) within the new EdS/EdD program (i.e., EDL 625, EDL 627, EDL 628, EDL 634, EDL 646). The course syllabi were revised slightly to address redesign requirements, and the titles of two courses were changed to reflect content more accurately.

Four courses, which were added to address new expectations for Kentucky principals, are among the six required courses in the leadership core (18 credit hours). EDL 661 School Technology Leadership presents an overview of principal responsibilities concerning technology adoption and utilization, which is a statewide initiative. EDL 706 Leadership for Learning-Centered Schools I (supervision of curriculum and instruction) and EDL 707 Leadership for Learning-Centered Schools II (supervision of assessment and accountability) assure candidates have content knowledge and skills to be effective learning leaders. The old program did not include courses about these two critically important responsibilities of principal leadership. To address new policy requirements, EDL 708 Organizational Learning in P-12 Schools replaced EDL 650 Leadership for School Program Improvement in the old program. EDL 703 Leading Organizational Change and EDL 704 Politics of Educational Leadership are required courses in the regular EdD program and serve as Level II courses in the new principal preparation program.

Formal performance assessments. All participants in the Principalship Program must defend their capstone project (i.e., report of action research about an authentic school leadership issue) before a committee composed of university professors and P-12 practitioners, which is a new policy requirement. Those who successfully defend their capstone project receive a letter of eligibility for provisional certification, provided they achieved passing scores on the two required professional examinations. Defense of the capstone project serves as the EdS oral examination. Graduates awarded the EdS degree must complete Level II courses within five years of program completion and assume an administrative position to qualify for professional certification.

For those seeking the EdD degree, the capstone project becomes Chapter 1 of their three-chapter dissertation, a format approved by the University of Kentucky for professional doctorate programs. Upon successful completion of the required 45 credit hours of coursework and with approval from their dissertation chair, doctoral students are allowed to sit for the qualifying examination, which is based on Chapter 2 of their dissertation (i.e., intervention plan to address the issue reported in Chapter 1). Doctoral students advance to candidacy status by passing their qualifying examination. While enrolled in the two academic semesters of required dissertation residency credit, doctoral candidates study the implementation of their proposed intervention and then write Chapter 3, which is the report of findings from another cycle of action research. Once a complete dissertation is approved by candidate's dissertation chair, the doctoral candidate is eligible to sit for an oral examination based on the three-chapter dissertation. The EdD oral examination is conducted by the candidate's advisory committee as specified in University of Kentucky regulations.

Common Program Features

Both the Teacher Leadership Program and Principalship Program offered by EDL evidence all elements that define high quality preparation programs (Orr & Pounder, 2011). Both are framed by relevant leadership theory and professional standards. Courses in each program are delivered in a sequence that assures candidates' development of requisite knowledge and skills, which is enhanced through use of active-learning strategies, collaborative work, and field-based projects as well as independent reading and writing. Web-based communication sites (e.g., AdobeConnect, Blackboard, Canvas) are utilized in all courses to enhance candidate's learning and support peer collaboration. Both programs are delivered through cohorts in order to develop communities of practice that extend beyond candidates' engagement in formal preparation. Both programs utilize a continuous assessment checkpoint system designed to support candidates' ongoing skill development. Candidates' performance on the standards framing the program is assessed at program admission, at program midpoint, and near program completion. Evidence of continuous progress is collected and documented in online portfolios framed by appropriate professional standards. Candidates in both programs must successfully defend the contents of their electronic portfolios and reports of their action research during oral examinations conducted by university faculty and educational practitioners. Program faculty includes tenure-track, full-time university professors and part-time adjunct instructors who are experienced educational leaders with expertise in the content area taught. Prospective adjuncts coteach with full-time professors prior to assuming responsibility for teaching a course.

Program Implementation

The first cohorts for both the Teacher Leadership Program and the Principalship Program launched during the Fall 2012 semester. At this writing, candidates are completing their second year of coursework, which makes it impossible to report on the impact of program implementation.

LESSONS LEARNED

As a leadership preparation scholar and professor at the University of Kentucky, I was an invited participant in almost all statewide activities related to principal preparation redesign that spanned three years. The process began in April 2005 with the *Leading Change* conference sponsored by the Commonwealth Collaborative of School Leadership Programs, a grassroots organization whose members were professors and instructors in the then-approved 11 principal preparation programs. The redesign process concluded during the May 2008 executive board meeting of EPSB when the *Continuum for Principal Preparation and Development* notebook, developed by the Kentucky Cohesive Leadership System (KyCLS), was adopted as the primary resource for use by universities and colleges during redesign activities. I became disillusioned about the potential outcome of the statewide initiative when a compliance mindset emerged during a Principal Redesign Summit held in January 2006. Most participants at that event were not directly involved in principal preparation either inside or outside of Kentucky. Then while participating in the monthly two-day meetings of the KyCLS design team between February 2007 and April 2008, my disillusionment transformed into frustration: Important decisions about program design elements and proposed assessments were made without analysis of data gathered from program graduates or without critical feedback from recently prepared principals.

Changed Attitude about Program Redesign

My attitude about program redesign changed as I participated in meetings of the College of Education' Masters Redesign Steering Committee. We functioned as a community of practice (Wenger, 1998; Wenger, McDermott, & Snyder, 2002) whose goal was to develop high quality graduate programs for teacher leaders. We accomplished that by providing critical feedback (Costa & Kallick, 1993; Handal, 1999) to our colleagues throughout development of several programs. Unlike the statewide initiative for principal program redesign, the Steering Committee sought input from university professors and P-12 practitioners—those most closely involved in teacher preparation. Our Teacher Leadership Program reflects the value of those Critical Friend reviews.

Experience gained by EDL faculty while participating in the Steering Committee and developing the Teacher Leadership Program expedited the development of our Principalship Program. We developed the curricular framework during an impromptu faculty meeting on a Saturday morning in late September 2011 and then utilized information technology for discussing ideas and drafting documents, which minimized our need for face-to-face meetings. Because we had already developed Critical Friendships with P-12 personnel while developing the Teacher Leadership Program, they were able to provide feedback on principal program redesign through electronic mail and phone calls. Our formal proposal, which included letters of support from eight superintendents, took only two months to prepare. It was submitted to EPSB for review in November 2011 and approved in May 2012. The collective engagement by EDL faculty and P-12 practitioners stimulated thinking about other possibilities; thus, today our department offers a range of program offerings for individuals seeking leadership development (http://leadership.uky.edu).

Implication for Program Development or Redesign

Writing this chapter required me to reexamine the statewide redesign effort and reflect critically about what unfolded over several years. Rather than using a policy mindset, which I did while writing a related journal article (Browne-Ferrigno, 2013), this time I viewed the process of program development and redesign using a Critical Friend mindset. That changed perspective provoked new thinking about critical feedback.

During the last two decades in the United States, active advocacy by external forces (e.g., private foundations, professional organizations, accreditation agencies, federal government) has generated the perception that universities and colleges are not adequately preparing P-12 educators, particularly school leaders (Adams & Copland, 2005; Fry et al., 2006; Hess, 2003; US Department of Education, 2005). This active agency is most notable by the investments of millions of dollars by the US Department of Education and the Wallace Foundation through block grants to regional centers and state departments of education or through individual grants to school districts and a few university professors. The powerful influence of foundations and granters on policymaking through agitation by special interest groups is not often discussed or challenged (Wirt & Kirst, 1997). The recent principal redesign initiative in Kentucky is such an example, particularly because considerable time and effort was spent gathering input from individuals not directly involved in principal preparation—or even residing within Kentucky. Nonetheless, university professors and their P-12 constituents redesigned the programs in use today by adapting to what works within the local context as suggested by Roach and colleagues (2011) and Young (2013).

The two advanced preparation programs described in this chapter resulted from imaginative thinking by University of Kentucky professors committed to renewal and innovation. Although policy mandates guided the development of program structures, the design work and revisions were informed through external conversations and Critical Friendships (Foulger, 2010; Gibbs & Angelides, 2008; Swaffield, 2007) with P-12 practitioners and university colleagues. Questions and critical feedback that followed reviews of course syllabi and program proposals during each phase of the approval processes was necessary to assure high quality preparation. The reviewers and evaluators were Critical Friends who provoked new thinking through their questions and suggestions for improvement (Costa & Kallick, 1993; Rallis & Rossman, 2000; Swaffield & MacBeath, 2005).

An implication from this secondary review of the case study I conducted earlier is that feedback and evaluation by Critical Friends were an essential component of the successful development and redesign activities at the University of Kentucky. Thus, whether conducting formal Critical Friend reviews or engaging in external conversations with those not directly involved in the activity, Critical Friendships are important.

REFERENCES

Adams, J. E., Jr., & Copland, M. A. (2005, December). *When learning counts: Rethinking licenses for school leaders.* Seattle: Center on Reinventing Public Education, University of Washington. Retrieved from http://www.wallacefoundation.org/knowledge-center/school-leadership/state-policy/Documents/When-Learning-Counts-Rethinking-Licenses-for-School-Leaders.pdf.

Andrews, R., & Grogan, M. (2005, Spring). Form should follow function: Removing the Ed.D. dissertation from the Ph.D. straight jacket. *UCEA Review, XLVI*(2), 10–13. Retrieved from http://www.ucea.org/storage/review/spring2005.pdf.

Bellamy, T., Fulmer, C., Murphy, M., & Muth, R. (2007). *Principal accomplishments: How school leaders succeed.* New York, NY: Teachers College Press.

Björk, L. G. (2002, March). *SAELP: Survey research summary report* [Internal progress report for research team]. Lexington, KY: University of Kentucky.

Björk, L. G., Keedy, J., Rinehart, J. S., & Winter, P. A. (2002, April). *State Action for Education Leadership Policy (SAELP) preliminary superintendent survey result: The principal search process* [Research report submitted to the Kentucky Department of Education]. Lexington, KY: University of Kentucky.

Browne-Ferrigno, T. (2009). Case study: Kentucky. In B. C. Fusarelli & B. S. Cooper (Eds.), *The rising state: How state power is transforming our nation's schools* (pp. 27–45). Albany, NY: SUNY Press.

Browne-Ferrigno, T. (2011). Mandated university-district partnerships for principal preparation: Professors' perspectives on required program redesign. *Journal of School Leadership, 21*(5), 735–756.

Browne-Ferrigno, T. (2013). Mandated preparation program redesign: Kentucky case. *Journal of Research on Leadership Education, 8*(2), 168–190.

Browne-Ferrigno, T., & Fusarelli, B. C. (2005). The Kentucky principalship: Model of school leadership reconfigured by ISLLC Standards and reform policy implementation. *Leadership and Policy in Schools, 4*(2), 127–156.

Browne-Ferrigno, T., & Jensen, J. M. (2012). Preparing Ed.D. students to conduct group dissertations. *Innovative Higher Education, 37*(5), 407–421.

Clements, S. K., & Kannapel, P. J. (2010). *Kentucky's march to the top: The past and future of education reform in Kentucky* [White paper]. Charleston, WV: Edvantia.

Commonwealth Collaborative of School Leadership Programs. (2005, April). *Leading change*. Louisville, KY: Shaping the Future/LEAD.

Costa, A. L., & Kallick, B. (1993). Through the lens of a critical friend. *Educational Leadership, 51*(2), 49–51.

Council of Chief State School Officers (CCSSO). (1996). *The Interstate School Leaders Licensure Consortium: Standards for school leaders*. Washington, DC: Author.

Council of Chief State School Officers (CCSSO). (2008). *Educational leadership policy standards: ISLLC 2008*. Washington, DC: Author.

Education Professional Standards Board (EPSB). (2008, February). *Kentucky teacher standards*. Frankfort, KY: Author. Retrieved from http://www.kyepsb.net/teacherprep/standards.asp.

Foulger, T. S. (2010). External conversations: An unexpected discovery about the critical friend in action research inquires. *Action Research, 8*(2), 135–152.

Fry, B., O'Neill, K., & Bottoms, G. (2006). *Schools can't wait: Accelerating the redesign of university principal preparation programs*. Atlanta, GA: Southern Regional Education Board. Retrieved from http://www.wallacefoundation.org/knowledge-center/school-leadership/principal-training/Documents/Schools-Cant-Wait-University-Principal-Preparation.pdf.

Gibbs, P., & Angelides, P. (2008). Understanding friendships between critical friends. *Improving Schools, 11*(3), 213–225.

Golde, C. M., & Walker, G. E. (Eds.). (2006). *Envisioning the future of doctoral education: Preparing stewards of the discipline*. San Francisco, CA: Jossey-Bass.

Guthrie, J. W. (2009). The case for a modern Doctor of Education degree (Ed.D.): Multipurpose education doctorates no longer appropriate. *Peabody Journal of Education, 84*(1), 3–8.

Hale, E. L., & Moorman, H. N. (2003). *Preparing school principals: A national perspective on policy and program innovations*. Washington, DC: Institute for Educational Leadership. Retrieved from http://www.iel.org/pubs/preparingprincipals.pdf.

Handal, G. (1999, Fall). Consultation using critical friends. *New Directors for Teaching and Learning, 79*, 59–70.

Harrison, C., & Killion, J. (2007). Ten roles for teacher leaders. *Educational Leadership, 65*(1), 74–77.

Hess, F. M. (2003, January). *A license to lead? A new leadership agenda for America's schools* [Policy report]. Washington, DC: Progressive Policy Institute. Retrieved from http://www.aei.org/article/education/a-license-to-lead/.

International Society for Technology in Education. (2009). *National educational technology standards for administrators*. Washington, DC: Author.

Kentucky Cohesive Leadership System. (2008, May). *Continuum for principal preparation development*. Frankfort, KY: Author.

Kentucky Education Reform Act, Kentucky Revised Statute, KRS 160.345 (1990).

Muth, R., Browne-Ferrigno, T., Bellamy, T. Fulmer, C., & Silver, M. (in press). Using teacher instructional leadership as a predictor of principal leadership. *Journal of School Leadership.*

National Center for Evaluation of Educational Leadership Preparation and Practice. (n.d.). *School Leadership Preparation and Practice Survey.* Charlottesville, VA: University Council for Educational Administration. Retrieved from http://edleaderprep.org/.

Orr, M. T., & Pounder, D. (2011). Teaching and preparing school leaders. In S. Conley & B. S. Cooper (Eds.), *Finding, preparing, and supporting school leaders: Critical issues, useful solutions* (pp. 11–39). Lanham, MD: Rowman Littlefield.

Perry, J. A. (2011, Fall). The Carnegie Project on the Education Doctorate: Phase II—A quest for change. *UCEA Review, 52*(3), 1–4. Retrieved from http://ucea.org/storage/review/UCEAReview_Fall2011_web.pdf.

Rallis, S. F., & Rossman, G. B. (2000). Dialogue for learning: Evaluator as critical friend. *New Directions for Evaluation, 86,* 81–92.

Roach, V., Smith, L. W., & Boutin, J. (2011). School leadership policy trends and developments: Policy expediency or policy excellence? *Educational Administration Quarterly, 47*(1), 71–113.

Sanders, N. M., & Kearney, K. M. (Eds.). (2008). *Performance expectations and indicators for education leaders: An ISLLC-based guide to implementing leader standards and a companion guide to the Educational Leadership Policy Standards: ISLLC 2008.* Alexandria, VA: Council of Chief State School Officers.

Schulman, L. S., Golde, C. M., Bueschel, A. C., & Garbedian, K. J. (2006). Reclaiming education's doctorates: A critique and a proposal. *Educational Researcher, 35*(3), 25–32.

Swaffield, S. (2007). Light touch critical friendship. *Improving Schools, 10*(3), 205–219.

Swaffield, S., & MacBeath, J. (2005) School self evaluation and the role of a critical friend. *Cambridge Journal of Education, 35*(2), 239–52.

US Department of Education. (2005). *Innovative pathways to school leadership.* Washington, DC: Office of Innovation and Improvement. Retrieved from http://www.ed.gov/admins/recruit/prep/alternative/index.html

Wenger, E. (1998). *Communities of practice: Learning, meaning, and identity.* Cambridge: Cambridge University Press.

Wenger, E., McDermott, R., & Snyder, W. M. (2002). *Cultivating communities of practice: A guide to managing knowledge.* Boston, MA: Harvard Business School Press.

Wirt, F. M., & Kirst, M. W. (1997). *The political dynamics of American education.* Berkeley, CA: McCutchan.

Young, M. D. (2013). Is state-mandated redesign an effective and sustainable solution? *Journal of Research on Leadership Education, 8*(2) 247–254.

Applying the Critical Friends Group Model to the EdD Program

Critical Friends Groups and Their Role in the Redefinition of the Online EdD in Higher Education Administration at Texas Tech University

Stephanie J. Jones

The use of Critical Friends Groups (CFGs) is more common in the K-12 environment, and has "been shown to make valuable contributions to learning and school improvement in a range of contexts" (Swaffield, 2004, p. 268). There is limited discussion in the literature of the use of CFGs in the discipline of higher education or within higher education organizations themselves. The purpose of this chapter is to explore the use of CFGs in the reform efforts of redefining an online education doctorate (EdD) in the discipline of higher education at Texas Tech University (TTU). Of specific focus in this discussion is how CFGs have been and continue to be instrumental in the redefinition of the online EdD at TTU. The redefinition of the EdD in higher education at TTU utilizes the Carnegie Project on the Education Doctorate (CPED) framework. CPED, in itself, serves as a CFG to all members of the project, who work together and discuss how to redefine and enhance the EdD. TTU's College of Education—higher education program—is a second wave member of CPED and is one of the few that is redefining its EdD in higher education, based on the CPED framework, within an online environment.

Costa and Kallick (1993) identify a Critical Friend as one that "takes the time to fully understand the context of the work presented and the outcomes that the person or group is working toward" (p. 50). Storey and Richard (2013a) identify, "At the core of a Critical Friendship is constructive, purposeful dialogue which is distinct from conversation or discussion" (p. 16). Others have noted that Critical Friends can help organizations make sound decisions by challenging expectations and shaping outcomes, but never overstepping boundaries by determining the outcomes (Brighouse & Woods, 1999; McDonald 1989; Stoll & Thomas, 1996; as cited in Swaffield, 2004). These statements describe the relationships of the CFGs and the higher education program at TTU, and frame the following discussion.

This chapter will present an overview of the higher education program within the College of Education at TTU, a brief history of its EdD and PhD degrees, the program's membership in the second wave of the CPED project, the use of and the roles of CFGs in the program's reform of its online EdD, as well as a description of the redefined online EdD. The benefits and challenges of utilizing CFGs in the redefining of an online EdD will also be discussed.

History/Purpose of the Education Doctorate in Higher Education at Texas Tech University

The higher education program in the College of Education at TTU is a standalone program that consists of a master's in higher education administration, an on-site EdD in higher education administration, an online EdD in higher education with an emphasis in community college administration, and an on-site PhD in higher education research. Prior to 2012, all doctorate degrees were 66 hours beyond the master's degree. If reviewing the doctoral degrees—EdD and PhD—side by side, one would find that the only thing that distinguished one from the other was that the PhD had a 12-hour research core while the EdD had a 9-hour research core plus an internship. From this point forward, reference to *the program* will infer the higher education program.

The student population in the program is working professionals in higher education organizations, with 100 percent of EdD students working full time and attending school part time. This is typical of most EdD programs. Many of the students take three to six hours per semester. Many students do not proceed through the doctoral program in a perceived timely manner, oftentimes taking six to eight years to graduate. This is stimulated by the ad hoc manner that students enroll in courses and the inability for some students to make progress on their dissertation. As the literature supports, dissertation experiences can be isolating when there is no longer the camaraderie felt from being in classes with other students.

Prior to spring 2011, most of the doctoral students in the higher education program were from Lubbock, Texas, or its surrounding region, with a large number of the students employed at TTU. The goal of most of the students in the program is to complete their doctorates so that they can advance in their careers as higher education administrators.

As with many programs that offer both the EdD and PhD, there has traditionally been little difference between the degrees. Most students seeking a doctorate in higher education apply to the PhD program, even though their career goals are to be higher education administrators. Many perceive, which anecdotally appears to be from talking to those with PhD's, that the EdD is an inferior degree and that an EdD would not enable them to obtain a job in a university or as an executive leader in any type of higher education institution. This is similar to the dilemma faced at other institutions, in which there exists "implicit biases that treated the EdD as a 'low-end PhD'" (Shulman, Golde, Bueschel, & Garabedian, 2006, p. 25). This was a concern to the program faculty, two who held EdDs, and who were prior college administrators. It was apparent that the conversations occurring at the university about the value of an EdD were inaccurate and it was important to the program to address this inaccuracy. It became a goal of the program faculty to have two distinguishable degrees that served separate and necessary purposes in higher education (Stephanie J. Jones, personal communication, November 6, 2012)

At the time that the discussion among the program occurred about distinguishing the two degrees, work began on creating an online EdD in higher education with an emphasis in community college administration to support the needs of the state of Texas, for qualified higher education administrators in the community college environment. The program also saw this as an opportunity to diversify its student population. Though the higher education program has multiple doctoral degrees, from this point forward the discussion will focus on the online EdD unless otherwise noted.

The curriculum for the online EdD was representative of the on-site EdD, with the exception that the focus of the curriculum was on community college environments versus general higher education. It was recognized that an online EdD would provide the program many opportunities to recruit from a wider geographical location, but most importantly it provides access and flexibility for those who desire to attain a doctorate degree. Though the purpose of delivering the degree online was to serve the needs of the state of Texas, it was recognized that there were limited barriers to serving the needs across the United States., as long as TTU had state authorization to do so. In fall 2011, at the same time that the program was implementing its new online EdD, TTU's College of Education was invited to join the second wave of the CPED. Perry (2012) identifies the goal of CPED is to redesign the EdD to "make it the highest-quality degree for the advanced preparation of school practitioners and clinical faculty, academic leaders, and professional staff for the nation's schools and colleges and the organizations that support them" (p. 42)

This provided a significant opportunity for the program to *peel back the layers* of its fairly new online degree, to see if it actually met the needs of community colleges, as well as to spend time determining how the program could set the EdD apart from its PhD.

Reform of the Online Education Doctorate through the CPED Process

In fall 2011, a representative of the program attended the first convening of CPED as a second wave member. This coincided well with the implementation of the online EdD, which was now in its second semester with its first cohort.

Attending the CPED convening was beneficial to the higher education program for two reasons: (a) it allowed the program to immediately see that what it was doing was not forward thinking enough or innovative enough to be competitive as a national higher education program; and (b) it allowed the program to see that there were esteemed institutions that were already doing things differently, and they were having success with redefining their EdD. What specifically caught the program's attention was the focus of CPED member institutions on incorporating authentic problems of practice into their curriculum, which was what the higher education program was seeking to do as it attempted to distinguish its EdD from its PhD. Seeing examples of authentic applications of projects that students who were working full time and attending school part time were able to accomplish, proved that these curriculum challenges could be implemented with success. Having access to the work of the first wave of CPED members and the knowledge base that had and was being created, also proved to be useful on many fronts. From this knowledge base, the program was able to establish a clear definition of the EdD that could be used as a foundational basis for the development of the redefined EdD. The definition now used by the program was developed by CPED members and is, "The professional doctorate in education prepares educators for the application of appropriate and specific practices, the generation of new knowledge and for the stewardship of the profession" (Carnegie Project on the Education Doctorate, 2013, p. 1).

Being a part of the discussions at CPED—seeing how wave one members were redesigning the EdD to be delivered in an accelerated format, as well as focused on problems of practice within the field of the discipline—enabled the program to push forward quicker with innovative enhancements to the degree than if it had had to pave its own way. What gave the program faculty extensive credibility with the other faculty and administration in the College of Education was the ability to showcase what other quality institutions were already doing in their redefinitions of their EdD. Examples of the California system's higher education and K-12 programs who had already successfully completed group dissertations focused on problems of practice, and the University of Nebraska-Lincoln who had already reformed their EdD with success, indicated that redefining the traditional EdD could be done and done in the highest of quality. Knowing that others before us had laid the framework for how to turn a degree program upside down with success led us to consider how the CPED framework could be implemented in an online environment. It is strongly perceived by the program that whether the curriculum is delivered online or on-site, the expectations of rigor and quality must be in line with what can be done in the on-site environment. The program did not want the online degree to be considered inferior or a *diploma mill* because it was online.

At the same time that the program became involved with CPED, the College of Education at TTU was also going through administration transition. The new dean of the College of Education arrived on campus in summer 2011. Coming from Arizona State, a wave one member of CPED, the dean immediately began creating his vision for the College—one of reform. He commonly states that Colleges of Education are in trouble and are at risk of being closed due to their national low performance. He is adamant that if Colleges of Education reform themselves—they will establish their place in higher education and can be instrumental to the education of qualified professionals who can be change agents and influencers in many educational settings (Dr. Scott Ridley, personal communication, August 22, 2011). His strong statements are supported in the literature with dialogues such as the problem with Colleges of Education are "chronic and crippling"—unless the problems are faced and dealt with, "schools of education risk becoming increasingly impotent in carrying out their primary mission—the advancement of knowledge and the preparation of quality practitioners" (Shulman, Golde, Bueschel, & Garabedian, 2006, p. 25).

The dean of the College of Education is an avid supporter of the program's involvement in CPED. His reform agenda aligns very well with the CPED framework for the redefinition of the EdD. A college in reform and strong allies in CPED members were instrumental in the success the program has had with applying the CPED framework to an online EdD. Since the college was in a period of extreme change and innovative thinking—the CPED framework provided a data-supported avenue to do things differently. Since the environment was already one of change, the program was able to openly discuss the CPED framework with all colleagues at the College of Education, which helped all to *rethink* the future of the EdD and what this future looked like in serving the needs of a changing society. In addition—this conversation encouraged the programs within the College of Education at TTU to think about how to set themselves apart competitively from other College of Education programs across the nation.

As mentioned previously, the EdD in higher education at TTU had been perceived to be an inferior degree to the PhD by many at the university and to the potential students who inquired about the degree. Comments identifying the EdD as a PhD lite or a low-end PhD are common in the literature, as well as around TTU. In addition, as noted by Shulman et al. (2006), nationally "the purposes of preparing scholars and practitioners are confused; as a result, neither is done well" (p. 26). This was no different in the program. Many students within the program prior to spring 2011 were employees at the university. TTU is categorized as a Research University (high research activity) by the Carnegie Classification of Higher Education Institutions ("Carnegie Classification," n.d.). TTU has also been identified as an emerging research university within the state of Texas. The issue that this brings is that most students that want to pursue a PhD at TTU are working full time and have no desire to be researchers or professors, but they perceive they must get a PhD to be promoted in an emerging research university. When they describe their goals and future career aspirations, it is to move up through the ranks of administration. These motivations are in line with a replication study conducted by Storey and Richard (2013b), in which enrolled students in an EdD program in the United States noted their interest in pursuing a structured, part-time program that would lead to career advancement. This causes a dilemma as what potential students describe is a practitioner-based career, but they want a research-focused degree. One of the challenges faced by the program was how to educate potential students of the value of the EdD and the PhD, without undermining the value of either. The CPED framework for the EdD focuses on developing scholarly practitioners, which is a cited need throughout the research for higher education leadership (Perry, 2012; Shulman et al., 2006). Being part of a national discussion of the magnitude of like-minded individuals at the first convening of CPED, enabled the program to redefine its discussions with potential students about the EdD, as well as also provided the program with information to help it educate potential students and others at the university that a national conversation was occurring on the value of the EdD.

TTU is also unique among CPED institutions due to the fact that prior to the program's affiliation with CPED the delivery of an online EdD program had been approved by the Texas Higher Education Coordinating Board and the Southern Association of Colleges and Schools. The challenge now became how to take a degree program that had been implemented for one semester, and start redefining it for the fall 2011 cohort.

CFGs and Roles in Redefining the Online Education Doctorate

The online EdD was purposefully created to serve the needs of community colleges in the state of Texas, who are experiencing a declining pool of qualified individuals to take over the helm of these organizations. As Shults (2001) and others have found, many senior level higher education administrators, staff, and faculty are retiring in crisis-level numbers. This crisis in retiring senior leadership has been predicted to last until around 2015. These massive retirements leave institutions without qualified leadership. The EdD is the doctorate that is designed to educate and train individuals with the practical skills needed to lead these organizations.

The first step in redefining the EdD entailed finding out what was going on nationally in the field of higher education. What did the research show was happening with the retirement of leadership and faculty? What competencies were being discussed as needed by future leaders? What were other doctoral programs in higher education doing? These types of questions were easy to answer by turning to the literature or reviewing institution websites. What was missing was the practical aspect of these areas—what was truly occurring in higher education organizations on a day-to-day basis, and what skills and knowledge were missing from those leading the way. One way to get these answers was to use CFGs to help broaden the discussion of what the future EdD should look like and who it should serve. There are five CFGs that are instrumental to the redefinition of the online EdD at TTU: (a) community college presidents and administrators; (b) higher education program faculty; (c) program coordinators for other programs in the College of Education at TTU; (d) College of Education administrators; and (e) current cohorts of online EdD students.

CFs in community colleges are instrumental to the success of the online EdD. This CFG helps the program identify the necessary skills and competencies needed in future leaders in community colleges. These individuals see, on a daily basis, the issues and challenges that community colleges are faced with, and they can help identify the skills and competencies that need to be incorporated into the curriculum to ensure graduates have the *toolkit* to lead these institutions forward in the future. The CFG of community college presidents and other administrators, whose primary roles were initially to help the program understand the needs of community colleges today and in the future, evolved into key consultants who help ensure the program curriculum is up-to-date and dynamic. These individuals are also leaders in partnering community college institutions who supply the program with institutional problems of practice for practitioner-based dissertations. The program faculty recognize that though they teach the courses and conduct research in higher education—they are not in the field. It is important to the success of the online EdD to have this CFG help the program determine what a graduate of the program should look like. This CFG has been instrumental in helping the program to identify what the *ideal future community college leader* looks like and to work backward to determine the skills and competencies that need to be taught in the curriculum. This process is supported by CPED, who from 2007 through 2009, examined the EdD—"starting with the end in mind—the graduate" and asking "what knowledge, skills, and dispositions should professionals working in education possess and be able to use" upon graduation (Perry, 2012, p. 42). This community college CFG brings a critical piece to the dialogue—and that is the practitioner side of the role that the program is educating students to fill. They are also instrumental in asking challenging questions that promote deeper discussions (Storey & Richard, 2013a) among the program faculty and other CFGs within the College of Education.

The program faculty is a second and extremely important CFG. The faculty are committed 100 percent to the redefinition of the online EdD and seldom disagree on how to move the degree forward. But this does not mean that critical dialogues are not occurring. The CFG framework is instrumental to the dialogues that are held—with all faculty open to constructive criticism—understanding that the questions posed will help to move the program forward. Though the program of discussion is delivered online—this is not a factor when discussing what skills and competencies graduates of the program need. It is recognized that the situation within the program and its commitment to this project may be an unusual situation—in that all faculty are supportive of the efforts to redefine the degree at the same time that the College of Education at TTU is going through reform initiatives—but the faculty understand and are committed to the idea that the redefined EdD will ensure that graduates are prepared for the higher education workplace of today and in the future—and that is the reward that they seek for the time and effort that they have committed and will continue to commit to this endeavor. The CFG of program faculty have been the instrumental group in redefining the EdD. As a program, it is fortunate that no one sees the redesign of the EdD as threatening "to existing policies and practices" or "to the role of professors" (Storey & Richard, 2013a, p. 7). The faculty are all assistant professors who have previously served as college and university administrators and who have fully committed and embraced the CPED framework for developing scholarly practitioners. The program has led the way for the college in promoting problems in practice dissertations and working with collaborative partners to help not only advise the program on the curriculum, but also to incorporate these partners into class assignments and experiences (e.g., service learning projects and individual authentic labs of practice), as well as dissertation committees.

Two other CFGs who have been and will continue to be instrumental to the redefinition of the EdD in the program, are the program coordinators of all other programs in the College of Education at TTU, and the administrators of the College of Education. These groups meet bimonthly to discuss reform efforts of the college and each program, all the while challenging the thought process and curriculum changes being discussed. The curriculum changes that have been proposed by the higher education program faculty have undergone significant critiques and multiple approval processes from the College of Education CFGs, with continuous improvement occurring. The program has been able to share the CPED framework with all of the other programs at these meetings. This has been useful in helping others reframe their thoughts on what doctoral programs and degrees should accomplish today and in the future. In addition, it has been useful to have groups outside of those affiliated with the discipline of higher education to critique and question the program's thought processes and assessments of the curriculum.

The final CFG that has been instrumental in the redefinition of the online EdD have been the current cohorts of students in the online EdD program. There is limited discussion in the literature of students being seen as Critical Friends. What sets the program's students apart from many—but not necessarily unusual in EdD programs—is that the students are already professionals in the field in which they are studying—they are practitioners (Shulman et al., 2006; Storey & Richard, 2013b). It is not unusual for some of the students to have more practitioner experience than the faculty who are teaching them. The online students as a CFG have contributed to significant dialogue, questions, and critiques of curriculum of the online EdD, as well as the online format it is delivered in. This CFG has challenged the faculty to consider how closer integration of curriculum between faculty members could produce more powerful learning experiences for the students. This aligns well with the signature pedagogy of learning communities—but is conducted in the online environment. Faculty have spent numerous hours discussing and critiquing with this CFG on what this looks like and how it can be integrated into the online format. Incorporation of case studies that apply learning outcomes of two classes into one response has not only encouraged students to think more critically, but has also helped them to build their skills of working across boundaries in higher education where they have normally been focused very narrowly. It took some time for the faculty to be receptive to students' critique of the curriculum and the faculty members' teaching styles and pedagogies, but through critical reflection and dialogue, the student CFG and the faculty have developed a trusting relationship where faculty are receptive to the student CFGs' challenges, and the student CFGs' development and understanding of purposeful curriculum and faculty intentions of skill and competency development are better understood.

The second contribution of the student CFG is focused on the online delivery of courses and the program. Each semester, the program obtains feedback from each online cohort to evaluate what changes, if any, need to be made. Once the feedback has been analyzed by the faculty, the faculty meet with the cohorts of students in their on-site summer session in Lubbock, Texas, to dialogue on how to make the online experience better and more effective. The contributions that the student CFG has made to the program has advanced it beyond what was initially thought doable by the program faculty and the College of Education, and these contributions have been integral to the redefinition of the EdD.

The Redefined Online Education Doctorate

Through the work of the five CFGs and the CPED framework, the online EdD has been redefined with the following program objective:

> Graduates of the online EdD in Higher Education with an emphasis in community college administration will be scholarly practitioners with the skills and competencies to name, frame, and solve problems of practice, using empirical evidence to evaluate impact. Understanding the importance of equity and social justice, they use applied theories and practical research as tools of collaborative change and influence (Texas Tech University, 2011).

The students in the online EdD are working professionals in community college environments. Their workplace is their *laboratories of practice*. Students are admitted as cohorts of 15 to 20 students that begin in the fall semester each year. One of the requirements to be admitted into the program is five years of professional experience in a community college and the student must be currently working in a community college or state organization that interfaces with them.

The redefined online EdD is one that is purposefully designed to enhance the skills and competencies of its students beyond knowledge level. The degree has been redesigned with the help of all five of the CFGs. It is a 60-hour doctorate (above the master's degree), and is designed to be completed in three years; two years of coursework and one year in an accelerated dissertation format. Students are required to attend a one-week intensive session in Lubbock, Texas, in the summer I semester for each of the three years of the program. Students' progress through three phases of curriculum with assessment and remediation occurring within each phase to ensure that students have the skills and competencies needed to move forward. Phase 1 of the curriculum is knowledge base. The main focus of this phase is to ensure that students have the ability to write at the professional level. It has been noted that higher education administrators spend a lot of their time writing (Munger, 2010). If students' assessments indicate they are not writing at the doctoral level—they are remediated prior to their moving to Phase 2. Phase 2 is guided practice. Signature pedagogies such as case studies and service learning are incorporated into the curriculum and students have extensive amounts of *guided practice* in both hypothetical and authentic environments. Courses that are sequenced in Phase 2 are required to have hypothetical and authentic problems of practice. Again, if students' assessments indicate deficiencies in their abilities to name, frame, and solve problems of practice using data, students will be remediated prior to moving to Phase 3. Phase 3 is authentic practice. Students are engaged in individual and independent practice through coursework and the practitioner-based dissertation. Practitioner-based dissertations are themed. The program identifies problems of practice within partnering community colleges as possible dissertation topics for the students. Though students are formed into groups by themes of dissertation topics, students do produce individual dissertations. The dissertation process is a one-year experience, where students work in small groups with partnering community colleges to provide solutions to problems of practice at these institutions. A member of the partnering institution is a member of the dissertation committee, and has equal input on the success of the student in the dissertation process (Texas Tech University, 2011).

Analysis and Evaluation of the Uses of CFGs in Redefining the Online EdD

Working with CFGs in redefining the EdD has been beneficial to the higher education program, and has enabled it to develop an EdD that will have direct impact on the field of higher education. As discussed by Swaffield (2003), CFGs allow groups to move beyond simple interactions with Critical Friends to relationships that foster trust, advocacy, critique, and questioning—all in a constructive environment with the goal of developing an EdD that prepares students with the skills and competencies needed to move higher education institutions forward. The CFG of community college administrators bring a practitioner perspective to the curriculum that would not have been possible if only the faculty within the program had determined what was needed. The program faculty have not worked on a college campus for four or more years. During this time, the financial crisis that is affecting higher education today due to state funding cuts, institutions experiencing record enrollments—especially community colleges, as well as the stirring need for crisis management, are all issues that have come to the forefront after the faculty moved into the professoriate. The ability to engage with a group of higher education practitioners about what skills and competencies are needed for the job has been extremely beneficial on two fronts. First, it ensures the program faculty—when developing the curriculum for the program—is aware of the skills and competencies that are needed in today's higher education institutions. Second, the long-term benefits of the relationships that have developed between the higher education program, the College of Education, and Texas Tech University and the CFGs in our partnering higher education institutions cannot be measured. As one CFG member called it—it is a "win-win" for both.

Evaluating the Motivations, Biases, and Level of Trust with CFG Stakeholders

Having the student CFG to provide the program with dialogue and critique of the rigor of the courses and the number of courses required each semester, has encouraged the faculty to continuously assess the program for improvement. But, this has not gone without turmoil. Faculty perceive that students often try to find ways to *cut corners* and perhaps are not dedicating enough time and effort into their doctoral studies. CFGs open up dialogue and critique—and this is not generally a role that students take—or faculty accept—especially in the EdD. The faculty spend a tremendous amount of time working with students in the online environment to help them acclimate to the expectations of the program and the commitment they need to bring to their coursework. This is difficult to do in an online environment—where all students cannot be brought into a room where an open discussion can ensue. Students are very independent and isolated in this environment and this has required the faculty to consistently have to discuss and dialogue about how to create an environment where the students can be successful, while also ensuring that students understand the expectations to meet the standards and be ready for the challenge.

At this time, the redefined online EdD in higher education with a focus on community college administrations appears to be progressing, but not without challenges. It has been difficult to get the right order of course sequencing down for the cohorts. The EdD is very different from the rigor of master's and undergraduate. Many of the students who are in the online EdD find out very quickly that adding a rigorous doctoral program to an already busy schedule is challenging and overwhelming.

Partnering With Your CFG Stakeholders to Coproduce Program Redesign

There have been many successes with working with CFGs. The community college CFG consistently praises the higher education program for the work they are doing to make the doctoral experience meaningful and useful—at a time when doctoral programs are under scrutiny by many external constituents. The members of the CFG recognize the role that doctoral programs hold in their future abilities to hire qualified leadership at their institutions. Other successes include the ability of the College of Education at TTU to reform its entire college through the use of CFGs—supporting programs and generating critical dialogue that will enable the college to reestablish itself as a critical player among Colleges of Education across the nation. The higher education program has benefited and will continue to benefit from these ongoing dialogues as it continues to redefine its online EdD. Student CFGs has also been instrumental to the redefinition of the online EdD. Students who are professionals in the field they are studying bring both practitioner and student influence into the program. Critical dialogues and questions among the program faculty and students have enabled the program to redefine the EdD to one that is more innovative and useful than could have been possible without the students' input. This type of partnership is not unique, or limited to the field of education. Companies take similar actions, seeking out their customers to assist them in the coproduction of their products. Coproduction, the inclusion of both the company and the customer, or in this case the program and future students, is a win-win for both parties. It allows the customer (future students) to contribute to their success, and the company (program) benefits as a result (Ford & Dickson, 2012).

There is minimal discussion in the literature on the use of CFGs in the redefinition of online EdDs or in the reform of higher education environments. Much of the literature discusses CFGs and their use in teacher education. The experiences discussed above will further the discussion of CFGs in environments outside of teacher education and show how collaboration can lead to redefined EdDs.

References

Carnegie Classification of Higher Education Institutions. (n.d.). Texas Tech University. Retrieved from http://classifications.carnegiefoundation. org/lookup_listings/view_institution.php?unit_id=229115&start_ page=institution.php&clq=%7B%22first_letter%22%3A%22T%22%7D.

Carnegie Project on the Education Doctorate. (2013). *Design concept definitions*. Retrieved from http://cpedinitiative.org/design-concept-definitions.

Costa, A. L., & Kallick, B. (1993). Through the lens of a critical friend. *Educational Leadership, 51*(2), 49–51.

Ford, R. C., & Dickson, D. (2012). Enhancing customer self-efficacy in co-producing their service experiences. *Business Horizons, 55*(2), 179–188.

Munger, M. C. (2010, September). 10 Tips on how to write less badly. *The Chronicle of Higher Education*. Retrieved from http://chronicle.com/article/10-Tips-on-How-to-Write-Less/124268/.

Perry, J. A. (2012, September). To EdD or not to EdD? *Kappan*, 41–44.

Shulman, L. S., Golde, C., Bueschel, A. C., & Garabedian, K. (2006). Reclaiming education's doctorates: A critique and a proposal. *Educational Researcher, 35*(3), 25–32.

Shults, C. (2001). The critical impact of impending retirements on community college leadership. *Research brief leadership series*, no. 1, AACC-RB-01–5. Washington, DC: American Association of Community Colleges.

Storey, V. A., & Richard, B. M. (2013a). Carnegie Project of the Educational Doctorate: The role of critical friends in diffusing doctoral program innovation. *National Council of Professors of Educational Administration (NCPEA) reviewers and the 2013 International Editorial Advisory Panel of Global Scholar*.

Storey, V. A. & Richard, B. (2013b, April). Why do students choose a professional doctorate in education: A comparison of motivations, perceptions, and outcomes between the U.S. and the U.K. Presented at the 2013 International Conference on Doctoral Education. Orlando, FL.

Swaffield, S. (2003, October). Critical friendship. [Inform No. 3] *Leadership for learning*. Cambridge: University of Cambridge Faculty of Education. Retrieved from http://www.educ.cam.ac.uk/centres/lfl/current/inform/Inform_3_Critical_Friendship.pdf.

Swaffield, S. (2004). Critical friends: Supporting leadership, improved learning. *Improving Schools, 7*(3), 267–278.

Texas Tech University (2011). Higher Education Doctoral Programs. Retrieved from http:// http://cms.educ.ttu.edu/academic-programs/psychology-and-leadership/higher-education/doctoral-programs.

CHAPTER 9

Using a Cohort Approach to Convert EdD Students into Critical Friends

Edmund "Ted" Hamann and Susan Wunder

A steadfast but not previously examined feature of our department's six-year (and counting) experience with a Carnegie Project for the Education Doctorate (CPED)-influenced Doctor of Education (EdD) program is the successful implementation of a cohort model and, in turn, the utilization of practitioners' sense of belonging and familiarity to become each other's Critical Friends. Looking across the experiences of three cohorts of University of Nebraska-Lincoln (UNL) CPED students—a first cohort that graduated eight EdDs, a second cohort with twelve students who attained candidacy just three months before this writing, and a new cohort of ten students also composed largely of educators who have not known each other prior to enrolling in CPED—this chapter considers the action steps pursued and the formative evaluative processes that compel minor redirections of course that have helped convert a collection of advanced graduate students into enduring Critical Friends Groups (CFGs). Data include program design elements, including syllabi, but the main sources of information are the accounts of the practicing professionals who have completed their EdD journey as members of our first cohort.

BACKGROUND

UNL was one of 25 institutions that began participation in CPED during Phase I in 2007. Two departments in UNL's College of Education and Human Sciences were and continue to be involved, albeit largely separately—Educational Administration and Teaching, Learning, and Teacher Education (TLTE). It is the latter department in which we authors are faculty members and about which we are writing here. At the time of our application, the national conversation about distinguishing the PhD in education from the EdD that has informed CPED (Perry, 2012; Shulman, Golde, Bueschel, & Garabedian, 2006; Watts & Imig, 2012) had an echo in our intradepartmental conversations about the same topic that stemmed from both an academic program review (APR) and our university's twin charge to be both a land-grant and research intensive institution. CPED provided the encouragement and vehicle for figuring out how best to proceed.

With knowledge of the emerging CPED initiative, our working group of interested graduate faculty met throughout 2007 and 2008 to develop a program for EdD students. As our report at the October 2007 CPED meeting in Nashville explained, these regular meetings "served to cultivate commitment to this initiative and to make more visible our teaching, research, and service commitments to each other. These meetings also enabled us to articulate why the CPED is a worthwhile venture for ourselves as faculty, our students, the context and the work of teacher education more broadly." Since well prior to this CPED conversation, our department had offered an EdD degree (as well as a PhD), but the graduation rate from it was not high and there was no single clear-cut delineation between what it proposed to be versus the PhD, beyond nine fewer credit hours of graduation requirements.

By the conclusion of the 2008 spring semester, we had determined intended programmatic outcomes, a preliminary coursework structure, core principles and pedagogies, and other program features. Per our first publicity about the new program, we were focused on the commitment to preparing scholars of educational practice "within a collegial and supportive environment." Noting that our EdD students were full-time practitioners who intended to continue to self-identify as practitioners (even as they built new knowledge, gained capacity as researchers and policy interpreters, and qualified to become teacher educators), we identified *epistemology, praxis, efficacy, problems of practice,* and *reflectivity* as key words and phrases that described both what we hoped to draw participants' attention to and how we were to guide our own program coordination.

Critical Friends was not one of our key words, but it could have been, as an emphasis on collegiality is evident in several of these founding documents. For example, we asserted as a core principle of our program that, "cohort learning offers opportunities to learn from each other and foster ongoing dialogue and connections beyond the degree." Descriptions of program coursework included the intent to "cultivate a culture of collaboration among scholars and practitioners across disciplines and roles, drawing upon the experiential ground of multiple concrete teaching/learning situations." Programmatic outcomes included to "cultivate a community of learning professionals invested in enlarging all understandings of the work of teaching and learning" and "build professional connections that sustain and nurture educator well-being."

CRITICAL COLLEGIALITY IN PRACTICE

Yet these were just intriguing ambitions until we admitted a first cohort of EdD students into this newly conceived program in January 2009. While we did not at any point in the ensuing semesters use the formal protocol associated with Critical Friends (Storey & Richard, 2012), our approaches were consistent with important aspects of it. For example, early in their programs, CPED EdD candidates read Brian Lord's (1994) account of critical colleagueship. For most, that was not their first encounter with the idea of professional learning communities and the related sensibility of professional peers as resources; indeed experience with these elements in professional practice is one reason our students have matriculated in the CPED program. However, the Lord article often was the first place where students actively considered the word "critical" as part of their expected and prospectively productive relationship with colleagues and it was also one of the early places where they have seen the design of their CPED program find an echo in professional literature that program faculty ask them to consider.

Lord (1994) begins his piece quoting at length from a study by David Cohen (1990) that highlights an individual practitioner—a math teacher from California—attempting to change her practice in response to new standards. While this is a scenario easily understood by our CPED students, it is the questions Lord (1994) poses reflecting upon Cohen that we really draw their attention to:

> Cohen's images [of the teacher] raise several questions for those who are concerned about teachers' professional development: In what ways might professional development contribute to a more reflective stance toward instruction? How will teachers be helped to move beyond "relatively superficial" interpretations of national content standards? From whom might [the teacher] get critical feedback on her teaching,

and how might constructive criticism be built into the very fabric of professional development? (p. 177).

It is not difficult to segue from questions like these (about a teacher they have never met who teaches 1500 miles from Nebraska), to questions that are far more overtly about our students' professional practice. We have asked: How and from whom do you get professional feedback? How do you know if your practice is responsive to ever-rising expectations? And how do you cajole, push, and collaborate with colleagues? In the No Child Left Behind-era, the question is not just "how well am I leading my own practice?," but rather "how do we assure that our whole school or district moves forward successfully?"

Conceptually important as Lord (1994) has been, the cultivation of critical collegiality has been more substantively advanced by three key features at the start of our program: the reinvention of existing course descriptions for new, more cumulative purposes; the continuation of certain courses for longer than a semester (which has permitted longer time frames for activities like honing a group paper); and our expectation that 30 of the minimum 45 new credit hours that CPED students were expected to take for the program were to be pursued as "cohort classes"—that is, required for members of the cohort and, with very limited exception, not open to other UNL students.

As an example of all of these features, one of the first two courses that CPED students are asked to enroll in is a spring and summer-spanning, six-credit hour, doctoral seminar that is accurately and vaguely subtitled "Challenges and Opportunities." (Our CPED cohorts have all started in the spring.) This seminar, which has been taught in each of its first three incarnations by one of your authors [Hamann], has fit within the similarly vague but flexible UNL guideline that requires six credit hours of "doctoral seminar" for EdD students. It has been the venue for students reading the previously referenced Lord (1994) article, as well as where they first start building a common shared knowledge of American educational history's link to present conditions by considering titles like William Proefriedt's (2008) *High Expectations: The Cultural Roots of Standards Reform in American Education* or David Labaree's (2010) *Someone Has to Fail: The Zero Sum Game of Public Schooling.*

More importantly, however, each rendering of that class has included a multicomponent group assignment that has them not only studying and critiquing a selected example of a practitioner-turned-scholar describing taking on a "problem of practice," but also critiquing each other's first forays in critiquing the selected example. Below is a quote from the first cohort's syllabus and then the more expansive

description of the same assignment to the third cohort to illuminate this complex, critical collegiality-building assignment:
From the first syllabus (Spring 2009):

GROUP PROJECT

The class will be divided up into three groups. Each group will have the task of reading Heaton (2000), Wilson (2007), *or* Wilhelm (2008). The group will then prepare a presentation and a paper that answer the following questions:

- What is the problem(s) that the author is attempting to solve?
- What appears to be the author's sense of what should be (i.e., their philosophical posture)?
- How does the author collect data germane to the identified problem?
- Do you find the research strategy compelling? Why or why not?
- If you were studying this problem, would you pursue it the same way?
- Are there relevant problems in play that the author is not acknowledging?

Note, in the summer you will read the two other books that you did not read for this spring final project.

The imprint of the first syllabus remains visible in the third, although there are a few clarifications and additions, for example overt connection to the challenging but important Deyhle, Hess, and Lecompte (1992) article "Approaching Ethical Issues for Qualitative Researchers in Education" and to our department's organization of our curriculum into five partially overlapping curricular *areas of emphasis*. Also the third syllabus more clearly specifies the second and third phases (the summer phases) of the activity that are crucial for assuring both the iterative nature of the project and its critical orientation.

From the third syllabus (Spring 2013):

ACTION RESEARCH GROUP PROJECTS

In early February, the class will be divided up into three groups. Each group will have the task of reading Heaton (2000), Herrera (2010), *or* Wilhelm (2008). For the final spring class, the group will then prepare a presentation and a paper that answer the following questions:

1. What is/are the problem(s) that the author is attempting to solve?
2. How does the author collect data germane to the identified problem(s)?
3. What about the author/researcher's research strategy did your group find generally compelling? How or why was it compelling?
4. What appears to be the author's sense of what should be (i.e., their philosophical or pedagogical posture)? What seems to be the author's research posture(s)? Per Deyhle, et al., (1992) what seems to be the ethical stance in which the author/researchers carried out his/her project? Would you label this effort as positivist? Interpretivist? Critical realist?
5. If we used the language and lens of design research, what would you say is the author's design that he/she is implementing and refining?
6. Are there relevant problems in play that the author is not acknowledging? What decisions did the author/researcher make that you think you might make or avoid (b/c of the author/researcher's experience and the nature of the research you are starting to consider)? If you were studying this problem, would you pursue it the same way?
7. Often schooling is about knowing—for example, knowing *what* to do and *why* to do it as a teacher, knowing academic content and behavioral norms of students. Whose knowing mattered in this action research project? What counted as knowing?
8. Overtly linking this text, to TLTE's Areas of Emphasis (i.e., (a) Curriculum, Teaching, and Professional Development, (b) Education Policy, Practice, and Analysis, (c) Literacy, Language, and Culture, (d) School, Society, and Reform or (e) Teaching and Learning with Technologies), explain how your book ties in to at least two of these areas.

The first action-research project presentations will occur in 40-minute blocks on April 24, for which the orthodox assumption is 20–25 minutes of presenting and 15–20 of Q & A. However, groups have control over how they organize this 40-minute segment and more interactive departures from the orthodox model will be welcome. A laptop and LCD projector will be available. Presenters should account for the fact that not everyone present for their presentation will be familiar with the text that is being analyzed (the audience could include classmates, CPED faculty, members of earlier CPED cohorts, and perhaps other grad students or guests). Given the time constraints, it is not expected that presentations will cover all eight of the questions. The papers that are part of the group project should be 10–20 pages and are due shortly after the presentations (the first group paper after April 24 presentations is due 29 April).

On June 4 and 11, the presentation and paper cycle will be repeated. For the first paper (April 29), groups have discretion over the way they organize the paper, but are responsible for assuring that all eight questions are answered. For the second paper (i.e., June 4), the group will take the earlier "April 29 paper" from their peers and revise/refine/ supplement it using the track changes and comment functions. In this instance, if the "Heaton group" for the April 29 assignment becomes the "Herrera group" for June 4, then the former-Heaton group needs to get to modify the original "Herrera" paper that was prepared for April 29. If the original Herrera group becomes the Wilhelm group, then for their June 4 assignment they would work with the original Wilhelm group's paper as a starting point. In other words, the products of the first groups become the source material for the second. Second papers can be 12–25 pages long and will be due June 11 (one week after the second presentation). I am anticipating that three to six net new pages worth of material will be added. Second paper groups should expect to share their papers with all classmates (just as first and third groups will too).

For the third presentation/paper, action research groups will read the remaining action research book that they have not yet reviewed. They will also review the "twice-drafted" paper about that book that emerged from the second cycle on June 4–11. However, the third presentation and paper will differ substantively from the first two. It should look across the three examples of action research and the nascent problems of practice research ideas of each group member to address considerations for your future research design. More specifically, it should include ten recommendations and/or cautions related to problems of practice. Returning to the four ideas emphasized at the beginning of this syllabus—epistemology, praxis, efficacy, and iterative [practice]—at least one recommendation/caution needs to address each of these themes (so this accounts for at least four of the ten total). The intent, quite literally is for each group to generate a checklist that can be used by all in the CPED cohort going forward. After each recommendation, there should be text (a paragraph, a page, or two pages) that clarifies the recommendation or caution and that justifies/rationalizes its inclusion. As a final component of this third paper, each group should generate three pages (total) worth of verbatim quoted recommendations or cautions from the three action research authors. Other authors from the 995 reading list can also be included in this three-page compilation, but each of the three action research authors must be represented at least once. Thus your third paper should have the following structure:

I. Ten recommendations and cautions related to studying problems of practice (8–12 pages)
II. Direct sage advice from the three action researchers and other 995 authors (3 pages)

The third paper will be presented July 1 and submitted as a final document by July 8.

As the two figures just presented suggest, our syllabi can be complicated and there is not space here to illustrate each of the intended dimensions, but we can point to a few key ones. First, building collegiality requires creating circumstances for that building to occur. By dividing cohorts into thirds (which has created groups of three, four, or five in every cohort) and then giving each team a series of required group tasks (planning a presentation, crafting a paper) team members have to collaborate. In that collaboration different propensities emerge: some reveal themselves as careful readers and good questioners; others warm to the task of preparing a PowerPoint or, more in keeping with their practitioner background, a different strategy for gaining the attention and comprehension of their peer audience; and still others agree to lead the paper writing task. In short, participants learn each other's comforts and discomforts, their weaknesses and strengths, and the ways to optimize the value of this intragroup variation.

This is an important step that occurs concurrently with and intertwined with the prospectively critical analysis asked for regarding each book and author. So as the new-to-each other cohort members are learning to be collegial and then collaborative with each other, they are also learning to be critical. This critical lens manifests itself in questions like: "Who's knowing mattered in this action research project? What counted as knowing?" (from the seventh question on the third syllabus) and "Are there relevant problems in play that the author is not acknowledging? What decisions did the author/researcher make that you think you might make or avoid (b/c of the author/researcher's experience and the nature of the research you are starting to consider)?" (from the sixth question on the third syllabus). But the critical lens also comes from each group having to rewrite and expand a previous group's paper. This is unusual work. Rarely are practitioners called upon to substantively review their colleagues' work, let alone find any of it wanting. Yet the point is not to tear down, but rather to show how critique can be an iterative vehicle of advance and improvement.

With Critical Collegiality Established, It Could Be Accessed and Developed

Not surprisingly, through the intense, multifaceted, and sometimes critical collaboration pursued during the "Challenges and Opportunities" class, affinity, common cause, and intragroup reliance all began to emerge. The third cohort's creation of a cohort members-only Google circle is a routine exemplification of this, but multiple manifestations as perceived by CPED students are shared here in later paragraphs. For now, the next point is that, with norms of critical collegiality established, these could be both drawn upon and deepened in subsequent course work.

During the remainder of their programs, CPED students were frequently required to interact with the entire class and sometimes again aggregate in smaller pairings and groups during class sessions and in Blackboard discussion forums. The notion of Critical Friendship was a regular aspect of this work. For example, during the final class in the program taught by one of your authors (Wunder), students worked on their comprehensive examination portfolios for the first several weeks. During each class session, small groups of three students would read and critically reply to each other's abstracts of each of the four identified portfolio strands in peer-review-type discussions.

Throughout their EdD programs, we regularly have the CPED students respond to a questionnaire that is directly related to our stated program outcomes. There are two items that relate directly to the emphasis on Critical Friendship and, the responses of a first-cohort student, Elise, are illuminating, suggesting the trajectory of her growth. Early in the program (July 2009) she remarked on the importance of the cohort as her community of learning. One year later (July 2010) she had incorporated the cohort into a larger network of learning professionals and had decided that community was so important to her that it would become the focus of her problem of practice. Her responses over three cycles to the prompt "I cultivate a community of learning professionals invested in enlarging all understandings of the works of teaching and learning" follow. The first was recorded just as she finished "Challenges and Opportunities."

> July 2009: *The cohort is a strong community. I relish the conversations that we have and I see myself employing the same conversation skills and visiting the same topics with colleagues at my school.*
> January 2010: *The cohort is my community right now.*
> July 2010: *Community is emerging as my research focus. Through experiences with the cohort, PLCs, and the Nebraska Writing project I see its pivotal value in education.*

The responses of Emily, another member of the first cohort, to another prompt—"I build professional connections that sustain and nurture educator well-being"—illustrate how she too she became increasingly involved with and invested in the cohort and its critical collegiality.

> July 2009: *It isn't something that I'm currently doing, but I hope to build more professional connections by way of this cohort.*
> July 2010: *The cohort group's mutual support of all members is why I've stayed in this program. I feel very comfortable discussing questions (& doubts) with the other members of the cohort.*

Graduate education can be lonely and exhausting, particularly when, for a part-time student, it comes on top of responsibilities to one's family and job. Emily's observations echo a refrain that we have heard from most cohort members (and that we have never heard challenged or dismissed) that the collegiality and related accountability to peers has helped them persevere and persist.

After completing their EdD degrees, Cohort One students were asked to participate in an "exit interview" and five agreed to do so. A graduate student not associated with the CPED EdD program conducted the interviews and asked questions related to reflecting on experiences in the program. None of the prompts (shared below) explicitly asked about the cohort model per se, so that it frequently was referenced voluntarily is particularly striking. The following guiding questions grounded the program's exit interview:

1. Please offer recollections and reflections on how you proceeded through the EdD program courses and experiences. What stands out as particularly memorable? Why? Particularly difficult? Why? Tell a story about a time you struggled. How did you get through this?
2. How did you decide and define a problem of practice to research?
3. As you proceeded through the program, how did you develop associations between and among theory and practice?

4. Describe the impact of the program on your professional trajectory as a scholar of practice.
5. Looking at all of the questionnaires completed in your classes over time, how do you explain the changes and consistencies?
6. Have you revised/changed the professional role(s) you are seeking?
7. What recommendations do you have for the CPED faculty as instructors and advisers for their future work with future cohorts? If you could do anything differently, what would it be?
8. What is your overall impression of the program?
9. Is there anything you would like to add?

The notion and importance of moving through the program with a set of trusted colleagues was something the graduates referenced repeatedly. Their reflections can be clustered into two themes: the cohort as a knowledge source; and the cohort as a source of encouragement.

KNOWLEDGE SOURCE

In all of the cohort classes, instructors valued and included discussion during class meetings and often on Blackboard discussion boards as well. These were events to which the students brought their wide range of personal and professional experiences as examples and/or contrasts with the class topic and readings. Cohort One members included two high school English teachers, an algebra coach, a religious educator, a middle school business and technology teacher, an elementary teacher, a district special education coordinator, and a child care center owner. They came from our state's two largest cities, but also suburbs and small towns. By coincidence rather than design, all were women.

A participant named April viewed the cohort as "a tremendous support for discussion and understanding." As Elise explained, there is "a humungous amount of background knowledge [among the cohort members] as you work through the courses." She added that "you have your teachers and you have your reading that you're learning from, but I probably learned as much [when] each [cohort member] became a textbook for me." The stories of cohort members that infused the readings and course discussions, was the "the cool part" she added.

Kristen was very involved with Elise throughout the program. They even organized a project in which Elise's then-high school students met and communicated with Kristen's elementary students. The challenging part of colleague work was when it became "critical" during peer review assignments. As she exclaimed, "I read eight-year-old writing!" Her level of comfort with peer review expanded over the program years, as she and Elise made and kept to a plan to meet regularly to review each other's work and talk as they wrote their dissertations. By that point, Kristen was referring to Elise as her "Critical Friend."

During the dissertation phase of the program when each student worked on her dissertation with no regular cohort meetings, the cohort members took it upon themselves to stay in touch mostly through email. As Kristen recalled, "missing [the cohort members] was hard" but regular electronic contact helped them work through what they saw as "mixed messages" from their different advisers.

Encouragement

During their exit interviews, all five EdD graduates who participated in them reflected on the importance of the cohort in times of doubt, fatigue, or personal and family misfortune. As Emily remembered, "if there hadn't been those other people who really understood what it was like to go through this experience, I might not have made it … they understand" in ways beyond what nonparticipating family, friends, and school colleagues do. April, too, believed that she "couldn't have done it without this cohort … they picked me up more than a few times." Sometimes describing herself as a bit disassociated from other cohort members' settings, Cindy nonetheless found the cohort to be a "support network [that] can't even be described in words. [It is] so powerful."

In her interview, Kristen remembered the nights at home telling her husband that she was going to quit because "it's too hard." Then she would gather herself, go to class the next Wednesday night and her cohort colleagues would challenge her doubts, telling her to "Stop it! We feel that way, too." Later, when Kristen dealt with a serious family medical situation during the program, she recalled how the cohort students and the CPED faculty "drew their wagons and circled around [her]" with a "sense of family that was above and beyond what [she] expected."

What had developed across the program and within the cohort was what Drago-Severson (2012) describes as a "holding environment." Borrowing from a concept originally related to healthy child development and later to adults, Drago-Severson defines a holding environment as one in which individual growth and experiences are regarded and supported. She finds the most effective ones: (a) meet and accept members at their current development point; (b) "let go" when the person is ready to move ahead; and (c) adapt to individual changes and growth in an ongoing manner.

At all stages group members are supported and challenged to grow. That is, the holding environment is "a context in which adults feel held well psychologically, supported and challenged developmentally, understood in terms of how they make sense of their work and the world, and accepted and honored for who they are" (p. 48). Not only, then, is high support necessary, but there must also be high challenge for adult growth, be that at the individual, group, or institutional level. It is what April described in the CPED cohort when she stated, "We had this experience together, but at the same time we were on our own journeys ... the paths they took were very different from the paths I took ... we identified ourselves as being cohort, but yet we had these individual paths that we took."

O'Connell Rust and Freidus (2001), too, have recognized and incorporated the necessity of challenge as they worked with a reform partnership project. As they organized the various members and activities of a large learning community of school and university personnel, they worried that "they might either gravitate uncritically toward a shared perspective, or, on the other hand, be stymied by competing opinions." (p. 143). Therefore, O'Connell Rust and Freidus intentionally configured partners in multiple levels, with one defined as a "critical colleagueship." Among their conclusions about the importance of partnerships that they learned from this project, the authors note that experience in the partnership including that with critical colleagues "provided a glimpse of the light at the end of the tunnel ... [where] seeing others succeed gives hope that success is possible" (p. 152). Success was indeed possible for the members of our first CPED-influenced EdD cohort with nearly 90 percent of them graduating within three and one-half years. Elise acknowledged that "[the] cohort is kind of a magic ... [it's] a lot of work for [the professors], but it is something that works."

Our colleague Elaine Chan (2012) studied several of our EdD students' experiences as practitioner researchers and the challenges of conducting research in one's own workplace. She found that our CPED students identified their involvement in a cohort as essential for both academic and emotional support. Chan explains that the cohort structure provided a "collective memory of course work and academic experience on which to draw" and an "intellectual space in which to draw upon a common body of theoretical knowledge built through the experience of having gone through their doctoral course work together as a group" (p. 191).

FINAL THOUGHTS

While the purpose of this chapter has been to focus on our CPED-tied EdD program, we should add that because of the success of CPED our department has also made some changes to our PhD program based on our experiences with the reshaping of our EdD program (a hope of the national CPED initiative is to strengthen both degrees). A clear example is that we now require a first-year seminar for incoming PhD students that features weekly sessions with departmental faculty members related to their research agendas, something the EdD faculty introduced with Cohort Two. We also keep the "generations" of cohort students in contact with each other through inviting the previous cohort to attend end-of-semester class sessions with the current students.

As CPED-influenced EdD cohort faculty members, we are encouraged and supported by the accomplishments of our students and their obvious support for the cohort program structure. Two of the Cohort One students included in their dissertation acknowledgments the following two statements:

> "Thanks to my cohort sisters for being my human textbooks."
> "To my cohort 'sisters' and colleagues, thank you for the fun, laughter, and your friendship during our CPED time together."

Dedications such as these boost our commitment to follow the advice of Kristen to

> "keep pushing this cohort 'cause it's awesome."

Of course that makes us proud and renews our own energy and engagement, but the task is not just to feel good about what we do or the EdD students think. As a member of the second cohort explained to us:

> The cohort design has tremendous practical value, but also reflects, I believe, an important theoretical position regarding both the conditions necessary for professional learning and but also the nature of knowledge and expertise related specifically to educational practice.

On the one hand, for full-time working professionals, the cohort helps avoid feelings of isolation, frustration, or stagnation and offers a community that off-campus graduate students may lack. Traditional on-campus doctoral students have regular access to faculty and often take many courses with the same students in their field—CPED students would totally lack this sort of social continuity if not for the cohort design. In the simplest sense, your cohort colleagues are your friends, for better or for worse, because you are all doing it together.

More importantly, the cohort provides a core group of individuals who are familiar, in a more than cursory way, with one's problem of practice, professional interests, and areas of expertise. Over time, this allows for deeper and richer conversations than one can manage with less familiar colleagues or classmates. When we are able to converse beyond a cursory overview of our ideas or problems, it is easier to engage critically and constructively; my familiarity with my cohort members' prior thinking and the evolution of their ideas, helps me to listen, praise, suggest, recommend, and advise with greater wisdom. At the same time, the relative heterogeneity of expertise and interests in the cohort ensures that we are always able to articulate our ideas to the interested lay-professional and not merely experts in our own fields.

Critical collegiality is at the heart of the CPED philosophy and certainly at the heart of what most of us imagine as good professional practice in education. The cohort design respects the conditions necessary to foster true critical collegiality—time, trust, continuity, plus shared knowledge, practices, and goals. From a program that purports to create the next generation of practitioner-scholars, the cohort helps us to build a network of like-minded, reform-oriented practitioners and allows us to tap in to one another's "funds of knowledge" about practice, theory, and local policy. The diversity within my cohort has allowed me to glimpse educational practice in a variety of contexts and appreciate more fully the size and scope of issues faced by practitioners. This vicarious knowledge has allowed me to broaden my understanding of the educational topography and serves a better advocate for sound practice in my professional life.

References

Chan, E. (2012). From teacher to researcher, researcher to teacher: Examining teachers' experiences of conducting research in their education settings. In M. Macintyre Latta & S. Wunder (Eds.), *Placing practitioner knowledge at the center of teacher education: Rethinking the policies and practices of the Education Doctorate* (pp. 179–197). Charlotte, NC: Information Age Publishing.

Cohen, D. K. (1990). A revolution in one classroom: The case of Mrs. Oublier. *Education Evaluation and Policy Analysis, 12*(3), 311–329.

Deyhle, D. L., Hess, G. A., & LeCompte, M. D., (1992). Approaching ethical issues for qualitative researchers in education. In M. D. LeCompte, W. Millroy, & J. Priessle (Eds.), *The Handbook of qualitative research in education* (pp. 597–641). San Diego, CA: Academic Press.

Drago-Severson, E. (2012). *Helping educators grow; Strategies and practices for leadership development*. Cambridge, MA: Harvard Education Press.

Heaton, R. M. (2000). *Teaching mathematics to the new standards: Relearning the dance*. New York: Teachers College Press.

Herrera, S. (2010). *Biography-driven culturally responsive teaching*. New York: Teachers College Press

Labaree, D. F. (2010) *Someone has to fail: The zero-sum game of public schooling*. Cambridge, MA: Harvard University Press.

Lord, B. (1994). Teachers' professional development: Critical colleagueship and the role of professional communities. In N. Cobb (Ed.), *The future of education: Perspectives on national standards in education*. New York: NY: College Entrance Examination Board.

O'Connell Rust, F., & Freidus, H. (2001). *Guiding school change: The role and work of change agents*. New York, NY: Teachers College Press.

Perry, J. A. (2012). What history reveals about the Education Doctorate. In M. Macintyre Latta & S. Wunder (Eds.), *Placing practitioner knowledge at the center of teacher education: Rethinking the policies and practices of the Education Doctorate* (pp. 51–72). Charlotte, NC: Information Age Publishing.

Proefriedt, W. A. (2008). *High expectations: The cultural roots of standards reform in American education*. New York: Teachers College Press.

Shulman, L. S., Golde, C. M., Bueschel, A. C., & Garabedian, K. J. (2006). Reclaiming education's doctorates: A critique and a proposal. *Educational Researcher, 35*(3), 25–32.

Storey, V. A., & Richard, B. M. (2012). Carnegie Project for the Educational Doctorate: The role of critical friends in diffusing doctoral program innovation. Unpublished manuscript.

Watts, E., & Imig, D. (2012). Why we need the EdD to prepare new faculty. In M. Macintyre Latta & S. Wunder (Eds.), *Placing practitioner knowledge at the center of teacher education: Rethinking the policies and practices of the Education Doctorate* (pp. 27–49). Charlotte, NC: Information Age Publishing.

Wilhelm, J. D. (2008). *You gotta BE the book* (2nd ed.). New York: Teachers College Press.

Wilson, S. (2007). *"What about Rose?" Using teacher research to reverse school failure*. New York: Teachers College Press.

CHAPTER 10

Criterion-inspired, Emergent Design in Doctoral Education: A Critical Friends Perspective

R. Martin Reardon and Charol Shakeshaft

> *The freedom to be intellectually subversive and challenging of received wisdom lies close to the heart of the Critical Friend's value and purpose*
>
> —*Swaffield & MacBeath, 2005, p. 251.*

The Carnegie Project on the Education Doctorate (CPED) is focused on encouraging Schools of Education to reclaim the education doctorate (EdD) (Shulman, Golde, Bueschel, & Garabedian, 2006) by developing EdD programs that refine the leadership skills of practitioners of educational leadership who wish to remain in practice. The creation of such programs implies a set of courses and emphases that are distinct from those conventionally offered in the PhD. As Mezirow (1990) asserted, "we learn differently when we are learning to perform than when we are learning to understand what is being communicated to us" (p. 1). This is not to say that the CPED-aligned EdD is devoid of learning to understand, but the emphasis on practice suggests that the identical course will not conform well to both EdD and PhD programs. In this context, the EdD has to overcome an "80-year history of confusion" (Perry, 2011, p. 3)—a history during which it has sometimes been referred to as "PhD-Lite" (Shulman et al., p. 27)—on its way to being known as "the highest professional degree in education" (Shulman et al., p. 28). To facilitate the process, Shulman et al. (2006) proposed "a 'zero base' approach to design, without any of the assumptions that characterize the status quo" (p. 28). Perry (2011) pointed out the enormity of the task of moving the EdD beyond its history by asserting that "before the EdD can change, schools and colleges of education and their constituents need to change" (p. 2).

TIME FOR CHANGE

The consensus that it was time to consider the need to change the PhD program in the School of Education at Virginia Commonwealth University CU School of Education PhD program underpinned the decision of the dean to commission a Task Force on the PhD in Education Program in the fall of 2006. At that time, the PhD program (which was founded in 1982 as a PhD in Urban Services, but was renamed a PhD in Education in 1996) was a 60-hour School of Education-wide degree with 15-hour concentration tracks in each of six department areas (Adult Education and Human Resource Development, Educational Leadership, Instructional Leadership, Research and Evaluation, Special Education and Disability Policy, and Urban Services Leadership). The dean charged the Task Force "to review the current program within the current climate in higher education and to outline where we want to go as a School of Education" (personal communication, *Notes and Minutes*, September 11, 2006, p. 1). The dean also encouraged the Task Force to examine ways to decentralize the program administration—effectively giving greater autonomy to the departments in terms of admission policies and course demands. At that same meeting, the dean of the Graduate School raised the possibility of an EdD degree (particularly for off-campus cohorts), alluded to the existence of competitive PhD programs with fewer credit-hours, and suggested that departmental boundaries were not always necessary (personal communication, *Notes and Minutes*, September 11, 2006).

The broad scope of the charge to the Task Force invoked critical reflection in the sense that term was used by Mezirow (1990) who drew a compelling distinction between reflection and critical reflection: "Reflection enables us to correct distortions in our beliefs and errors in problem solving. Critical reflection involves a critique of the presuppositions on which our beliefs have been built" (p. 1). The Task Force was invited by both deans not so much to correct distortions (the School of Education's Office of Doctoral Studies reported the PhD program to be in excellent condition) but to critically reflect on the presuppositions that underpinned the original PhD program, the later change in focus, and the nature and context of EdD in the twenty-first century. The recommendation from the Task Force regarding the establishment of the EdD was only the first phase of the process. Other phases included the establishment of an EdD Task Force (distinct from the initial Task Force) to design the program, the creation of a curriculum design process, the visit of a CPED review team, and the creation of an ongoing curriculum redesign process. All these phases are informative when discussed in terms of the Critical Friend concept. However, before proceeding to this discussion, it is appropriate to consider the operational definition of Critical Friendship in this context.

CRITICAL FRIENDSHIP

Costa and Kallick (1993) drew an analogy between a visit to the ophthalmologist and the way that Critical Friendship benefits both the one critiqued and the one offering the critique. When a patient visits an ophthalmologist for a vision check-up, the ophthalmologist works through a process of changing lenses and asking the patient whether one lens is better or worse than its predecessor in terms of the patient's perception. The ophthalmologist is unable to judge objectively which lens is better or worse. The patient's view is obviously of the highest importance in the context of ophthalmology. Similarly, the enlightened eye of accumulated wisdom that the Critical Friend brings (MacBeath, 1999) is an invaluable asset to the "befriended" (Swaffield, 2005, p. 44). Members of the Task Force represented each of the departmental tracks, and were committed to the best interests of their departments as well as the School of Education, and there were instances where well-intentioned colleagues' perceptions diverged—leading to healthy debate. As Eisner (1991) pointed out:

> The way in which we see and respond to a situation, and how we interpret what we see, will bear our own signature. This unique signature is not a liability but a way of providing individual insight into a situation. (p. 34)

It was in the context of this divergence of insights that the Critical Friend comparison was most relevant in this context. From time to time, one member or another of the Task Force from a different department would provide other lenses on an issue on which a befriended Task Force member felt strongly.

In the public school context, Costa and Kallick (1993) defined a Critical Friend as a trusted person who asks provocative questions, provides data to be examined through another lens, and offers critique of a person's work as a friend. A Critical Friend takes the time to fully understand the context of the work presented and the outcomes that the person or group is working toward. The (Critical) Friend is an advocate for the success of that work. (p. 50)

Costa and Kallick went on to describe a Critical Friends meeting—both among teachers and students—as comprised of a six-step process involving (a) description of a practice by the learner, accompanied by a request for feedback from the Critical Friend, (b) the seeking of clarification by the Critical Friend, (c) the declaration of the desired outcomes by the learner, (d) the provision of feedback about what seems noteworthy in the practice by the Critical Friend (this is the first stage in which different lenses come into play), (e) the Critical Friend prompts the learner to see the project through a different lens (this is the second stage in which different lenses come into play), and (f) both learner and Critical Friend write reflections on the conference, to which the learner gives due consideration (without defending a position to the Critical Friend).

Such a formal process was not implemented at any stage of the emergent design process described in this chapter, but Critical Friendship is a robust process, and has been applied in a wide range of contexts that have freely interpreted the concept. For example, in a less constrained way, MacBeath (1999) referred to the Critical Friend in the context of school reform in England as "a supportive yet challenging facilitator, aiding and encouraging the evolution of a process uniquely tailored to the values of the school community, where the concerns of the various clients are closely aligned" (p. 247). Both Swaffield and MacBeath (Swaffield, 2005, 2008; Swaffield & MacBeath, 2005) also referenced Critical Friendship in the context of school reform in England. Ralston (2011) referenced Costa and Kallick's (1993) six-step process in the context of Critical Friendship as a strategy for teaching deliberative democratic theory at undergraduate/graduate levels in the United States. Burke, Marx, & Berry (2011) utilized a Critical Friends approach to improve student achievement and learning in a small mid-western United States school district.

In the context of this chapter, a Critical Friend is a member of the team in the phase under discussion who acts as a supportive yet challenging facilitator by proposing different lenses through which to view the emergence of a process uniquely tailored to the needs of the participants of the EdD program at the Virginia Commonwealth University (VCU).

Phase 1: Task Force Recommendation

Having received its brief, the PhD Program Review Task Force commenced meeting on a biweekly basis through the fall of 2006. While the data provided to the Task Force by the School of Education (SOE) Office of Doctoral Studies indicated the health of the existing PhD program, Critical Friends highlighted the more than one hundred participants in the Educational Leadership Department track who had completed or almost completed their course work in a department that, at that time, was not able to provide enough dissertation advisement to cope with that number of students. Despite the fact that faculty in other departments were happy to chair dissertations for Educational Leadership Department track participants where their expertise extended to the interests of those participants, the Critical Friends pointed out that, usually, any department is expected to provide for the needs of participants in its own track.

This awkward situation had come about as the result of the highly effective recruitment efforts of the entrepreneurial arm of the SOE. As a way of ensuring high-quality leadership succession, recently retired high-profile educators had for some years collaborated with school divisions in the Richmond area to encourage cohorts of teachers who wished to enroll in masters and postmasters programs leading to building-level leadership endorsement. Highly effective outreach had resulted in a relatively large number of masters and postmasters graduates who were interested in extending their cohort experience to the PhD. Over a few years, PhD cohorts of approximately 20 participants were accepted to the Educational Leadership track.

In the context of the invitation to revisit the suppositions upon which the PhD rested, Critical Friends focused on the uneven quality among the many participants in the Educational Leadership PhD track. Few of these participants, Critical Friends pointed out, had any intention of entering the academy—leading to varying levels of disinterest in discussing theoretical approaches in some of the PhD classes (some of which were also uncomfortably large for classes at this level). In addition, Critical Friends pointed out, the appropriately practical emphasis of the masters and postmasters courses did not effectively prepare Educational Leadership track participants for the type of writing expected of students in terminal degree programs. In this context, other Critical Friends in the Task Force highlighted the urban legend that some academics do a poor job of teaching while laying the blame for poor performance at the feet of the individual participants.

The upshot of this discussion was that a subcommittee of three (chaired by the first author) was appointed to research the recently published literature on the CPED, and review examples of CPED programs. The subcommittee members were familiar with the writing of Shulman and his colleagues, and focused particularly on the programs in place at Vanderbilt and the University of Southern California. Prior to developing its report, the subcommittee invited the input of the associate dean for Academic Affairs as a Critical Friend. The associate dean's critique was encouraging, and a brief report was prepared for submission to the Task Force (private communication, *Minutes of Meeting*, November 16, 2006). In brief, the subcommittee presumed that more than one department would be involved in implementing a practice-oriented doctorate, and proposed a 42+-credit framework that incorporated research, concentration, core, cognate, and thematic dissertation components (see Table 10.1).

Since the Critical Friends in the Task Force were highly focused on the ramifications of the changes being proposed to the PhD program itself, the EdD subcommittee report was accepted with appreciation but little comment, and the basic recommendation that the EdD be established was incorporated into the Task Force report.

Phase 2: Task Force for Program Design

The recommendation to establish the EdD received support from the dean of the School of Education and the appropriate VCU administrative officers. The dean of the School of Education invited the deans of the Vanderbilt and the University of Southern California Schools of Education to campus to discuss their respective implementations of the EdD with the entire faculty of the School of Education. The implementation of the EdD was an item that was discussed during the spring of 2007 with the applicants for the department chair's position to

Table 10.1 Initial proposed framework for EdD

Research	Logic of Systematic Inquiry Decision Analysis: Quantitative Approach Decision Analysis: Qualitative Approach	9 credits
Concentration	To be decided by tracks	18 credits
Core	To be taken by both PhD and EdD students	9 credits
Cognate	Focusing on technology uses	TBD
Dissertation	Thematic approach	6 credits

commence in the fall of 2007. The incoming department chair (Dr. Charol Shakeshaft, second author) cochaired the Task Force on the EdD in Leadership together with the first author (Dr. Martin Reardon).

By the time this Phase 2 Task Force commenced its work, it was clear that the presumption of the EdD subcommittee that more than one department would be interested in creating a practice-oriented doctorate was incorrect, and that only the Educational Leadership Department would be involved. However, all concerned were keen that as wide a range of interests as possible be represented in the discussions about the program design. Consequently, the Task Force included (in addition to the ex officio director of Doctoral Studies, and associate dean for Academic Affairs) two other department chairs, four faculty members from other departments, one PhD student, one Richmond-area superintendent, and one assistant superintendent. The Phase 2 Task Force met every second week, and began from the zero-base recommended by Shulman et al. (2006), with Critical Friendship underpinning every aspect of the discussions.

One of the most far-reaching decisions made by the Task Force was that the EdD would be an *EdD in Leadership* (as opposed to Educational Leadership)—the intention being to make it clear that applicants from outside the public school environment would be welcome to apply. This was particularly relevant in the context of the School of Education that included a department focused on sports management. Highlighting the role of Critical Friends with respect to the title of the program, Reardon (2013) commented,

> We understood the bold step we were taking when we drew this distinction, and we were encouraged by our Critical Friends to formulate clearly the degree to which faculty in an Educational Leadership Department could speak effectively to leadership issues in educational settings outside the PK-12 domain. Our claim, which has since been validated, was that participants involved in the practice of leadership in educational settings outside the school house deal with issues that are so closely analogous to those encountered by leaders in customary educational settings, that discussion of similarities and differences would enrich the learning of all. The substantial commensurability that we anticipated across the broader educational spectrum has been born out specifically in the second and third Learning Communities. In these two Learning Communities, diversity of field of practice is more evident among the participants than in the inaugural Learning Community. As we prepare for the admission of our fourth Learning Community, we have welcomed to the program leaders in educational settings from universities, community colleges, and PK-12 schools, as well as from the business and non-profit sectors. (n.p.)

Critical Friends in the Phase 2 Task Force collaborated in refining the initial conceptual schema for the EdD, which envisaged linked program threads leading like spokes to the central capstone project (see Figure 10.1). In this early, highly abstract conceptualization, the links between the program threads (data and decisions, reflective practice, systems theory, and so forth) were conceptualized as being the laboratories of practice discussed by Shulman et al. (2006).

After four months of meetings and with many individual members of the Task Force taking on the role of Critical Friend at various times, the conceptual schema had evolved into a much more concrete form (see Figure 10.2). Two aspects of Figure 10.2 are of particular relevance: (a) the three analytical lenses that are envisaged as setting the context for the program (the lens analogy is particularly relevant in the context of the development of the operational definition of Critical Friendship adopted in this chapter), and (b) the case-based design envisaged for Year 1 and Year 2. At the time of this design (February, 2008), there was much discussion in the Richmond area of a second report that had released toward the end of the previous year

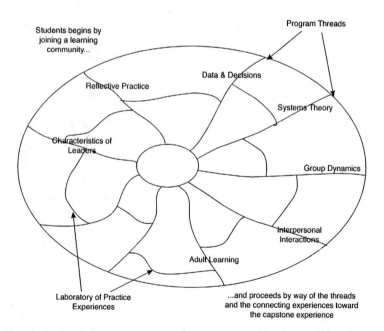

Figure 10.1 An early conceptualization of the relationship among proposed program elements.

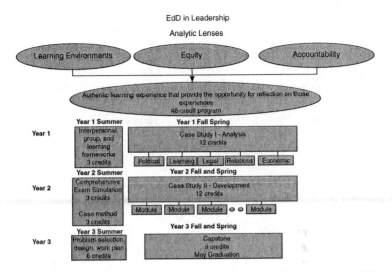

Figure 10.2 Late-stage, linear conceptualization of key elements of the program.

by a consultant focusing on the opportunities and challenges facing the greater Richmond area (Crupi, 2007). After much discussion, it was decided that whether driven by that report or not, the basic focus of the first year should be the analysis of a case study, and the basis of the second year should be the development of a case study. The expectation was that these two experiences would effectively prepare participants for a team-based capstone project along similar lines.

THE CURRICULUM DESIGN PROCESS

As it transpired, the superintendent who was a member of the Task Force offered to support a cohort of 20 participants from his large school district as the initial Learning Community for the EdD. This offer was accepted, subject to the admission requirements of the program—which included having fulfilled a leadership role for at least three years, a score on the *Miller Analogies Test* at the fiftieth percentile or above, three references, the submission of appropriate written responses to key questions related to leadership for learning, leadership for equity, and leadership for accountability, and a portfolio of leadership artifacts. In deference to the fact that this district had recently completed the Phi Beta Kappa (PBK) School District Audit process, the decision was made to use the extensive PBK Audit Report as the basis for the case study aspects of both Year 1 and Year 2.

In the summer of 2008, the first Learning Community of the EdD Program commenced its path to graduation. The Educational Leadership Department chair was intent on ensuring that the EdD establish its credentials as a practitioner-focused doctorate from the outset. One key way in which this focus was evidenced was the decision to allocate two instructors to each course. This was operationalized by breaking the relatively large number of participants into two sections while honoring VCU's minimum size requirements for doctoral classes. This ensured that the Critical Friend concept was built-in to the instructional delivery decisions made in each course. The two instructors were expected to share the content and concept development aspects of each course, and provide feedback to each other in a way that exemplified the collaborative team approach envisaged for the capstone. In addition, the intention was that, wherever possible, one of the two instructors would be a current practitioner so that a focus on current issues confronting leaders would be a hallmark of the class sessions.

The Educational Leadership Department chair invited Dr. Cheri Magill to be the first director of the EdD Program, and she set about leading the extensive design process that would produce the syllabus documents for the 17 courses of the 48-hour EdD. Each of the syllabus documents was drafted in the context of a Critical Friends framework. At that time, the Educational Leadership Department met for administrative purposes every Tuesday morning. Among the other business of the day, Dr. Magill took the opportunity at each meeting to keep the faculty apprised of progress in elaborating the big picture of the conceptual schema into syllabus titles, descriptions, texts, and recommended readings, and invited faculty to remain after the administrative meeting for follow-on meetings at which the details of each class session were clarified. In this regular Critical Friends context, faculty members who were currently teaching in the EdD, or who were interested in contributing to the emergence of the program were integrally involved in the emergent design process.

Some of the highlights of the design that emerged included commencing the program in the first summer (see Figure 10.2) with an exploration of the relationship among personal characteristics, preferred learning modalities, and effective team processes. This opening course set the tone for each participant's subsequent empirical approach to investigating and analyzing his or her own leadership approaches and characteristics as a leader. Also in this first course, the participants were required to establish an online portfolio to which they would continue to add throughout the program. The portfolio consists of two components: a professional blog, and an online collection of digital artifacts that relate to each participant's ongoing leadership experience.

For later semesters, two formative assessment processes were implemented—one each at the end of the first and second spring semesters. These formative assessments were designed as 30-minute formal presentations to a committee of three faculty members, in which each individual participant presented each of the sections of his or her digital portfolio. In both these formative assessments, the faculty committee members take the role of Critical Friends. Both of these evaluations are strictly formative, but the feedback provided by each participant's committee constitutes a dispassionate assessment of the leadership presence of each candidate and—in the case of the second formative assessment process—a response to the growth in leadership competency that each participant has exhibited since he or she commenced the program.

Lastly, an extended field experience was designed to form the backbone of the fall and spring semesters of the second year. This field experience engages participants in conducting a program evaluation for a client in the context of their local leadership environment. This extended field experience provides the opportunity for every participant—in a suitably low-stakes environment—to gain individual experience of every aspect of the program evaluation process. The capstone process was designed as a team-based process, but the individual learning experience was regarded as critical in ensuring that every team member is in a position to contribute from his or her own perspective to the high-stakes, client-based process of the capstone evaluation in the third and final year of the program.

Visit of a CPED Review Team

The members of the first Learning Community of the EdD Program quickly found their feet, and, although details were being worked out in the weekly Critical Friends session (the phrase "building the plane while flying" was mentioned from time to time), the program was well supported by the Educational Leadership Department and the School of Education. (As an indication of support from the school, two faculty members of other departments collaborated in the teaching of a course in the first year.)

Early in its history, CPED had received a grant from the federal Fund for the Improvement of Postsecondary Education (FIPSE) to sustain a research program into the effectiveness of the CPED endeavor. In March 2011, CPED invited the Educational Leadership Department to host a visit from two CPED-FIPSE researchers. As Perry (private communication, June 27, 2011) put it in introducing the final report to the department,

> Each research team wore two "hats" during their visit. The first and primary hat was that of researcher. In this role, researchers collected data about the changes that have taken place in your school of education at the institutional, programmatic, and individual levels … The researchers also wore the "hat" of Critical Friends. The notion of Critical Friends has been vital to the CPED process and has contributed to the improvement of programs across members. Valuable input—shared both at and outside of our convenings—has been crucial in the Ed. D. design process. (p. 1)

Each Critical visited for two days. The final Critical Friends report drew attention to "the commitment to thorough planning and (the) success of the students" and "the regular weekly meetings of faculty to collaborate on the co-teaching" (Perry, private communication, June 27, 2011, p. 2). In their report, the CPED Critical Friends went on to comment that

> the program benefit(s) from collaborative strategic planning, and there is currently a strong sense of mission and focus. There was some evidence that this cohesion may be difficult to maintain as faculty revise the program to meet the needs of the newly recruited cohort; particularly as faculty become more cognizant of the program's learning outcomes. Overall, the university has implemented the CPED-influenced EdD program with fidelity, and is to be commended for the institution's vision, innovativeness, and diligence. (Perry, private communication, June 27, 2011, p. 3)

Another aspect of the EdD program that the Critical Friends commended was our decision to refrain from admitting a second Learning Community until the first Learning Community members had graduated. We had made this decision very early in the design process, as we felt that this step was necessary to avoid overcommitting our personnel resources.

THE ONGOING CURRICULUM REDESIGN PROCESS

The upshot of not admitting another Learning Community during the three years that the first Learning Community participants were completing the program was a sense of heightened expectation among prospective participants who had heard about the program and were keen to apply. In addition to this pent-up demand, a smaller university about a two-hour drive away that was known for its fine teacher preparation program negotiated an arrangement whereby their faculty would act as professors of practice and host a satellite site for a subset of participants admitted to the second Learning Community from their local area. In addition, it became clear that there was the potential for another satellite site centered in a school district a similar distance to the north of Richmond. Consequently, the second Learning Community consisted of 41 participants who meet in two remote sites as well as the Metro site.

Due to the retirement of the program director, the second Learning Community participants began the program under new faculty leadership. Because the PBK District Audit had no relevance to the vast majority of the second Learning Community participants, one major task in terms of curriculum development for the new program director encompassed the redesign of the courses that had been constructed to align with that document for the participants in the first Learning Community. A second major task involved keeping all three sites "on the same page" in each of the courses. In order to facilitate these tasks, the program director instituted a process of Critical Friend peer review of projected course content, followed by the creation of detailed lesson plans on a consolidated Blackboard site. Each week, a Word document (referred to as "the Private Label") was circulated among all those interested in the EdD program outlining a proposed framework for the upcoming class session. The Private Label replaced the weekly meetings used during the first Learning Community—sessions that were not feasible in the context of faculty teaching across three widely dispersed sites. Comments and suggestions were incorporated into the Private Label, which was then elaborated into a class session plan and redistributed for Critical Friend peer review. Finally, the class session plan was fully expanded into the one consolidated Blackboard site to which all assignments and course-related announcements and assignments were also posted. While this process involved a major commitment of time and resources, the advantage was the creation of a common understanding across all three sites of the focus of each class session—along with an audit trail of what was taught that provided the basis for the course structure for the third Learning Community (and, potentially, also for subsequent Learning Communities).

Part of the feedback from Critical Friends focused on the benefit of repositioning some of the courses in the light of faculty experience with the first Learning Community. There were few of these changes, but they represented notable revisions (see appendix; the courses whose numbers are out of sequence have been changed). One notable revision concerned the sequencing of the two writing-intensive courses that had originally been placed in the fall and spring of the third year. Our experience with the first Learning Community indicated that these courses were optimally situated much earlier in the program. Another notable change repositioned the course that was designed to engage participants with the intricacies of making meaning of data. This was repositioned to coincide with participants' preparation of the final report for their individual client, rather than when they were working as a team to deal with their capstone data.

CRITICAL FRIENDS: FINAL THOUGHTS

The concept of Critical Friendship relates conceptually to many aspects of the design process that formulated the EdD program within the School of Education at VCU. Critical Friendship also played out specifically in the formal program review conducted by two Critical Friends that was sponsored by CPED in 2011. Critical Friendship continues to underpin the design and revision of the courses in the EdD, and the sequence in which these courses are offered.

There is one final way in which the concept of Critical Friendship is relevant to this program: It describes the spirit in which we commission small teams of EdD participants to collaborate in the conduct of the capstone. We expect our participants to collaborate closely but to be forthright in addressing their colleagues' performance in the capstone Project (referred to in current CPED terminology as the dissertation in practice) with which the EdD program concludes.

The lessons learned from this criterion-inspired practical application of emergent curriculum design in higher education suggests a useful framework for institutions that are similarly motivated "to quell resistance to an innovation (which is sometimes manifested in anxieties and fear), and facilitate the adoption of a (re)designed professional practice education doctorate" (Storey & Richard, 2013). In the spirit of Critical Friendship, the authors wish to declare their openness to feedback on this chapter, and welcome comments and suggestions for program improvement.

REFERENCES

Burke. W., Marx, G. E., & Berry, J. E. (2011). Maintaining, reframing, and disrupting traditional expectations and outcomes for professional development with critical friends groups. *The Teacher Educator, 46*, 32–52. doi: 10.1080/08878730.2010.530342.

Costa, A. L., & Kallick, B. (1993). Through the lens of a critical friend. *Educational Leadership, 51*(2), 49–51.

Crupi, J. (2007). *Putting the future together.* Plano, TX: Jim Crupi Strategic Leadership Solutions.

Eisner, E. (1991). *The enlightened eye.* New York, NY: Macmillan.

MacBeath, J. (1999). *Schools must speak for themselves: The case for school self-evaluation.* London: Routledge.

Mezirow, J. (1990). *Fostering critical reflection in adulthood: A guide to transformative and emancipatory learning.* San Francisco, CA: Jossey-Bass.

Perry, J. A. (2011, Fall). The Carnegie Project on the Education Doctorate: Phase II—A quest for change. *UCEA Review,* 1–3.

Ralston, S. (2011). Deliberating with critical friends: A strategy for teaching deliberative democratic theory. *Teaching Philosophy, 34*(4), 393–410.

Reardon, R. M. (2013, Spring). Team-based program evaluation dissertation in practice at Virginia Commonwealth University. *CPED Newsletter.* Retrieved from https://docs.google.com/a/vcu.edu/document/d/1VA U4esHRkgbdj1HfgYXJF6lt3iWAk5s5pdS6M8LxqXA/edit.

Shulman, L. S., Golde, C. M., Bueschel, A. C., & Garabedian, K. J. (2006). Reclaiming education's doctorates: A critique and a proposal. *Educational Researcher, 35*(3), 25–32.

Storey, V. A., & Richard, B. (2013). Carnegie Project for the Educational Doctorate: The role of critical friends in diffusing doctoral program innovation. In C. A. Mullen & K. E. Lane (Eds.), *Becoming a Global Voice—the 2013 Yearbook of the National Council of Professors of Educational Administration.* Ypsilanti, MI: NCPEA Publications.

Swaffield, S. (2005). No sleeping partners: Relationships between head teachers and critical friends. *School Leadership & Management, 25*(1), 43–57. doi: 10.1080/1363243052000317082.

Swaffield, S. (2008). Critical friendship, dialogue and learning, in the context of leadership for learning. *School Leadership and Management, 28*(4), 323–336. doi: 10.1080/13632430802292191.

Swaffield, S., & MacBeath, J. (2005). School self-evaluation and the role of a critical friend. *Cambridge Journal of Education, 35*(2), 239–252. doi: 10.1080/03057640500147037.

APPENDIX

CURRENT COURSE SEQUENCE FOR THE EdD IN LEADERSHIP

	Summer	Fall	Spring
Year 1	3 hours EDLP 700, Effective Learning Networks (3 credits) Key Features: Metacognitive processes Leadership	6 hours EDLP 702, Understanding Self as Leader: Theory and Data Analysis (2 credits) EDLP 703, Understanding Self as Leader: Practical Applications (1 credit, on campus) EDLP 715, Principles for Professional Writing I (3 credits) Key Features: Leadership Team-building Research literacy	6 hours EDLP 704, Frameworks for Decision making: Legal Perspectives (3 credits) EDLP 705, Frameworks for Decision making: Ethical Perspectives (3 credits) Key Features: Theory and policy related to decision making Formative Assessment I
	6 hours ELDP 708, Leadership Presence (3 credits) EDLP 709, Equity and Leadership (3 credits)	6 hours EDLP 711, Evidence-informed Perspectives on Practice I (3 credits) EDLP 716, Principles for Professional Writing II (3 credits)	6 hours EDLP 713, Evidence-informed Perspectives on Practice II (3 credits) EDLP 717, Communicating Research Findings (3 credits)

Year 2	Key Features: Laboratory of Practice • Application of learning • Summary of results • Organizational context	Key Features: • Orientation to research, program evaluation, and qualitative analysis • Selection of and immersion in local laboratory of practice • Renewed focus on writing in a range of genres pertaining to practice, particularly related to interim and final reports to evaluation clients	Key Features: • Facilitating closure of evaluation research and local laboratory of practice • Data management and effective communication of research findings • Formative Assessment II
Year 3	*6 hours* EDLP 712, Planning for Sustainable Change I (3 credits) EDLP 790, Capstone Development (3 credits) Key Features: Capstone Development • Background • Writing Response to RFP • Research design • Meetings with clients Candidacy	*6 hours* EDLP 714, Planning for Sustainable Change II (3 credits) EDLP 798, Capstone Plan Implementation (3 credits) Key Features: • Capstone plan implementation • Finalizing design • Data collection • Data analysis Data management, analysis, portrayal	*3 hours* EDLP 799 Capstone Completion (3 credits) Key Features: Capstone completion • Data analysis • Portraying data results • Conclusions, recommendations for implementation • Presentation and defense Graduation

Epilogue

Jill A. Perry and Rachael L. Hoffman

INTRODUCTION

The Carnegie Project on the Education Doctorate (CPED) is a change effort. It is an effort to engage schools of education in distinguishing the Education Doctorate (EdD) as *the* professional practice doctorate for the field and in rethinking the content and structures that prepare PK-20 educational leaders. Unlike change efforts of the past, however, CPED is designed to create change from inside schools of education and to be led by faculty. Though change is not a new concept in schools of education, change led by education faculty has historically been less likely. Since their inception, schools of education have endured numerous efforts to refashion, refocus, and redesign them. The primary stimulus for many of these change efforts has most often been the need for qualified teachers to staff America's schools. Throughout the twentieth century, change efforts came in the form of commissions, study groups, and professional societies all created to promote the change efforts to improve schools of education.

A brief sample of twentieth-century change efforts notes the overwhelming role of outside bodies—from foundations to the US Federal government—in attempts to change the way schools of education function. In the early 1900s, the Carnegie Foundation for the Advancement of Teaching sponsored a major initiative to transform normal schools at the start of the century (Learned & Bagley, 1920/1965). During the 1930s and 1940s, philanthropic foundations advanced most reform efforts. The 1950s and 1960s saw a greater effort to establish education as a profession with reforms that sought to create standards, advance research, and establish a professional presence in education. During this time, many professional associations collaborated with the Federal government to develop accrediting bodies to standardize programs while other associations like the American Association of School Administrators (AASA) collaborated with the Kellogg Foundation to develop a research base for school administration. During the 1970s, the US Education Department pushed to move forward the notion of performance-based criteria and educational objectives and worked with professional organizations to clearly define what performance-based meant. In 1983, the Federal government published *A Nation at Risk*, a national report that described the poor state of American education. This publication set the course of educational reforms in the 1980s and beyond, which saw the establishment of large-scale networks of educators funded by philanthropic organizations coming together to respond to this harsh document. In the 1990s, foundations like the Philip Morris Foundation invested monies to transform education schools. In 2001, the No Child Left Behind Act (NCLB) reauthorized the Elementary and Secondary Education Act (ESEA) of 1965, which was the main federal law overseeing education from kindergarten through high school. Also in 2001, the Carnegie Corporation, with the support of the Annenberg and Ford Foundations, launched the Teachers for A New Era initiative. This initiative represented the culmination of a century-long effort to transform and change education schools.

In much of these efforts, schools of education and their faculty are largely absent, playing minimal or no role in the redefining of their institutional purposes and processes in preparing school professionals. This might be because we do not typically think of the academic profession as working *for* higher education, rather faculty members have traditionally worked *at* higher education, focusing on specialized research areas and teaching specialized courses. The faculty member's "job" asks them to be experts in what they know, not necessarily to be team players in the running of an institution. In an effort to counteract how reform has taken place in schools of education, the CPED has asked the faculty from member institutions to work *for* higher education, locally in their own context as well as nationally in collaboration with peers from 56 schools of education, to "reclaim" the EdD and to develop cohesive, outcomes-oriented professional preparation programs. However, before we consider this innovative process to change, it is necessary to first understand the history of the EdD and describe the factors that converged to birth the CPED initiative.

CPED Background

Since the creation of the EdD at Harvard College in 1921, the purpose and goals for this degree have been murky, leaving it commonly referred to as the "PhD lite" (Shulman, Golde, Bueschel, & Garabedian, 2006, p. 27). Eighty years of scholarly inquiry (Anderson, 1983; Brown, 1966; Clifford & Guthrie, 1990; Deering, 1998; Denemark, 1985; Eells, 1963; Freeman, 1931; Levine, 2005; and Osguthorpe & Wong, 1993) investigating the differences between the EdD and the PhD degrees resulted in little distinction or understanding of the purpose of the EdD. Despite this considerable attention, very little reform of either degree has resulted other than to call for elimination of one (Clifford & Guthrie, 1990; Deering, 1998) or both (Levine, 2005).

In January 2007, the CPED was launched as a response to the Shulman, Golde, Bueschel, and Garabedian (2006) call to schools of education to clearly define each degree or "risk becoming increasingly impotent in carrying out their primary missions—the advancement of knowledge and the preparation of quality practitioners" (p. 25). Their plea came at a culminating point in this debate. Work being undertaken at the Carnegie Foundation for the Advancement of Teaching under the then leadership of President Emeritus Lee Shulman was focused in two areas—the Carnegie Initiative on the Doctorate (CID) sought to better understand research doctoral preparation across six disciplines, and the Preparation for the Professions Program (PPP) investigated professional preparation in six fields.[1] Findings from both these projects confirmed the need to distinguish the EdD from the research doctorate (PhD) in education and to clarify the purpose of the EdD.

Nationally, around this same time, the debate was once again reopened. The American Education Research Association (AERA) and the National Academy of Education (NAEd) came together to "conduct a systematic assessment of education research doctorate programs using the methodology of the National Research Council (NRC) Assessment of Research Doctorate Programs . . . to improve education research doctorate programs nationally" (National Academy of Education, n.d.). At the start of this work, the EdD was removed from the taxonomy because of its confused nature. Also at this time, Art Levine (2007) had published his third policy report that investigated American education schools and called for the elimination of the EdD on the grounds that educational leaders could be best prepared with a "master's degree akin to the master's of business administration" (p. 92). Finally, the Council of Graduate Schools (CGS) had released its *Taskforce Report on the Professional Doctorate*, which described professional doctorates as the highest degree for the "preparation for the potential transformation of that field of professional practice, just as the PhD represents preparation for the potential transformation of the basic knowledge in a discipline" (p. 6).

The timing was right for action, prompting the Carnegie Foundation for the Advancement of Teaching to issue a request for proposals to members of the Council of Academic Deans from Research Education Institutions (CADREI) to participate in a national, interinstitutional dialogue aimed at improving the preparation of advanced educational practitioners. Deans brought the request back to their institutions and invited their faculty members to submit proposals. The idea being that though CADREI deans were the recipients of the invitation, the work would be developed and led by school of education faculty who had an interest in and commitment to making these distinctions. Twenty-one schools of education (additional members were invited in 2010) were selected based on their potential for change in their current and intentional work on redesigning their EdD (either within a program or schoolwide) as well as their commitment to support a faculty leader in an experimental, intellectual process that called for sharing across national contexts and testing ideas locally (Perry & Imig, 2008).

The CPED Recipe

Shulman and his colleagues laid the groundwork for the birth of CPED. In their 2006 article, the authors suggested:

> Ultimately, this kind of change will occur from the bottom up, institution by institution, program by program. No institution can be expected to pull it off in isolation. Therefore, even as change occurs locally and experimentally, it must be supported by the progressive networking of individual sites prepared to form consortia that experiment with such efforts in collaboration (p. 30).

Lee Shulman, then president of the Carnegie Foundation for the Advancement of Teaching, Robert Yinger, a Carnegie Fellow, and David Imig, the founding director of CPED, worked together to envision ways to bring together a group of like-minded institutions that were "committed to working together to strengthen every facet of their current doctoral programs" (CPED communication, 2007). The original design of CPED proposed a three-to-five-year process mapped out in three stages: Conceptual and Design Stage, Experimental Stage, and Deliberation and Dissemination Stage. In Stage I, members would "organize an intellectual community that engages seriously and in a sustained way with one another over the course of the project" (CPED communication, 2007). Member institutions would send both faculty and graduate students who would share the work undertaken on their campuses and work across institutions to identify "the challenges and central issues that confront education schools as they transform programs and a set of design principles for further work" (CPED communication, 2007). During Stage II, it was anticipated that "individual campuses [would] pilot new experimental programs, [while] inter-institutional partnerships and other configurations of institutions [would] enable participating institutions to have and be critical friends." In Stage III, Imig saw "CPED institutions engaging with one another in the critical examination of goals and outcomes, determined to work collaboratively to produce new programs that can serve as models for other education schools" (CPED communication, 2007). This design was grounded in the Shulman et al. (2006) vision and aimed to allow members to develop ideas from inside their own institutions and share across a national context in a vetting process that would result in definitions and frameworks for others to learn from and follow.

Imig's vision stemmed from reading the inaugural address given by then New York State commissioner James E. Allen's for James A. Perkins, new presidency of Cornell University, in 1963. Allen described the tension that always exists in any friendship between being candid, constructive, thoughtful, honest, and helpful and the temptation to praise while holding deep reservations, of "the pat on the back" while privately saying "this doesn't measure up." Allen carved out the distinction between Critical Friends and friendly critics and urged Dr. Perkins and his board members to aspire to become Critical Friends—not shallow or callous friendly critics. Coming off a 25-year tenure as president and CEO of AACTE, Imig suggested that education had far too many friendly critics and an insufficient number of Critical Friends. What he, Shulman, and Yinger aspired to achieve within CPED was a network of Critical Friends—participants who were committed to examining every facet of program design and conduct with the intent of making both their program and other programs better. They believed that they could create such a network and participants could engage one another in such conversations.

As Imig opened the first CPED convening in Palo Alto in June 2007, he noted:

> The difference between *friendly critics* and *Critical Friends* is significant. The latter are essential in any good relationship—they play a helpful and significant role in a relationship. While the former can be destructive, the latter are important, helpful and promote forward movement. We are hopeful that partners who join in this conversation play the role of good friends who can be candid, thoughtful, and helpful.

When asked what the intention of this statement was, Imig responded, "We [Imig, Shulman, and Yinger] believed because of the seriousness of the effort and the commitment of this selected list of participants that we could realize a network of Critical Friends."

During the first few years of the CPED initiative, Phase I members (the original 21 plus 4 additional institutions) were mindful of the environment that had been set by Imig's leadership and as a group they sought to maintain this environment. In 2009, when seed money from the Carnegie Foundation ran dry, founding members provided support to sustain the effort until new funding was secured. It was felt among the group that the work of redefining the EdD had not been completed and that the cooperative nature of the consortium was the best means to reach that goal. A year later, CPED was awarded a $700,000 grant from the US Department of Education Fund For the Improvement of Post-Secondary Education (FIPSE) to investigate how institutions and programs had changed as a result of the consortium's work. As part of Phase II of CPED, additional members were added (and four left) to raise the membership to 55 schools and colleges of education. New members were partnered with founding members in loose mentor-mentee relationships as a means to enculturate new members into the CPED environment of Critical Friends and help them adapt to the open and collaborative nature of the convenings and the work of the consortium.

In the building of the CPED consortium during Phase I and into Phase II, a formal use of Critical Friends and Critical Friends Groups (CFGs), as defined by Costa & Kallick (1993) and those that have expanded upon their work, has not been central to the CPED process, though as the consortium grows and our work is expanded upon in an upcoming Phase III, there is a clear place for such formality. Instead, what has guided the CPED consortium to date comes before formality—the building process—and can be explained through research on the developmental process of collaborations and structures of networks for change.

A COLLABORATIVE NETWORK

Wood and Gray (1991) define organizational collaboration as "a process in which a Group of autonomous stakeholders of an issue domain engage in an interactive process, using shared rules, norms, and structures to act or decide on issues related to that domain" (p. 437). In 2007, individual institutions came together to collaborate and examine the EdD. The format for this work was the "convening," a signature activity of the Carnegie Foundation for the Advancement of Teaching, which provided the right process for this collaboration. According to Walker, Golde, Jones, Bueschel, and Hutchings (2009), the term convening is "meant to convey not only that these meetings are different from traditional conferences, but also that the central feature is coming together" (p. 168). Five key features make the convening unique:

1. Idea Centered: key questions and proactive ideas focus each convening and engage participants in discussing and defining the future of the EdD.
2. Mix of Pedagogies: plenary sessions, campus teamwork time, structured small groups, presentations, and social occasions make up the structure of a convening and promote intellectual community.
3. Multiple Voices: A crucial component of the convening is the voices of multiple stakeholders—faculty, deans, and graduate students.
4. Unstructured Conversations: convenings include the all-important social components to build personal connections and strengthen intellectual connections.
5. High Expectations: each institution team is asked to complete several assignments in advance, which often involve consulting widely with leadership and other members of their institution (adapted from Walker et al., 2009).

CPED convenings are held twice a year, in June and October, and bring together one to two faculty members (and occasionally a graduate student) from each institution to work in this collaborative process.

For a group to be considered a collaboration, Kezar (2005) explains, the group work must "entail an interactive process (relationship over time) and [be guided by] shared rules, norms and structures" (p. 834). As noted above, the convening model provided space and structure for an interaction between institutional representatives (faculty participants known as PIs). In Phase I, the rules and norms were guided not only by the expectations of the three stages of the project but also by the convening model that provided the ingredients for democratic engagement that focused on "purpose and process" (Saltmarsh, Hartley, & Clayton, 2009). Elements of this type of engagement include reciprocity, inclusive collaboration, multidirectional flow, and cocreation of knowledge, and change that result from this cocreation of knowledge (Saltmarsh, Hartley, & Clayton, 2009). Democratic engagement was the justification for implementing the convening model, which created a safe space for members to build working relationships.

Kezar's (2005) study of collaborations in four institutions of higher education found that relationships are a central thread in collaboration building because they help to build trust that then fosters commitment to the work. The building of commitment in higher education is different, however, from building commitment in corporations where collaboration can be "mandated form the hierarchy" (p. 846). Instead, in universities, faculty members need to be "convinced of the importance of the commitment" (p. 846). In the first year of CPED, faculty participants at convenings represented an array of commitment to the task of rethinking the EdD. Deans had originally committed to joining this effort but had then turned the process over to their faculty members to allow for an organic design process owned by the very people that would teach in these programs. The faculty representatives that participated in the beginning needed to be convinced that the work was necessary and doable.

Kezar (2005) outlines three stages that take place in the development of collaborations. Stage I is the building of commitment, which centers on a set of shared values, external pressures, and learning. In the context of CPED, the shared values came from common belief that the state of US education was in disarray and that schools of education had a critical role in resolving the issues that face our education system. As described above, the national environment provided the kinds of external pressures that warranted the birth of the CPED initiative. These pressures "emerged as an important area that facilitated and enabled" (Kezar, 2005, p. 853) CPED faculty members' willingness to collaborate around this work, though some faculty members may have been unsure of the direction of CPED in these early days. To temper their uneasiness, the faculty members looked to CPED convenings as a learning environment where they could consider how to address these pressures.

Lee Shulman stimulated this learning. He presented to the consortium a set of loosely defined design-concepts—signature pedagogy, laboratory of practice, and capstone—and then engaged conversations about how such concepts might serve as foundations for a new professional practice degree in education. Over the course of Phase I, faculty members expressed that learning about and defining these concepts together and sharing ideas at CPED convenings in this democratic fashion reinforced their thinking about and development of programs on their own campuses.

The second stage in the development of collaborations is grounded in mission, support from senior executives and networking (Kezar, 2005). Though the hows of reclaiming the EdD were not clear from the beginning, the mission was—to redesign the EdD to prepare those who would steward the practice of education as distinct from the PhD, which prepares those who are stewards of the discipline. After commitment to the initiative was established, members were more willing to buy into and own the mission and, as they progressed in doing this work, they sought support from their deans (senior executives) for the testing of ideas on their home campuses. Developing ideas together, testing them in their local context, reporting results to each other, and receiving feedback from peers created a process that served as the foundations for CPED to become a network.

Lieberman and McLaughlin (1992) describe networks as professional communities that work together to shape their own learning. Such networks, they say, are powerful because they "embrace diverse activities and participants" (p. 674) and successful because they share common features and provide "support, knowledge and encouragement" (p. 675). Though their work described PK-12 teacher networks, the fundamental components of networks can be applied to the CPED consortium. In particular, the components that resonate with CPED are *focus, variety, discourse,* and *leadership* (Lieberman & McLaughlin, 1992). The authors define focus as having a clear emphasis of activity and a sense of identity that CPED has established with its mission to distinguish the EdD and its branding of CPED-influenced EdD programs. Variety "provide[s] opportunities for colleagueship and professional growth by engaging members in varied activities" (p. 674) that blend personal and professional, social and work. This variety, found in the biannual CPED convenings, is an "important ingredient in establishing a climate of trust and support" (p. 674). Another central aspect of the CPED convening is a "discourse community" or "exchange and respect for knowledge which fosters commitment to change, willingness to take risks, and dedication to improvement" (Lieberman & McLaughlin, 1992, p. 674). Finally, networks require "clear assignments of responsibility" (Lieberman & McLaughlin, 1992, p. 676) that will allow members to take leadership and ownership of the network. Within the CPED consortium, faculty leadership has taken forms of scholarship, committee formation, and individual initiative. Many members have published the results of implementing the designs that the consortium promulgates, others have organized committees around organizational needs such as publication, quality, funding, and awards, and several individuals have brought forth ideas for improving communication and function of the organization.

The progression by which CPED had developed into a network fits precisely with Kezar's findings. She explains, "higher education institutions do not appear to advance through development based on learning, but based on well-developed relationships" (p. 856). Faculty members are both influenced and persuaded by peers (Birnbaum, 1991; Kezar, 2001) making the give and take of relationships central to collaborations. Bringing together faculty members from 56 institutions to collaborate in this interpersonal manner, as CPED has, results in a productive network. Maintaining this momentum is another story.

Stage III of Kezar's (2005) model focuses on sustaining collaboration. She explains that the three main elements needed to sustain a collaborative network are "integrating structures, creating rewards and formalizing the network" (p. 850). The CPED consortium is entering a place where sustainability and formality are needed if the network it is to continue. Over the coming years of Phase III, the consortium will be working to create the structures necessary to become sustainable entity. This includes the development of rules and governance systems, more formal structures for collaboration and rewards, adding new members, and long-term visions for the purpose and impact of the work.

As we embark down this path, we need to be mindful of the problems of networks and heed the advice of Lieberman and McLaughlin (1992). These authors suggest networks are "outside of the norms" (p. 675) of traditional institutions, and therefore warrant questions about outcomes and structures. First, questions about the outcomes of the network might ask about the quality of new ideas, the means for applying new ideas at home institutions, and the role of the faculty member in translating these ideas from the network to the home institutions. Second, questions about the structure of the organization arise and include future stability, ownership of the agendas and objectives, leadership that identifies clear responsibilities and balances between member ownership and hierarchical leadership, and development of long-term goals that serve both the network and the individual and the evaluation of the network. One final caution that Lieberman and McLaughlin (1992) stress is the possibility of overextension of the network. They note that as networks succeed and become popular, they create a demand from outside. Such demands may stretch the abilities and directions of the network creating a "fundamental problem" (p. 676) for the managing success of the network.

The CPED consortium has offered a new way for reforming schools of education, one that crosses lines of competition between institutions and asks faculty members to work together to create a network of intellect that functions in an active, collaborative process. As Jones aptly points out in chapter 8 of this book, this is not common in higher education, particularly between faculty or between institutions. The original members of Phase I worked hard to establish an environment that would allow the important work of redesigning and improving the EdD to take place at a national level. Phase II members have welcomed that environment and entered the consortium willing to share and learn together. As CPED moves forward seeking to create structures that can formalize the consortium and maintain an equilibrium between member ownership and hierarchical leadership much can be learned from the works in this volume (as well as the extant literature) about the structures, the roles, and the processes of Critical Friends and CFGs. In addition, formalizing this framework might enhance the nature of and expand CPED as a collaborative network crossing boundaries and reaching out to multiple stakeholders as a means to improve the EdD.

Structured Collaboration Is Key

To date, CPED structures have been best explained by the theoretical work of Kezar, Lieberman, and McLaughlin, and others; however, looking forward, the Critical Friends framework may serve as a way to continue building relationships and collaboration toward productivity and success in improving the EdD. Institutions, organizations, and even individuals rely on structure to guide action and to monitor progress. The Critical Friends framework provides a dynamic structure that can not only be applied across settings but that also contains elements necessary to keep participants on track. Critical

Friends protocols include a specific schedule of events that include straightforward and honest feedback, along with time for reflection. This enables participants to move through the steps without spending an excessive amount of time, for example, glorifying the negative aspects of a problem.

The Critical Friends process serves not just as a tool for the development of individual students or faculty members, but also as an instrument for improvement across organizations. As Andreu, Canós, De Juana, Manresa, Rienda, and Tarí (2003) discuss, a Critical Friends framework can benefit large entities such as universities by providing a structure for evaluation, feedback, and discussion. In order to do this, CFGs must include a clear structure and an environment of trust and respect, and the Critical Friends involved must value and consider the perspectives of others (Andreu et al., 2003). The chapters of this book and the evolution of the CPED consortium suggest several important lessons with regard to this structure and environment, as well as the roles and processes of Critical Friends and CFGs.

Lessons Learned: Structure

Several chapters in this book have provided particular insight into the structure of Critical Friends and CFGs, and the ways in which these structures can be important to the EdD redesign process in CPED. In particular, we can see intentionality of Critical Friends and the role of feedback as central to the benefits of CFGs.

Intentionality. Friendly critics are accidental in many cases. Critical Friends, on the other hand, are intentional. The examples in this book describe how faculty members looked to Critical Friends to gain input for their program, which helped shape their program and served as a tool within their programs. The notion of asking others to examine work done and provide feedback was intentional. For example, Taylor and Marsh note in chapter 2 the aim of the University of Central Florida faculty members to go beyond CPED and reach out to colleagues around the United States and abroad to provide insights to their design process. Similarly, at the University of Colorado Denver, Iceman Sands et al. describe in chapter 4 how the design of their educational leadership EdD was enhanced by purposefully conducting focus groups with practitioners as a means to gather ideas for their program.

Further, participation in CPED is intentional. All institutions represented in this volume as well as the full membership of the consortium intentionally applied to be members of CPED. In most cases, applications expressed the desire to join the consortium because of the benefits of sharing and learning among like-minded colleagues. In fact, in emerging findings from data collected across 21 founding member institutions in the CPED FIPSE research project, faculty (both PIs and institutional faculty) overwhelmingly cite the role that CPED has played through collaborative sharing and learning in the EdD design process.[2]

Feedback. Storey and Richard describe in chapter 1 how the feedback process works in CFGs. Though not always as formalized as the process they outline, the feedback process in CPED has provided "[a] fertile starting place" (p. 72) as Iceman Sands and her colleagues describe in chapter 4. Information gathered from those outside of the design process offered fresh perspectives and new ideas. Such feedback is valuable both from practitioners and outsiders as well as from institutions within CPED. Sawyer discusses in chapter 5, for example, how CPED convenings and meetings provide a place for scaffolded disruption of institutional narratives by prompting members to put their ideas in a new environment, outside of the structure of their university, where ideas can be analyzed and developed with the benefit of multiple perspectives. Strategic design of this kind of multi-faceted and multi-tier approach provides optimal benefit for those involved. In chapter 9, Hamman and Wunder, though describing the process of developing a professional Critical Friends network among their graduates, offer guiding questions that the CPED consortium might utilize going forward. They ask, "How and from whom do you get professional feedback? How do you know if your practice is responsive to ever-rising expectations? And how do you cajole, push, and collaborate with colleagues?" (p. 164).

Looking to the future role of CFGs inside CPED, Belzer has offered potential ideas for establishing the kinds of structures needed for this unique consortium. In chapter 3, she discusses the infrequency of CFG-focused meetings, time constraints, and a lack of deep familiarity with other institutions and with the Critical Friends process that are primary challenges to long distance critical friendships. However, Belzer posits that with greater direction and structure for ongoing relationships (i.e., rather than relying solely on brief activities at biannual meetings), these barriers could be overcome. As a model, Belzer and several of her CPED colleagues have successfully navigated through and met these challenges in a CFG focused on improving EdD candidate writing. The steps of success for this group include gathering a small group of critical friends, learning about each member's program and concerns, and maintaining contact outside of biannual convenings by meeting regularly via videoconferencing. For CPED, as the consortium grows, the creation of small CFGs focused on specific issues seems promising. The use of technologies such as videoconferencing for connecting in between convenings might also serve as a means to foster smaller CFGs among faculty members throughout the consortium.

Lessons Learned: Roles

Outstanding in this volume is the "who" aspect of CFGs among CPED members. In many cases, CPED itself was the primary CFG. In other institutions, without prompting from CPED leadership, members saw value in reaching beyond the consortium to garner input for their designs from their own faculty, non-CPED institutions, practitioners, and community members. As Taylor and Marsh suggest in chapter 2, Critical Friends across students, faculty, community representatives, and employers who live in different locations and have experience with different institutions provides a broad knowledge base with multiple perspectives.

CPED & Institutional faculty. As MacKinnon discusses in chapter 6, the principles of critical friendships were familiar ones for faculty at the University of Vermont, though they had never utilized Critical Friends language to describe them. For this group, a primary role of the Critical Friends framework was experienced in interactions with other CPED members. The nature of the Critical Friends relationships were "old habits of heart, mind, and hand" (p. ##) for UVM faculty, but the ability to have reciprocal relationships across a large network of institutions provided important opportunities for problem solving and discussion. Therefore, for UVM, the role of Critical Friends as a network was integral to the ongoing development of their programs. Reardon and Shakeshaft tell of Virginia Commonwealth University faculty members in chapter 10 (both those who were currently teaching in the EdD or those who were interested in contributing to the emergence of the program) who were integrally involved in the emergent design process.

Students & other stakeholders. Authors such as Jones (chapter 8) describe a systematic interaction of Critical Friends processes across multiple levels of stakeholders. Since CFGs typically consist of fewer than 12 people, multiple concurrent CFGs may be appropriate to target different components of a significant goal, or aspect of the EdD redesign. At the College of Education at Texas Tech University (TTU), the goal was to redefine the online EdD. During this process, five CFGs were utilized. Jones lists the following CFGs: "(a) community college presidents and administrators; (b) higher education program faculty; (c) program coordinators for other programs in the College of Education at TTU; (d) College of Education administrators; and (e) current cohorts of online EdD students" (p. ##). In this context, it is clear that the CFGs include a range of stakeholders with multiple perspectives on programmatic issues. Not only did TTU engage individuals within higher education that included students, they also went outside the university to learn from future employers of those students: community college presidents and administrators. These CFGs were systematically designed so that the processes of each CFG interacted and focused on particular design components.

Chapter 2 describes a way in which critical friendships were extended beyond CPED, beyond the field, and even beyond the United States. In this discussion, Taylor and Marsh allude to the importance of identifying Critical Friends who will contribute a broad spectrum of perspectives. It is important, they suggest, to consider the scope of experience and input necessary to address the goals of a CFG, and to ensure that those involved can meet these needs. In the case of the University of Central Florida, the scope of the challenges the faculty members faced and the goals they had in mind required a broader range of input. Therefore, they went beyond the population of individuals involved in CPED and engaged people from various fields and experiences to provide feedback and support during the design and implementation of their Educational Leadership EdD program. Similarly, the faculty at the University of Colorado Denver sought the input of five superintendents, three executive leaders from institutions of higher education, and seven community-based partners to ensure their program would address the problems of practice and professional needs of future practitioners.

Lessons Learned: Processes

The processes involved in Critical Friends relationships have been described at length throughout this book. However, important lessons can be learned from the ways in which these processes have manifested across contexts. This lesson is the sharing of ideas through collaborative learning. Though Kezar (2005) would suggest that learning is most important during the building of commitment to collaboration (Stage I) and takes a backseat to relationship building as collaborations grow, the evidence presented in this volume might suggest otherwise.

In chapter 5, for example, Sawyer notes the multiple levels of learning and influence that Critical Friends relationships can have. He cites the CPED convenings as prompting new ideas and perspectives, and discussions with colleagues. These interactions offered feedback on existing practices and plans that he brought forth from the institutional level. Following the convenings, Sawyer was able to take new ideas and critiques back to the institutional level at Washington State University. There, he engaged in sharing and learning with his departmental colleagues. For Sawyer, the Critical Friends processes offered sharing and learning across multiple levels to inform his program redesign. Browne-Ferrigno uses hindsight to look back upon the redesign process at the University of Kentucky in chapter 7. She explains that the process of interacting with multiple state-level stakeholders resulted in collaborative learning about the needs of practitioners; this learning led to the successful development and redesign activities of their EdD program.

Learning from CPED members what structures, roles, and processes have shaped and defined collaborative processes and CFGs is central to the future success of CPED. Putting such structures into place across the broader consortium will allow for greater learning and improvement of EdD programs. In the coming years, CPED will be testing the impact of CPED-influenced EdD graduates in practice. Collaboration in small groups and across the consortium will provide a network of sharing and learning that will inform designs, produce smarter educational practitioners, and improve schooling for our youth.

Critical Friends Framework as a Tool for Improvement

As Costa and Kallick (1993) note, "Every student—and educator, too—needs a trusted person who will ask provocative questions and offer helpful critiques" (p. 49). As discussed throughout this book, Critical Friends are particularly prevalent in the preparation and practice of education professionals. These relationships may take somewhat different forms depending on their nature and purpose; however, Critical Friends and CFGs are universally characterized by mutual trust, respect, and commitment to collaboration (Burke, Marx, & Berry, 2011; Curry, 2008; Law, 2005).

A key theme across Critical Friends relationships is the goal of improvement through systematic collaboration in a trusting environment. Improvement may occur within an individual, an organization, or across a network of organizations. Whatever the target, it occurs through a structured relationship among people who share a common goal. The signature activity of this relationship involves regular meetings during which the Critical Friends follow a specific procedure to share ideas or problems, question assumptions surrounding those issues, provide feedback, and collaborate to develop deeper understanding through which decisions can be reached. Critical friendships may involve just two individuals, or they may include a group of eight to twelve individuals who convene as a CFG (National School Reform Faculty, 2012). Within these groups, a framework offers specific protocols for interactions among Critical Friends that enable efficient implementation and maintenance of the relationship. This straightforward nature of communications that results from this process contributes to the ability of Critical Friends to lead to improvement.

While research has focused on Critical Friends among groups of students as a tool for knowledge and skill development, these relationships can be particularly fruitful when they cross the boundaries of institutional roles and disciplines. The CPED consortium has provided a loose platform for these kinds of relationships to develop by involving deans, faculty members, practitioners, and graduate students in interinstitutional dialogue and problem-solving efforts. However, the full potential of this Critical Friends network has yet to be realized. By integrating concepts of improvement science with Critical Friends theory, a direction for better incorporating a CFG protocol becomes clear.

Improvement science offers the meeting of collaborative networks and empirical research. Within improvement science, a methodology that promotes both these aspects is the Plan-Do-Study-Act (PDSA) cycle. PDSA cycles provide a systematic and iterative procedure for the design, implementation, and evaluation of solutions to problems. This process can be implemented in isolation; however, when utilized in the context of a diverse network of individuals and/or organizations, the process can occur with greater efficiency and impact (Bryk, Gomez, & Grunow, 2010; Langley et al., 2009). These cycles are often embedded within a Networked Improvement Community (NIC), which is an incorporation of individuals from diverse perspectives who contribute to the collective goals and actions of the community. An NIC has a clearly defined membership, similar to CFGs, which engages in activities that allow for individual expression while encouraging the dedication and accountability of members so that goals can be accomplished. It is a method for information sharing that facilitates efficient growth and learning, while providing monitoring and feedback from others to refine ideas, solve problems, and generate knowledge. This approach echoes the "designed serendipity" concept suggested by Nielsen (2011) in his book *Reinventing Discovery: The New Era of Networked Science*. He notes that structures that join individuals of varied expertise foster creative solutions to complex problems, because collective knowledge of a group far exceeds that of any one individual. This is the key value of Critical Friends: collective knowledge and multiple perspectives.

The chapters in this book demonstrate the importance of critical friendships and their role in changing schools of education and improving EdD programs. They also hint at the way in which CPED can take a greater role in facilitating the "designed serendipity" needed to ensure that Critical Friends serve as an *ongoing* feedback loop through which individuals can benefit from other perspectives to critically examine their own ideas and practices. Due to its dynamic nature, however, the Critical Friends framework does not and perhaps should not prescribe what stakeholders should be involved. Nonetheless, the authors in this book, members across the consortium and the tenets of an NIC offer suggestion of how to begin to organize CFGs within the consortium.

We suggest that CPED could serve as a "network hub" that assists in connecting members together around design concepts and problems to develop optimal groups of individuals and institutions (Langley et al., 2009) to improve EdD designs. As Fahey (2011) noted, participants view the presence of a facilitator as an important part of a CFG, and by serving as a "network hub," CPED could take on this role. A great deal of information about the characteristics of member institutions, faculty, and students is collected and managed by CPED, but only a portion of it is utilized for action. These data could potentially be used to bring particular institutions together for discussion and problem solving. Furthermore, CPED could facilitate communication among groups that are considering similar issues, thereby enabling multiple concurrent PDSA cycles and communication of the conclusions of each CFG.

Many different methods could be used to match up CPED members in an optimal manner. At past convenings, members have been paired or grouped based on a given institutional characteristic, level of experience, randomly, or simply based on personal preferences. However, to develop more fruitful and productive CFGs, a more complex structure may be needed. One approach that holds particular promise is Q Methodology, which is used in social science research to examine individual perspectives on a given topic. Participants sort a series of statements onto a forced distribution based on the way they value each statement, an inverted factor analysis is completed, and then participants are placed into affinity groups with individuals who sorted the statements in a similar way (Watts and Stenner, 2012). This process was used during a two-part session at the June 2013 CPED Convening. During the first part of the session, members were asked to sort a series of statements based on what they believed were the most important elements of the professional doctorate. Ultimately, each participant had a normal curve in front of them—either on a computer screen or composed of index cards with the statements—that described what they felt were the least important elements to those they felt were most important. A factor analysis was then conducted, which grouped people based on the similarity of their distributions. During part two of the session, participants met with their "affinity groups" to determine what shared personal and professional characteristics existed, and how these features may have influenced the way they considered the elements of a professional doctorate program.[3] While this activity was initially met with some resistance, participants ultimately engaged in rich and lively sharing and learning interactions. Given the potential for systematically grouping people together while appreciating the subjective perspective of each individual, Q Methodology seems to be one way in which optimal CFGs could be developed within the consortium. However, other options exist and will be considered as the consortium moves forward. Ultimately, the goal is to connect consortium members in a way that establishes a more structured Critical Friends network focused on testing design elements, assessing impact, and ultimately improving the field.

CONCLUSION

Up to this point in CPED's history, the consortium has been progressing through stages one and two of developing collaboration (Kezar, 2005). With products defined such as principles for EdD program design and design concepts, and data emerging about how to implement change in programs, the consortium is ripe for moving into Kezar's (2005) Stage III. Over the coming months, CPED leadership will work to formalize its structures and processes. In doing so, the Critical Friends framework will prove invaluable as membership is expanded to include a wider array of stakeholders—practitioners, national associations invested in educational improvement, and schools and colleges outside of the CADREI membership. CPED leadership will also look to improvement science as a means to foster cross-institutional research of EdD program designs and graduate impact. One thing will remain the same in this next phase and future phases of CPED: collaboration at all levels will continue to be integral to the success of this organic sharing and learning process.

NOTES

1. More information on this project can be found at http://carnegie foundation.org
2. More information on this project can be found at http://carnegie foundation.org
3. Data and results from this study will be published in the coming year.

REFERENCES

Anderson, D. G. (1983). Differentiation of the Ed.D. and Ph.D. in education. *Journal of Teacher Education, 34*(3), 55–58.
Andreu, R., Canós, L., de Juana, S., Manresa, E., Rienda, L., & Tarí, J. J. (2003). Critical friends: A tool for quality improvement in universities. *Quality Assurance in Education, 11*(1), 31–36.
Birnbaum, R. (2002). *Management Fads in Higher Education.* San Francisco: Jossey-Bass.
Brown, L. D. (1966). *Doctoral graduates in education. An inquiry into their motives, aspirations, and perceptions of the program.* Bloomington, IN: Indiana University.
Bryk, A. S., Gomez, L. M., & Grunow, A. (2010). Getting ideas into action: Building networked improvement communities in education. In M. T. Hallinan (Ed.), *Frontiers in sociology of education* (pp. 127–162). Netherlands: Springer.
Burke, W., Marx, G. E., & Berry, J. E. (2011). Maintaining, reframing, and disrupting traditional expectations and outcomes for professional development with Critical Friends Groups. *The Teacher Educator, 46*(1), 32–52.
Clifford, G. J., & Guthrie, J. W. (1990). *Ed school: A brief for a professional education.* Chicago, IL: University of Chicago Press.
Costa, A. L., & Kallick, B. (1993). Through the lens of a critical friend. *Educational leadership, 51,* 49–49.
Curry, M. (2008). Critical Friends Groups: The possibilities and limitations embedded in teacher professional communities aimed at instructional improvement and school reform. *The Teachers College Record, 110*(4), 733–774.
Deering, T. E. (1998). Eliminating the doctor of education degree: It's the right thing to do. *The Educational Forum, 62,* 243–248.

Denemark, G. (1985). Educating a profession. *Journal of Teacher Education, 36*(5), 46–51.

Eells, W. C. (1963). *Degrees in higher education.* Washington, DC: The Center for Applied Research in Education.

Fahey, K. M. (2011). Still learning about leading: A leadership Critical Friends Group. *Journal of Research on Leadership Education, 6*(1), 1–35.

Freeman, F. N. (1931). *Practices of American universities in granting higher degrees in education: A series of official statements* (Vol. 19). Chicago, IL: University of Chicago Press.

Kezar, A. (2001). *Understanding and facilitating organizational change in the 21st century: Recent research and conceptualizations,* ASHE-ERIC Higher Education Reports, Washington, DC Report 28:4.

Kezar, A. (2005). Redesigning for collaboration within higher education institutions: An exploration into the developmental process. *Research in Higher Education, 46*(7).

Langley, G. J., Moen, R., Nolan, K. M., Nolan, T. W., Norman, C. L., & Provost, L. P. (2009). *The improvement guide: A practical approach to enhancing organizational performance.* San Francisco: Jossey-Bass.

Law, B. (2005). Creating moral schools: The enabling potential of Critical Friends Groups. *Educational Horizons, 84*(1), 53–57.

Learned, W. S., & Bagley, W. C. (1965). Purpose of a normal school. In M. L. Borrowman (Ed.), *Teacher education in America: A documentary history* (pp. 122–140). New York, NY: Teachers College Columbia University. (Reprinted from *Carnegie Bulletin No. 14 ed.*, 1920, New York: Carnegie Foundation).

Levine, A. (2005). *Educating school leaders.* New York, NY: The Education Schools Project.

Levine, A. (2007). *Educating researchers.* Washington, DC: Education Schools Project.

Lieberman, A., & McLaughlin, M. W. (1992). Networks for educational change: Powerful and problematic. *The Phi Delta Kappan, 73*(9), 673–677.

National Academy of Education. (n.d.). *History and examples of research.* Retrieved from http://www.naeducation.org/NAED_080203.html.

National School Reform Faculty. (2012). Retrieved June 11, 2013, from http://www.nsrfharmony.org/faq.html#1.

Nielsen, M. (2011). *Reinventing discovery: The new era of networked science.* Princeton: University Press.

Osguthorpe, R. T., & Wong, M. J. (1993). The Ph.D. versus the Ed.D.: Time for a decision. *Innovative Higher Education, 18*(1), 47–63.

Perry, J. A., & Imig, D. G. (2008). A stewardship of practice in education. *Change: The Magazine of Higher Learning, 40*(6), 42–49.

Saltmarsh, J., Hartley, M., & Clayton, P. H. (2009). *Democratic engagement white paper.* Boston, MA: New England Resource Center for Higher Education.

Shulman, L. S., Golde, C. M., Bueschel, A. C., & Garabedian, K. J. (2006). Reclaiming education's doctorates: A critique and a proposal. *Educational Researcher*, 35(3), 25–32.

Walker, G. E., Golde, C. M., Jones, L., Bueschel, A. C., & Hutchings, P. (2009). *The formation of scholars: Rethinking doctoral education for the twenty-first century*. San Francisco: Jossey-Bass.

Watts, S., & Stenner, P. (2012). *Doing Q Methodological Research: Theory, Method & Interpretation*. SAGE Publications Limited.

Wood, D. J., and Gray, B. (1991). Toward a comprehensive theory of collaboration. *Journal of Applied Behavioral Science 27*(2), 139–162.

CONTRIBUTORS

Alisa Belzer is an associate professor in the Department of Learning and Teaching at Rutgers University in New Jersey. Prior to her appointment at Rutgers in 1999, she directed a statewide teacher research-based professional development initiative for adult basic education practitioners in Pennsylvania. She began her professional life working in adult literacy education and has been a program coordinator, tutor trainer, and classroom teacher and tutor. Her research interests have been in the areas of alternative assessment, professional development and teacher research, adult literacy education policy, adult learner beliefs, and adult reading development. She became director of the Education Doctorate Program at Rutgers in 2012. Her scholarly work related to doctoral education has focused on describing and analyzing the change process involved in launching a new professional practice doctorate and redefining the dissertation relative to this type of doctoral training.

Rodney L. Blunck is an associate clinical professor in the Administrative Leadership & Policy Studies and Executive Educational Leadership programs at the School of Education and Human Development, CU Denver. He teaches in the school's EdD program. His work covers the development of the next generation of educational leaders within our state, region, and nation. Dr. Blunck's content interests include emerging trends in educational leadership, incorporating job embedded experiences to address organizational issues and simultaneously fulfill degree requirements, and organizational measurements within a leadership context.

Tricia Browne-Ferrigno is a professor of Educational Leadership Studies in the College of Education at the University of Kentucky. Her primary research agenda centers on leadership preparation and development, specifically the lived experiences of those actively involved, program features and their impact on participant learning, and program evaluation. Her scholarship also examines educational reform and school improvement, professional mentoring, and innovations in doctoral education. The former director of two school-leadership development projects funded by grants from the US Department of Education, she currently serves as the coordinator of her department's new teacher leadership program. Her chapter in this book is informed by the case study she conducted for an article published in a special issue on state-mandated preparation program redesign of the Journal of Research on Leadership Education.

Alan Davis is an associate professor of Research, Evaluation, and Measurement at CU Denver and serves on the doctoral faculty in Urban Ecologies. His research focuses on the social contexts of education and the relationship of adolescents and schooling. His most recent studies have been on cultural contexts of identity formation, career aspirations of urban youth, resiliency and high school graduation, and effective high schools for English-language learners. Davis teaches courses on qualitative and statistical methods of research and evaluation, and is past president of the Association of Colorado Educational Evaluators.

Connie L. Fulmer is a professor of Administrative Leadership and Policy Studies in the School of Education and Human Development at CU Denver. She earned her PhD from The Pennsylvania State University and started her academic career at Northern Illinois University before coming to UCD. Dr. Fulmer's research efforts are focused on school administrators and their professional development. Her published scholarship is located in three inquiry-focused areas: (1) scholarship on technology and information systems for school administrators, (2) scholarship on developing quality preparation programs for principals, and (3) scholarship related to identifying leadership practices of principals leading successful highly impacted schools. The most rewarding research experience of her career has been working with five thematic dissertation students during this past year.

Edmund "Ted" Hamann is an associate professor in the University of Nebraska-Lincoln's (UNL), Department of Teaching, Learning, and Teacher Education. An anthropologist of education and longtime researcher of education policy development, notably school reform, in the face of diversity and demographic change, his first school-based research was as an undergraduate, under Ted Sizer's tutelage, as the Coalition of Essential Schools was first promulgated. At UNL since

2005, he has taught the introductory, two-semester, "Challenges and Opportunities" course to each of the three CPED EdD cohorts that have matriculated so far.

Rachael Hoffman is a graduate student currently enrolled in Duquesne University's School Psychology PhD program. She works as a graduate assistant for the Carnegie Project on the Education Doctorate and as a research developer for Psychology Software Tools, Inc. Her primary research interests involve neuropsychological assessment and intervention, efficacy of assistive technology, and understanding the interaction of experience and instruction in student learning outcomes.

Stephanie J. Jones is an associate professor and coordinator of the higer education program at Texas Tech University. She currently teaches graduate level courses in higher education administration and her research foci is women in higher education, community colleges, and distance learning. Dr. Jones has previously served in community college administrator roles in the areas of distance education, instructional technology, and instructional support. She has also served as the project director for a Title V Cooperative grant. Prior to her administrative roles, she served as faculty and department chairperson. Dr. Jones began her career in information technology as a software developer and project manager. She worked in many management level positions in IT, before moving into higher education.

Nancy L. Leech is an associate professor at CU Denver. Dr. Leech is currently teaching master's and PhD level courses in research, statistics, and measurement. Her area of research is promoting new developments and better understandings in applied qualitative, quantitative, and mixed methodologies. To date, she has published more than 65 articles in refereed journals, and is coauthor of three books: SPSS for Basic Statistics: Use and Interpretation; SPSS for Intermediate Statistics: Use and Interpretation; and Research Methods in Applied Settings: An Integrated Approach to Design and Analysis, all published by Taylor and Francis. Dr. Leech has made more than 70 presentations at regional, national, and international conferences.

Nicole Lea Marsh is the senior administrator for Evaluation Services in Orange County Public Schools, Florida, having previously been in management in the private sector, school district, and higher education. Currently, her research interests focus on development and implementation effectiveness of initiatives and of graduate programs. She was one of the first Carnegie Project on the Education Doctorate Fellows and holds an MBA from the Crummer Graduate School of Business at Rollins College, an MA in Communication, and an EdD in the Educational Leadership Executive Track from the University of Central Florida.

Colleen T. MacKinnon is the Director of Assessment and Accreditation in the College of Education and Social Services at the University of Vermont. Dr. MacKinnon's teaching and research interests include school governance, educational leadership, and the relationships among technology, schooling, and society. Her work in higher education has intersected with her active participation as a public school director for nearly two decades and she currently serves as chair of a supervisory union school board.

Jill A. Perry is a Duquesne University Research Faculty and codirector for the Carnegie Project on the Education Doctorate. She is a graduate of the University of Maryland, from where she also received her PhD in International Educational Policy. Dr. Perry's research focuses on professional doctorate preparation in education, organizational change in higher education, and faculty leadership in higher education. She has over 20 years of experience in leadership and program development in education and teaching experience at the elementary, secondary, undergraduate, and graduate levels in the United States and abroad. She is a Fulbright Scholar (Germany) and a returned Peace Corps Volunteer (Paraguay).

Brendan M. Richard is a doctoral student at the University of Central Florida enrolled in the Methodology, Measurement and Analysis program. He has taught several courses within the field of management at the university level including: strategic management, conflict resolutions and negotiations, human resources and business ethics. He has authored or coauthored book chapters and journal publications in the fields of educational leadership, mentoring, innovation, and hospitality management. His research focus is on innovation and its applications in the fields of higher education, and management.

Maria Araceli Ruiz-Primo is an associate professor of Educational Psychology, the director of the SEHD Research Center, and the director of the Laboratory of Educational Assessment, Research, and InnovatioN (LEARN) at CU Denver. Her work focuses on two strands: assessment of students learning at both large-scale and classroom level (e.g., item contexts effect on student performance), and the study of teachers' assessment practices (e.g., teachers' informal and formal formative practices such as the use of assessment conversations and embedded assessments). She coedited a special issue on assessment for the Journal of Research in Science Teaching. Her recent work and publications focus on the development and evaluation of assessments that are instructionally sensitive and instruments to evaluate formative assessment practices in the classroom.

R. Martin Reardon is currently an assistant professor in the Educational Leadership Department of the College of Education at East Carolina University, Greenville, North Carolina. He holds an MEd in Mathematics Education, and obtained his PhD in Educational Policy, Planning, and Leadership from The College of William and Mary in Virginia. He has held a wide range of administrative positions at the high school and college department levels. The chapter for which he is the lead author recounts the development of the Education Doctorate in Leadership program at Virginia Commonwealth University, which is aligned with the Carnegie Project on the Education Doctorate. Reardon was the director of that program for two years. His research focuses on learning-centered leadership, and quality and equality in education—both in the context of middle school enhancement models—and technology-infused learning—with particular interest in digital simulation-based learning in the context of educational leadership.

Deanna Iceman Sands is dean of the College of Education at Seattle University, and was formerly a professor and associate dean of Research in the School of Education and Human Development at CU Denver. There, she led the school's pre- and post-grant and contract awards, held continuing and professional education programs, led an Evaluation Center conducting national and international work, a Faculty Research Center, and the Center for Advancing Practice, Education and Research (CAPER)—home to national centers hosting research, technical assistance, PD, outreach and engagement, and policy advocacy. She led faculty mentoring and faculty affairs, supervised academic programs, and served as program director to the schoolwide PhD and EdD programs. Her research areas include formative assessment, student engagement/voice, and curriculum and instruction.

Richard D. Sawyer chairs the Masters in Teaching Secondary Program for WSU Vancouver and the Teacher Leadership EdD on three campuses of the university. His scholarship focuses on qualitative research and teacher education and development within a curricular theory lens. He is completing work on a 12-year longitudinal study comparing curriculum making and curriculum change of teachers prepared through either alternate route certification or college-based preparation. Recent publications include the following: R. D. Sawyer and J. Norris, *Understanding Qualitative Research: Duoethnography* (2013); and R. D. Sawyer and T. Liggett, *Shifting Positionalities: A Critical Discussion of a Duoethnographic Inquiry of a Personal Curriculum of Post/Colonialism* (2013).

Charol Shakeshaft is a professor of educational leadership. She is the author of four books and over two hundred referred articles and papers. Her research focuses on gender and race in leadership, educator sexual misconduct, and the effectiveness of technology for learning. Dr. Shakeshaft was the first female vice president of Division A. She is one of the original founders of the National Women's Studies Association and is currently international chair of Women Leading in Education. Charol often serves as an expert witness in federal cases. Over her career, Dr. Shakeshaft has received over 10 million dollars in federal grants.

Nancy Shanklin has been instrumental in both the first design and now redesign of CU Denver EdD Program. She co-led with Dr. Ron Tzur a thematic dissertation group from Cohort One of six members around STEM and professional development. She has taught the internship courses for Cohorts Two and Three. Her areas of expertise are in literacy, professional development and instructional coaching, teacher education, and literacy assessment.

Valerie A. Storey is an associate professor in the School of Teaching, Learning, and Leadership, College of Education at the University of Central Florida. She is the coordinator of the EdD Education Program and Executive Educational Leadership, EdD developed in partnership with the Carnegie Foundation. Storey earned her doctoral degree in Educational Leadership and Policy at Peabody College, Vanderbilt University. Her dissertation focused on the power struggle between social welfare agencies, that is, street level bureaucracy through the lens of Education Action Zones. She serves currently as a member of